SOCCER COACH'S SURVIVAL GUIDE

William E. Warren • George D. Danner

PARKER PUBLISHING CO.

Library of Congress Cataloging-in-Publication Data

Warren, William, E.
    Soccer coach's survival guide / William E. Warren and George D.
    Danner.
        p.   cm.
    Includes bibliographical references (p.   ).
    ISBN 0-13-907973-4
    1. Soccer—Coaching.   I. Danner, George D.   II. Title.
    GV943.8.W37   1999
    796.334'07'7—dc21   98-50402
                                                                    CIP

Acquisitions Editor: *Connie Kallback*
Production Editor: *Mariann Hutlak*
Interior Design/Formatter: *Dee Coroneos*

Printed in the United States of America

10 9 8 7 6 5 4 3 2 1

ISBN 0-13-907973-4

PARKER PUBLISHING COMPANY
West Nyack, NY 10994

On the World Wide Web at http://www.phdirect.com

Prentice Hall International (UK) Limited, *London*
Prentice Hall of Australia Pty. Limited, *Sydney*
Prentice Hall Canada, Inc., *Toronto*
Prentice Hall Hispanoamericana, S.A., *Mexico*
Prentice Hall of India Private Limited, *New Delhi*
Prentice Hall of Japan, Inc., *Tokyo*
Pearson Education Asia Pte. Ltd., *Singapore*
Editora Prentice Hall do Brasil, Ltda., *Rio de Janeiro*

DEDICATION

For
Dale, Dustin, and Mandi
and
Louise and Brandon

ACKNOWLEDGMENTS

It all starts with, and revolves around, the players. They are, after all, the reason why the game is played.

Listing the names of the hundreds of players who have come through our school and club programs in the past fifteen years is an obvious impossibility; suffice it to say that each of them has been special to us, touching our lives and enriching us with their dedication and commitment to the simple pleasure of kicking a ball around. We may not remember all of their names, but we will never forget their contributions or their impact.*

Then there are the coaches: Arthur Graves, our assistant coach and strength/ conditioning coach for the past five years; Jerry Fields, our jayvee coach and assistant varsity coach for ten years; Laughton Brown and Mike Criswell, longtime assistant coaches; Paul Gibbons, former director of the Griffin Youth Soccer Club; Wayne Stutes, who helped us to develop Griffin's club soccer program, and Wayne Gardner, president of the Griffin Excel Soccer Club and director of the Olympic Soccer Development Program in Georgia; Bain Proctor, who helped to pave the way for varsity soccer in Griffin and persuaded us to forsake basketball coaching for soccer; former Atlanta Chiefs and Atlanta Attacks pro player Adrian Brooks; Bret Simon, men's soccer coach at Creighton University; Kurt Swanbeck and Lorenzo Canalis, men's and women's soccer coaches, respectively, at Berry College; Jeff Ford, varsity boys' coach at McIntosh High School, who went out of his way to help a young coach getting started fifteen years ago; and last—but certainly not least—Mike Morgan, the outstanding coach and director of the Stone Mountain Soccer Club, whose friendship has extended to granting us permission to base much of the material in the latter portion of Chapter 13 on information supplied to us by him. Thanks, Mike—and thanks to the rest of the coaches cited above, without whose assistance and support neither this *Survival Guide* nor our own survival as coaches would have been possible.

Thanks, too, to Griffin High School principal Mike McLemore and acting athletic director Vic Barrick for allowing us to use the "GHS Athletic Packet" featured in Appendixes F, H, and I; and to Scott Rogers, photographer for the *Griffin Daily News*, for his very capable work on our behalf.

---

* We would be remiss, however, if we failed to acknowledge the contributions of the fine young men and women whose photos appear in Chapters 5 and 6: David Rice, Brantley Spillman, Dustin Danner, Daniel Wiser, Travis Gamble, Brent Parker, Erica Palmisano, Jeannette Joslin, Carolyn Knighton, Alexis McCarty, Rebecca Jenkes, Mindy Crow, Shannon Cliatt, and Jennifer Willis.

We have been fortunate to have enjoyed top-notch medical support for our teams over the years; every coach should be so lucky as to have medical support personnel such as Tim Marlow and Charlie Penny of Health South Therapy Clinic; Dr. Alan Davis of Whitewater Medical Clinic; Dr. Gerald Bohn of Griffin Internal Medicine Clinic; Dr. Tommy Hopkins of Griffin Orthopedic Clinic; and Dr. Tony Nicholas of Ellis Chiropractic Clinic. They were the glue that held our teams together for a decade and a half.

Finally, we should acknowledge the continuing support of Prentice Hall editor Connie Kallback and vice president Win Huppuch in bringing this project to fruition. Their concern for the authors'—as well as the book's—well-being has transcended telephone lines and words typed into a computer. Their friendship and encouragement have been invaluable to us at every step along the way.

George Danner
Bill Warren

ABOUT THE AUTHORS

George Danner knows what it takes to build a winning soccer program.

Starting from scratch with a new program and inexperienced players at Griffin (Georgia) High School in 1984, George first built a strong local club soccer program. Gradually, his varsity boys' teams began to improve toward their present status as a perennial powerhouse in the state. George's 132-76-8 record at GHS includes a 60-18-6 mark since 1992 and back-to-back second-place finishes in the AAAA state tournament in 1996 and 1997.

Named state Coach of the Year in 1996 by the Georgia High School Association, George also coached the Georgia high school senior all-stars vs. Tennessee's all-stars that year. Four of his players have earned All-South honors, eight have played in the GHSA All-Star Soccer Game, and twenty of his former players have received college scholarships.

George received his B.S. and M.S. degrees from Southwest Missouri State University in 1977. He lives in Griffin with his wife, Dale, and they have two children, Mandi and Dustin.

Dr. William Warren coached for nineteen years, and has written eighteen books in all—ten of them for coaches—including *Coaching and Motivation* (1983), *Coaching and Winning* (1988), and *Coaching and Control* (1996), all from Simon & Schuster. He also co-authored *Basketball Coach's Survival Guide* (1994). This is his first soccer coaching book.

Dr. Warren attended Armstrong State University, Georgia Southern University, Auburn University, the University of Kentucky, and the University of Georgia, earning his Ed.D. degree at UGA in 1970. He lives in Griffin with his wife, Louise.

ABOUT THIS RESOURCE

It's not always easy, and it's not always fun, to teach the fundamental skills of soccer—or *any* team sport, for that matter—but it *is* always important. As we'll remind you often in this book, coaching is *teaching*, and teaching begins with the basic skills that determine how the game is played.

Ours is an age of perceived shortcuts to success. In sports, youngsters see major league baseball players hitting .230 and going through arbitration to gain larger salaries, and pro basketball players receiving millions of dollars in annual salaries because they can change light bulbs in the ceiling without a ladder. The result is, in too many cases, young athletes who resist instruction because they think they can get by with natural talent alone.

Taught from early childhood that success is an entitlement rather than a responsibility or a product of hard work, some players regard learning as less important than simply executing skills in whatever manner feels natural to them. And because teaching skills can be difficult and time-consuming, some coaches take the easy way out, ignoring the fundamentals and concentrating on team strategies and scrimmaging. This is a mistake that no one who takes his or her coaching seriously can afford to make. You can get by with it for awhile if you've inherited a dynamite team that is loaded with experienced, talented players who have already mastered soccer's basic skills. If your team and your players are not of such high caliber, though, the only way to catch up with the rest of the pack is by training harder than other teams and focusing on the skills that better teams and players already have.

Many coaches contend that, because of factors such as those just cited, coaching is more difficult today than it has ever been before. We don't see it that way; in fact, we believe that exactly the opposite is true.

Yes, coaching soccer is difficult. It always has been, and always will be. If it were otherwise, every player would be an All-American and every coach would be Coach of the Year. That difficulty, however, works to the advantage of coaches and players who devote themselves to their teaching and learning responsibilities in a dedicated, conscientious manner. If you're committed to teaching your players the skills they need to learn in order to become good soccer players, that alone puts you ahead of those coaches—and there are many of them—who regard daily soccer practice as two hours of time to fill in the easiest manner possible. That's not coaching; it's babysitting—going through the motions of coaching. You can do better than that, and you *will*, if you believe that what you're doing is important.

Yes, it's true that many of today's young players would rather not go through the instruction and drills upon which all successful soccer is based. But if, through the process of elimination, you surround yourself with players who accept you and your coaching philosophy as compatible with their best interests, you'll eventually overcome whatever obstacles stand in your path to success in soccer coaching.

If you're just starting out in coaching, a good way to begin is by accepting the truth of the following statement:

You have within you the seeds of greatness in your soccer coaching.

You can be (and will be) as great a coach as you want to be, if—and this is a very important *if*—you're willing to pay the price that coaching demands. In fact, there are only three ways you can fail to become a successful coach: by dropping out of coaching before you've given yourself a chance to achieve all that you're capable of achieving; by remaining in a situation in which you fail to receive the support necessary to build a successful program; or by expecting great results without having given a total effort in your coaching. Our basic rules of thumb regarding how hard a coach should work are these:

1. To coach your team effectively, you must work harder than you expect your players to work; and

2. Your personal goal should be to outwork the coaches whose teams you play.

Of course, it's not quite that simple, and not merely a matter of putting in long hours on the job, since coaching is a difficult task, even when done badly. Striving for excellence in your coaching begins with *preparing yourself to coach* by taking the time to sit down and list your strengths and weaknesses, and then working to eliminate your weaknesses by turning them into strengths. Whatever shortcomings you might have as a beginning coach will be overcome by the same kind of diligent effort to improve yourself that you expect from your players. The purpose of *Soccer Coach's Survival Guide* is to show you how to build your program, your coaching skills, and your team from the ground up.

To that end, **Part 1,** "First Steps," tells you how to build a program that you, your players, their parents, and other supporters will be proud of.

Chapter 1, "Building a Successful Program," tells you how to build an effective feeder program that will keep your teams supplied with the kinds of players needed to produce and maintain consistently successful teams.

It all starts at the club level, with your willingness to work with local recreation department officials in organizing soccer teams and leagues for youngsters to get their kicks in. Without that necessary first step to draw children of early elementary ages into soccer (and, not coincidentally, to provide their coaches with the basic rudiments of effective teaching and coaching skills), you'll wind up teaching fundamental skills to high school sophomores that they should have learned ten years ago.

There's more to it than that, though; program building also refers to steps taken to extend the school soccer program downward through B-team or junior varsity, junior high, and possibly middle school as well. Chapter 1 offers practical advice on how to expand participation at all levels; improve facilities; train coaches and officials at the rec league level; acquire a club format and gain state affiliation; upgrade girls' and women's soccer; extend your school feeder program downward; gain administrative and community support; develop a soccer booster club and sponsorships; build a base of medical support personnel for your team(s); and gain the support of media personnel. Chapter 1 also describes ten personal qualities shared by successful coaches.

Chapter 2, "Surviving the First Year," tells how a coach can use goal setting as a motivational tool in forming positive attitudes toward hard work and individual improvement. Operating under the assumption that you're more likely to inherit an inexperienced or unskilled team than one that is state championship-bound, we'll also deal with such topics and problems as handling difficult players; extending your players' comfort zone; teaching players how to win; defining roles; scheduling; using losses as steppingstones to success; developing a positive and dynamic team ethic; and life in your second year at a school.

Chapter **3,** "You and Your Team," describes the ideal soccer team as one that functions as a second family for everyone involved. Family members may squabble and fight occasionally, but they are also bound together by powerful bonds of love, respect, and commitment. Chapter 3 shows you how to build a team atmosphere in which—secure in the knowledge that they are accepted, respected, and loved by their teammates and coaches—players feel a deep sense of obligation to their teammates and commitment to team goals.

These are more than idle words set down on paper to fill pages; love is the most powerful and positive force at your disposal in coaching. When players feel genuine affection for one another and their coaches, there is no limit to how hard they will work to keep from letting down their teammates.

You can, through effective leadership and the example of your personal and professional commitment to every player on the team—from budding superstars to the least-skilled benchwarmers—build such a team; if you do, you'll never regret it—and your players will never forget it.

Chapter **3** also offers two shortcuts in the pursuit of excellence; four ways to promote team unity via social settings; how to lead a team effectively; motivating your players; developing team leaders; using team captains, seniors, and assistant coaches to full advantage; and handling player problems and problem players.

Part 2, "Playing the Game," deals with preparing yourself and your players for competition.

Chapter **4,** "Developing an Understanding of the Game," begins at the beginning, introducing neophyte coaches to the world's most popular team sport. It includes the soccer field, or *pitch,* and its lines and dimensions; rules and playing procedures; and the players and their basic responsibilities.

Chapter **5,** "Soccer Fundamentals," briefly examines the various elements that combine to produce successful teaching, and analyzes soccer's basic skills—passing, shooting, dribbling, heading, receiving, tackling, defense, and goalkeeping—and offers teaching progressions and coaching tips to ensure that skills are understood and mastered as they are taught.

Chapter **6,** "Soccer Drills," offers a representative sampling of effective activities and drills for physical conditioning, and for teaching individual skills and team concepts. To be effective over the long run, drills must be challenging and enjoyable as well as repetitive, or else they will be merely boring. While this is not to say that daily practices should be laugh-a-minute frolics, it doesn't hurt to show your players that learning can be fun rather than hard work, or that *working hard* can be *fun.*

In its most basic form, soccer strategy is associated with imaginary thirds of the pitch—the defensive third, the midfield third, and the attacking third—that do not appear as lines or field markings. Beyond that basic consideration, the effective use of strategies as analyzed in **Chapter 7,** "Systems of Play and Their Associated Strategies," is not really so different conceptually from other team sports: positioning players in such a manner as to play to your strengths, hide your weaknesses, negate opponents' strengths, or exploit their weaknesses.

For example, a basic principle of team sports strategy holds that, without divine intervention or luck combined with a lack of motivation by the opponents, it is virtually impossible for a weak team to defeat a superior team *at what the superior team does best.*

It's nice to dream impossible dreams of outrunning a team of racehorses to defeat the defending state champions; but if all you currently have at your disposal is plowhorses, your best bet to remain competitive against faster, more highly skilled opponents is to (a) slow the game down as much as possible through careful ball control, (b) attack only when your team has a clear advantage, and (c) stack your defensive third of the field with enough defenders to hold off the Chinese army whenever the opponents have the ball. Even then, your strategy is unlikely to defeat a clearly superior opponent, but it at least gives your players their best chance of keeping the score relatively close, and avoiding the sort of crushing defeats that a more aggressive strategy would be likely to produce. And who knows? When scores are close late in the game, luck and motivation can cause strange and wonderful things to happen. But they *won't* happen if you're behind by ten goals at the half because you tried to defeat a superior opponent at its own game.

That's one example of team strategy; there are others, of course, that apply to other teams and other situations. The success you can expect from any playing strategy is directly related to your players' relative ability to master the skills and concepts involved. Chapter 7 also analyzes man-to-man and zone defense.

Chapter 8, "Basic Soccer Strategy," compares various playing systems (e.g., 4-4-2, 3-4-3, and 5-3-2) in terms of their effective use with teams of varying skills and experience.

Part 3, "Coaching Your Team," deals with the organizational techniques coaches employ to prepare their teams for an upcoming season, individual games, and the playoffs.

Chapter 9, "Team Tryouts and Squad Selection," tells how to conduct preseason tryouts: recruiting prospects within your school; conducting tryouts; qualities to look for in young players; five guidelines for player selection; the length of tryouts; and trimming the roster to regulation size in the kindest, gentlest manner possible.

Chapters 10, "Preseason Practice," and **11,** "Organizing Your Daily Practices," deal with time management—using your practice time wisely and efficiently to ensure that what *needs to be covered* in your daily practices *is covered.*

In both preseason and in-season practice sessions, the *daily practice schedule* and its preparation constitute the hub around which everything else revolves. Conducting daily practice sessions without a predetermined, detailed practice schedule is like driving cross-country on back roads without consulting roadmaps along the way; you may wind up where you thought you were heading—but then again, you may not. And even if you *do* make it, you'll have wasted a lot of valuable time and energy getting there in such a haphazard, disorganized fashion.

With limited preseason practice time available, and so much to be covered, it's obviously impossible to cover everything at once. The best solution to this problem lies in prioritizing your goals, a process that should be conducted before preseason practice begins. Chapter 10 tells you how to do it, beginning with the first team meeting and getting the paperwork out of the way. It also considers the problem of what constitutes a desirable ratio of time spent in conditioning and warmup activities, individual and team drills, and installing the team offense and defense during preseason.

Chapter 11 extends that analysis of priorities into the regular season by (a)considering the problem of what constitutes a desirable ratio in daily practice between *repetitive drills* to improve skills and *scrimmaging* to practice those skills under simulated game conditions; (b) describing a process known as *controlled scrimmaging,* which simultaneously incorporates features of drills *and* scrimmaging; (c) going through the process of installing your offense and defense via walk-throughs and breakdown drills; (d) analyzing time management and the mechanics and length of daily practices; (e) offering a new slant on breakdown drills; and (f) offering five guidelines for conducting dynamic, challenging sessions that will keep your players alert and eager to come back for more.

Chapter 12, "Game Preparations," deals with scouting and game plans. Regarding the former, it covers such topics as priorities in scouting with teams of varying ability; indirect scouting; techniques and tips for successful direct scouting; and preparing scouting reports. The latter portion of Chapter 12 deals with formulating a basic game plan for your team and making contingency plans or adjustments for situations such as these: wide or narrow playing fields; late-season play; and meeting teams for the second time or merely changing strategies when your basic game plan fails to contain or control the opponents. The chapter concludes with a series of questions and answers relating to game plans.

Chapter 13, "Filling in the Gaps," begins by outlining the off-season duties and responsibilities that school coaches (and sometimes club coaches as well) are expected to perform—such things as coaching other sports; conducting or working at summer camps; arranging post-season awards banquets; developing off-season strength and conditioning programs for your athletes; scheduling; budgeting; attending (or conducting) rules clinics and coaching clinics; officiating—and possibly coaching teams, as well—at the club level; and developing and supporting booster clubs and sponsorships. The chapter concludes with information for coaches and players alike regarding the college search and recruiting process, answering commonly encountered questions from student-athletes (e.g., "When and where should I start looking at colleges?" and "How many times can I take the SAT or ACT?") and offering a time line for involvement in the recruiting process that begins in the player's freshman year of high school.

SYMBOLS

———▶	=	Player movement (offensive or defensive)
∿∿∿▶	=	Dribbling
------▶	=	Path of ball
———⊣	=	Area of defensive coverage or denial at the end of a dribble or other offensive movement
W_2	=	Offensive player (in this case, a winger)
W	=	Offensive player with ball
FB_1	=	Defensive player (in this case, a fullback)
▼	=	Opponent (position unnecessary)
GK	=	Goalkeeper
SW	=	Sweeper
ST	=	Stopper
WB	=	Wingback
HB	=	Halfback
FB	=	Fullback
MF	=	Midfielder
F	=	Forward, or Striker
W	=	Wing

(NOTE: Player designations in some of the diagrams may be preceded by an **I** (inside), **O** (outside), **C** (center), **L** (left), or **R** (right) to further define or clarify positions.)

CONTENTS

Chapter 6
SOCCER DRILLS   108

PART 3
COACHING YOUR TEAM   205

Chapter 9
TEAM TRYOUTS AND SQUAD SELECTION   207

Chapter 10
PRESEASON PRACTICE   214

Chapter 13

FILLING IN THE GAPS   249

APPENDICES   257

Appendix A

ANNOTATED BIBLIOGRAPHY   259

Appendix B

COACHING TASKS AND PREPARATIONS   263

Appendix C

THE SOCCER PITCH   264

Appendix D

SOCCER STAT SHEET   265

Appendix E

PLAYER CHECKLIST—PREPARATION FOR GAMES AND DAILY PRACTICES   266

Part 1

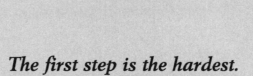

FIRST STEPS

The first step is the hardest.

—Marie de Vichy-Chamrond
Marquise du Deffand (1763)

Chapter 1

BUILDING AND MAINTAINING A SUCCESSFUL PROGRAM

You have to be hungry. You have to be dedicated
100 percent to play this game.

—Giorgio Chinaglia

"Succesful" programs are often identified with winning teams, and "unsuccessful" programs as being the other side of that coin, but as the old song says, *it ain't necessarily so.* We prefer to think of a successful program in more comprehensive terms, namely, *a program that the coaches, players, fans, and supporters can be proud of,* and *one that is progressing in the direction of the stated goals that the coach has laid down, whatever they may be.* Winning, although important and the most obvious feature of a successful program, is but one aspect of the total package. If you make it more than that, you're asking for more trouble than you ever thought existed.

In discussing the task of building a successful program, then, we aren't going to tell you how to win every game; no one could do that. We *will*, however, tell you how to build a program that you, your players, and your fans will be proud to be associated with. And we'll tell you how to ensure that your program makes steady progress toward what you want it to become. We can do that because there are no secrets to building a strong program, and there is no magical recipe for success that is known only to a few select coaches at the top of the ladder. You already hold the keys to success or failure in your head and hands; this chapter is intended to help you unlock the doors that would delay or deny your quest to reach your goals in coaching.

WHAT YOU NEED TO BUILD A SUCCESSFUL PROGRAM

If we're talking here only about short-term success, all you really need are four things: enough skilled players to win as often as you and your supporters will be satisfied with; the motivational skills to keep your players playing as a team; daily practices that are sufficiently rigorous to get your players in shape and keep them that way; and a game plan that will allow them to use their skills to maximum benefit. Anything more than that is overcoaching.

3

If we're talking about the sort of long-term success that will carry on when your current players are gone, however—well, the list of prerequisites is brief but, for the most part, vastly more difficult and time-consuming to satisfy. Those prerequisites are:

1. a vision of what your program can become, and a plan for accomplishing it

2. an effective feeder program

3. community support and administrative backing.

> *Where there is no vision, the people perish.*
>
> —Proverbs 29:18

> *Our plans miscarry because they have no aim. When a man does not know what harbor he is making for, no wind is the right wind.*
>
> —Seneca, a Roman statesman
> c 4 B.C. – A.D. 65

A Vision of What Your Program Can Become, and a Plan for Accomplishing It

There are two kinds of goals, *short range:* (i.e., day-to-day, weekly, monthly, a season) and *long range* (i.e., several seasons or a career). What you do on a short-term basis should relate directly to what you hope to accomplish on a long-term basis, or else the effort is wasted. But what do long-range goals relate to? They relate to the dreams or visions of accomplishment that everyone brings to his or her particular coaching situation.

Because they are long range, such visions may be grand (winning a state championship), or even grandiose (gaining national rankings or prominence), as long as they are not stated as specific goals to be achieved within a specific time frame such as "winning a state championship—*this year!*" When you pinpoint a specific time for a specific achievement, it ceases to be a vision and becomes a promise to be kept, and anything less than total success is likely to be perceived as failure.

Whether your dreams of great achievement are realistic is immaterial; the important thing is to have a dream and the desire to share and accomplish it with others. The "sharing" part is what we call *recruiting,* or *selling your program;* the "accomplishing" part is what we normally think of as *coaching.*

If everyone has such dreams, one might ask, what makes *me* so special? Why should I expect to be successful when there are so many other coaches out there who have their own visions of greatness?

To answer that question, let's turn it around: Why should you *not* expect to be successful? What could possibly hold you back? A lack of talented players? That could be true on a short-term basis, but as your program expands over several soccer seasons, you should be able to bring more and more athletically gifted youngsters into your program. (If you can't, either you aren't doing your job properly or you need to find somewhere else to coach.) Could a lack of (a) coaching experience, (b) understanding of the game, or (c) teaching skills hold you back? No, because all of those shortcomings can be overcome through hard work, the desire to improve yourself, and willingness to learn from your mistakes.

The only real limits on your potential for success in coaching are those you impose on yourself; they are, in fact, some of the same reasons that many players never achieve their potential: laziness; lack of commitment; unreasonable expectations of instant success without having devoted sufficient time and effort to mastering essential skills; and unwillingness to accept the conditions or roles upon which coaching is based.

If you possess an uncompromising work ethic, uncompromising commitment to your dream, and willingness to learn and to immerse yourself in the time-consuming task of becoming the best coach you can be, you *will* be successful—albeit not necessarily today, tomorrow, or next week. Henry David Thoreau put it nicely:

> If one advances confidently in the direction of his dreams, and endeavors to live the life he has imagined, he will meet with a success unexpected in common hours.

The same applies to women coaches, of course.

Don't expect it to be easy; it won't be. If you start out expecting coaching to be the most difficult task you've ever undertaken, you probably won't be disappointed—but you'll also be prepared to withstand the pressures of the task that lies before you. You start with a dream, or a vision of what can be accomplished by people working together. If you cling to that dream and cherish it, it will carry you through whatever hard times you encounter. But that's only part of the story.

You also need a plan for accomplishing your dream. Like skyscrapers, successful athletic programs aren't built by guesswork, but rather from blueprints that start at the ground level and work up.

Building a Feeder Program

If you're a high school varsity soccer coach, you'd probably prefer not to wait until their sophomore year to start teaching youngsters how to play soccer. Children must be brought into soccer as early as possible, not just to teach them how to play the game but also to avoid losing them to other sports or activities.

Our school has girls' and boys' B-team and varsity soccer at the high school level; by the time those players get to us most of them have extensive playing experience via our local soccer club. We have a strong high school soccer booster club, and we receive excellent backing from the business community. Many of our players play soccer year-round, including varsity soccer in the spring, club soccer in the late spring and fall, indoor soccer in the winter, and at camps in the summer. Nearly two dozen of our ex-players have received college scholarships, and some present and past players have been involved with top classic-level teams and the Olympic Development Program. Our club teams have won state championships, and our varsity boys have, at writing, finished second in the state and achieved national rankings in each of the past two years.

We say all this, not boastfully or to show you how "expert" we've become as coaches—as someone sagely observed, an "ex" is a has-been and a "spurt" is a drip that fizzled—but to show you how very far we've come since the early days of our coaching when *soccer* was a four-letter word in the United States.

Starting from Scratch: A Case Study in Persistence

We started out in coaching in 1977 with dreams of greatness—not in soccer coaching but in basketball. When our goal of moving up the ladder from B-team to the varsity level was eventually thwarted, however, and the possibility of starting a varsity boys' soccer team arose in 1984, we took the job with more than minor misgivings. After all, we were coaching in Georgia, where high school football reigns supreme, and what we knew about soccer could have been compressed into two or three sentences.

The local rec soccer program at the time was minimal, and participation was sparse, which meant that most of the kids coming to us would know as little about soccer as we did. We knew that catching up with the established soccer programs in our region would be a major undertaking. We considered writing the entire Brazilian national team, including Pele, to ask if any of them still had any high school eligibility left.

We read books and watched soccer films, talked endlessly with established coaches, borrowing their ideas and learning as much as we could about the game from them, and enlisted the assistance of a few locals who understood what the game was all about. Still, many of the first drills we used in our daily practices were basketball drills adapted for soccer. The year wasn't a total failure, though, since our previous coaching experience had taught us the need for organization and discipline. Too, we were blessed with players who, despite their inexperience, were hard workers and eager to learn. You can do anything with kids like that—anything, that is, except win the majority of your games. We were 2-8-1 in our first year of coaching soccer, and tied for last in our regional division. Those two wins and a tie were due to the fact that we weren't the only coaches in our region who were building a program from the ground up. To us, though, those three non-losses were solid gold.

There are many lessons to be learned from losing—not the least of which is that, with more and better players, you won't lose so often. Dynasties are built from the ground up, with young athletes-to-be entering the program early, rising through the program, and learning as they go—eventually to replace the current players, who have made their coaches look like budding geniuses or blooming idiots.

In our case, the local recreation soccer program had three leagues—PeeWee (ages 6-9), Junior (10-12), and Senior (13-16). There were no soccer fields in the county, so games were played on narrow rec league football fields. Originally, there were two soccer seasons, fall and spring, but the spring season had been dropped due to low participation and fear that it would interfere with the rec baseball program. Since rec league rules required that everyone play at least half of each game, coaching strategy consisted largely of pitting your 9-year-olds against the opponents' 6-year-olds at the PeeWee level, playing what we called "running kickball" at the Junior level, and playing a rugby-like, physical game with lots of body contact but little or no physical skills or team tactics at the Senior level. The coaches, almost all of whom were players' parents, knew nothing at all about soccer but understood football very well. We knew that, to build an effective feeder system, we would have to become intimately involved in every phase of local soccer at this formative stage.

Through determined efforts by a few local—and vocal—soccer supporters, we managed to persuade the local rec authorities to realign the youth soccer association program in ways that benefited the kids (e.g., Muppet Soccer for ages 5-6 with simplified rules, no winning and losing, fewer than seven players a side and coaches allowed on the field to instruct them; and Under 10, Under 12, Under 14, Under 16, and Under 19 leagues for older players).

Our influence within the GYSA grew as youth participation expanded, and we and our growing list of supporters were elected to its presidency and other offices. Eventually, the recreation department allowed us to take over the rec soccer program entirely when it became evident that we knew what it took to build a strong program in soccer and they didn't. They were, after all, recreation specialists, not soccer specialists. Two large land tracts were purchased for the construction of several soccer fields of various sizes, and we expanded our newly formed soccer club program to two levels, *recreational* (for the majority of youths who simply were interested in playing the game) and *club* (for the best among those players who sought the challenge of taking their game to higher levels of competition). Our 1990 Under 12 Excel Premier team became the first local soccer team to win a state title for our school.

Now, all that may not seem like much as you're reading this, but for us it was a mountain range of obstacles to be overcome when we were living it on a daily basis over a period of several years. It was—and we're not exaggerating here—virtually the equivalent of holding down three full-time jobs: teaching a full load of physical education classes, coaching our varsity teams, and training the club teams from which our future varsity teams would be stocked. During that formative period we also organized a volunteer coaches' association to teach the coaches how to coach soccer, and a soccer referees' association to ensure that games were being officiated by qualified, licensed officials.

Was it hard work? Unless you've lived through this sort of experience, you have no idea. Sometimes, in looking back on those early years, we wonder where we found the time to do all we did. But it's like everything else in life: *If it's really important to you, you'll find the time to do it.* Was it frustrating? Constantly. And most important, Was it worth it? Well, you tell us: *How much time and energy would you spend on building a comprehensive feeder program if you thought it might lead to your varsity teams' reaching the state playoffs in nine of the last ten years?*

Believe us, if there had been an easier way, we'd have taken it. But since we weren't blessed with the sort of coaching genius that instantly transforms ordinary players into Supermen and Superwomen, we opted for the next best thing, namely, taking matters one day at a time and focusing on what could be done *today* to improve our program in some small way. There were setbacks aplenty along the way, and delays that made it seem as if our program would never move into high gear—but because we knew what we wanted to accomplish and refused to admit that it couldn't be done, we eventually saw our goals being achieved, one by one.

And so it will be with you—success achieved partly by inspiration, but mostly by perspiration.

COMING TO GRIPS WITH YOUR PROGRAM

You may not be facing the sort of bleak prospects for success that we encountered in building our program from the ground up; let's hope not, anyway. But if you *do* face a long uphill struggle to establish your program, consider some of the specific areas of improvement that may require attention.

Expanding Participation

This is nothing more than plain, old-fashioned public relations. (Be advised, though, that *participation* refers to parents as well as children.)

When we started out coaching soccer, only 62 children in a community of 20,000 people were playing soccer. We enlisted the support of the parents and grandparents of those youngsters, and relied heavily on them to spread the word in the community regarding our vision of what an expanded soccer program would mean to everyone in our community. In a very real sense, we "sold" our vision to those parents, and to everyone else who would listen to us. We spoke at club gatherings, civic luncheons, PTA meetings, recreation meetings, board of education meetings, and elsewhere. We formed a soccer booster club at the high school, and solicited the influence of those parents in attempting to expand our influence downward through the feeder program at both the school and recreational soccer levels. We arranged to be interviewed by local radio and newspaper staff, and solicited their expanded coverage of *all* soccer in the community.

In short, we felt then (as we do now) that the strength and effectiveness of Dr. Martin Luther King's "I have a dream" speech lay as much in his desire and eagerness to proclaim that dream as in the message itself. Having a dream is critically important—but the importance of delivering your message to the people who matter cannot be overlooked.

Participation in recreational soccer gradually increased as parents and players alike spread the word to other parents and children that *Hey, soccer is fun! You ought to try it out!*

We now have about 800 children involved in girls' and boys' recreational and club soccer. Through their growing and continued participation they permit us to keep our varsity teams stocked with youngsters who are ready to play and eager to learn.

Improving the Local Soccer Facilities

This is at heart a financial problem that may not concern you, if the powers that be in your community have already (a) realized that *soccer games should be played on soccer fields* and (b) provided special recreational facilities just for soccer. Still, if yours is not one of those fortunate situations, don't despair. All is not lost. Your goal should be, as in all problem areas, *to do the best you can with what you have while laying a groundwork for future improvements.*

If you've been a soccer coach for longer than it takes to read this sentence, you're aware that football fields don't make good soccer fields; they're too narrow, and in many cases too short as well. If that's all you have, make the best of it and try to overlook the constant throw-ins that delay the action. When enough supporters, fans, and parents get tired of the constant interruptions in play to join their voices in protest, they'll enlist the support of local politicians and the school board in funding needed changes. Just remember: Unless you were born and raised in that community and know its people intimately, you probably don't have the sort of political clout to wage those protests by yourself. You need well-placed local connections to speak for you; enlisting those connections as soccer supporters should rank at the top of your priority list.

Training Coaches and Officials

Since (in our experience, anyway) many coaches at the rec league level don't know much about soccer, it behooves someone—guess who, if you're the varsity head coach?—to teach them how the game is played, coached, and officiated. Don't expect the recreation department personnel to do it—or if they *do*, don't expect them to do it well. Work with them; in 99 percent of the cases they'll be glad for your participation and assistance in this manner.

Having organized our soccer club, we made it mandatory for all participating coaches to attend our coaching seminars. You may not have that sort of clout initially, but even so, you should offer coaching seminars covering such topics as rules, playing procedures, basic skills, teaching and coaching tips, practice drills, and so on. The more handouts you give the coaches, the more they will benefit from your seminars.

One of the greatest benefits to be derived from doing coaching seminars in your feeder program is that the coaches who know little or nothing about soccer will learn the game the way *you* want them to learn it, as will the players who play for them. The implications of that statement are far-reaching. Just think: If every coach in your feeder program is using the same playing system and drills that your varsity team uses (with modifications, of course), by the time their players reach varsity age *they'll understand your system so well that you can concentrate on fine-tuning rather than starting from scratch*. The time saved will be enormous, and will free you to work on other aspects of your team preparation.

This is, in fact, the approach used by the legendary football coach Wright Bazemore of Valdosta (GA) High School. Every rec team in his county played football the Valdosta Wildcats way. By the time a youngster reached high school, he was almost as familiar with Bazemore's system as the assistant coaches were. The result was thirteen state championships for Valdosta under Bazemore and a career winning percentage upward of 90 percent for the coach. Do you suppose he'd say it's worth it for you to treat the local rec soccer program as part of your extended family?

We assume that there are other teams in your feeder system (i.e., middle school, junior high, and B-team or junior varsity). We'll address that aspect of program development shortly, but for now we'll note that, if your working relationship with those coaches is good, you can enlist their aid in conducting your seminars for the rec league coaches. And if your school feeder program is underdeveloped, you may be able to persuade one or more knowledgeable ex-players in the community to help you.

It's no exaggeration to say that *the quality of your recreational and club soccer will be no better than the officiating it receives*. If you're serious about your feeder program, you must ensure that games are officiated by qualified, certified personnel who understand the game and its rules. The easiest way to accomplish this is to become a certified referee instructor yourself in order to certify the game officials who call your club and rec games. Regardless, you and your supporters should lobby for certified officiating in all matches.

Finally, because fans must be educated, too, you may want to extend an invitation to everyone in the community to attend your rules seminars, if for no other reason than to clarify the offside rule.

Gaining State Affiliation and Acquiring a Club Format

If you are to develop a superior recreational feeder program, your best players need higher levels of competition than they get in regular rec league play. This means forming traveling teams to play other superior teams in your area and around the state; that in turn entails adopting a club format that offers dual levels of competition, and state affiliation that offers access to top-level competition in other areas.

In our state, the Georgia State Soccer Association encompasses three levels of competition: *recreational, premier,* and *classic,* the latter two of which correspond roughly to traveling all-star teams. In our case, our soccer club offers recreational soccer for the masses of young soccer enthusiasts and the Excel teams play premier and classic schedules. Such a format is obviously more expensive than simply lumping all of your players into one rec league format, but the experiences to be gained at the higher competitive levels cannot be duplicated at the recreational level. Club-level play is important to the overall soccer program in your community for the same reason that the Olympic Development Program is important to the United States Soccer Federation.

If your community already has a local soccer club, work within that club by helping to coach and train teams. In addition to developing the players who eventually will make up your varsity teams, your presence and involvement will show the coaches, players, and parents that your interest in them is genuine. It's a selling point for your varsity program that you can't afford to overlook.

If you don't have a local soccer club, start one. Your state association can give you guidelines for starting a local club. You'll need local support to start a club, but look at it this way: If there weren't at least a ground swell of support for soccer in your community, there wouldn't *be* a varsity soccer team for you to coach.

Upgrading Girls' and Women's Soccer

If men's soccer has been slow in catching on in the United States, its growth has been a rapid blur compared to that of women's soccer, which—Title IX notwithstanding—has progressed at a snail's pace, especially at the high school level. Some of the reasons given for excluding girls' soccer from high school athletic programs are as follows (with our responses in parentheses):

"We can't afford it. It's not a revenue-producing sport." (Neither is golf or wrestling—two predominantly male sports at the high school level.)

"There's no interest in girls' soccer in our school. We don't have enough girls who want to play to field a team." *(Build it [a girls' soccer program], and they will come* —"they" being players to fill the squad and spectators to fill the seats when a successful program is established. When we began coaching varsity boys' soccer in 1984, we had only about ten to fifteen spectators in the stands for our home games; now, we average between 1,000 and 1,200 paid admissions per home game. Give your soccer fans a quality program and your varsity teams a decent place to play, and you won't have to worry about player or fan interest, or about girls' or boys' soccer being a drain on the athletic department's budget.)

"We're saving the open P.E. teaching slot for a football coach." (If all you want is football coaches who teach P.E., who is monitoring your girls' P.E. locker rooms?)

There are at least four excellent reasons why a coach should support girls' soccer, and possibly even consider coaching a girls' soccer team:

1. *Soccer is soccer,* whether it be girls or boys playing it. Soccer enthusiasts always need to support each other because unity lends strength to their common cause—promoting the game. As Benjamin Franklin noted at the signing of the Declaration of Independence, "We must all hang together, or assuredly we shall all hang separately."

2. *Supporters are supporters;* having a girls' varsity soccer team will bring new supporters into the soccer booster club.

3. *Many of the high school girls who play soccer have younger brothers and sisters who may become involved in the game because of the older sister's interest.* The same is true of boys, of course, but having boys' *and* girls' teams in your school will impact more households in your community.

4. *It may be easier to build a competitive team and strong program in girls' soccer than in boys' soccer.* Unless yours is one of the only schools in your area that doesn't have an established girls' soccer program, you may not have as far to go to catch up with or surpass the other schools in your area that play girls' soccer. In our case, for example, most of the schools in our region had had varsity boys' soccer teams for seven years when we fielded our first varsity team in 1984; we were *seven years* behind the rest of the pack coming out of the gate.

Exceptions exist, of course, but in many areas, girls' soccer is still in its formative stages, and the disparity in experience and skills may not be so great as to require seven years of relentless toil to catch up with everyone else. We say that, not disparagingly or condescendingly of the girls' game, since we've always been strong advocates of *all* girls' sports, but to point out that, if you're looking for a possible shortcut to success in coaching, this may be it. The work will still be difficult and time-consuming, of course, since that's the nature of coaching; still, it may not take you nearly as long to build a competitive girls' program as it took us to build a successful boys' program from scratch.

Extending Your School Feeder Program Downward

We have a B-team girls' and boys' soccer program at our school, but no teams at the middle school or junior high levels; still, there are several reasons why it's not terribly important to us to extend our program downward within the schools. First, and most important, we've painstakingly developed a very effective local club soccer program, with premier and classic teams training our future varsity stars. Since those teams play traveling schedules, the schools are relieved of those and other related expenses (e.g., uniforms and equipment) that school teams would incur. The school system doesn't have to hire soccer coaches at those levels, and we don't have to train them or persuade them to use our system, drills, and so forth. Instead, we coach the club teams and develop players who will get their first taste of school soccer at the B-team level. This approach has worked very well for us, and we do not hesitate to recommend it to any coach who is developing a varsity program.

If you have a school feeder program that extends below B-team level, you should work closely with those coaches to facilitate their efforts to field winning teams. The more closely you are involved with their teams, the greater the eventual dividends for your varsity teams. You can and should attend their matches whenever possible; hold coaching seminars for them; give them full access to the books and instructional videotapes in your personal coaching library; talk with them at least once or twice a week regarding their teams' progress, problems they may be encountering, or simply maintaining professional and social ties that let them know that what they are doing is important to you; give them copies of your daily practice schedules to use as a basis for their own practice sessions, if you and they so desire; speak at their banquets and invite them to your own banquets; and generally make yourself available to help them in any way possible, on the grounds that whatever you do for them will be amply repaid with their loyalty to you and your program.

Seeking Administrative Backing and Community Support

As we've noted in other books, the coach *is* the team and the program, at least in the early stages of their development. While many people are ultimately responsible for the success of a team or program, it is the coach's vision and plan that shapes their destiny. Others can share your vision and support your plan, but they should not and cannot be permitted to direct your program except in broad terms (i.e., the sort of administrative guidelines to which all school athletic teams are expected to adhere). After all, it's your neck, and not theirs, on the chopping block if your team and program consistently fail to achieve what other people expect them to.

There are three keys to working with your administrative superiors (e.g., the principal and athletic director). First, there is *communication*—telling them exactly what you plan to do and what you'll need to do it. You can start by distinguishing in your own mind between what you *need* for your program and what you *want*. Second, there is *give-and-take*—your willingness to compromise as necessary on a short-term basis in order to achieve long-range goals. (Remember, though, that compromise has its limits: If you compromise away the basic principles you believe in, you're selling your soul, not your program.) And third, there is *patience*. Since even with full administrative support you aren't going to solve all of the problems associated with program building right away, it follows that patience is tremendously important, especially in dealing with administrators who may offer less than total support for your efforts to build a strong soccer program.

Administrators view sports differently than do coaches; this is true even of administrators who were—or are—head coaches. It's a matter of priorities: While coaches tend to think primarily of winning games, administrators tend to regard winning as nice but secondary in importance to getting the bills paid. What this means for you is that, if your soccer program isn't yet a high priority in your athletic department's pecking order, you should prioritize your needs and focus on the most important ones, setting aside the others until such time as your program becomes a high priority (or else seek alternative sources of funding for your other priority items).

Example: A new coach came into a school and, at the first budget meeting held in the athletic director's office, requested that shoulder bags be purchased for his players. "What for?" the athletic director asked. "They already have shoulder bags, and they haven't won a soccer game in two years." The coach fidgeted in his chair. "Well, I just think it would be a good way of showing the players that we haven't lost faith in them," he said. The a. d. shook his head. "We don't reward our athletes for losing games. Win a few games this year and we'll talk about it next year." If we'd been there, we could have told the coach that those shoulder bags were a lost cause, at least for the present. He'd have been better off talking to the president of the soccer booster club or seeking a sponsorship from a local merchant, if indeed shoulder bags were high on his list of priorities.

Example: "I coached soccer at my high school for *five years* before my varsity boys were allowed to use the football stadium for our home games," the coach told us. "Before then, we played our home games on a seventh-grade P.E. field or a local recreation softball field. I used to say that we always had standing-room-only crowds at home, because those fields didn't have any bleachers."

Why didn't you look for another coaching job somewhere else? we asked.

"Because I knew I could build a good program there," he replied. "We had good kids; they just weren't very good soccer players at the time. But I knew things would change sooner or later, and I wanted to be there when they did.

"When we entered the football stadium for the first time, we felt like we were treading on holy ground. And then we lost the game, 6-2. I just knew the athletic director, who was also the football head coach, was gonna send us back to the softball field, but he didn't. By then, though, we had enough support for our program that he probably couldn't have."

Our conversation with that coach highlighted a crucial question in program building: Assuming that you have within yourself what it takes to build a successful program (i.e., a vision, a plan, and willingness to work as long and hard as necessary to achieve your goals), *when do you accept the harsh realities of a really bad situation and take your coaching elsewhere in search of happier surroundings?*

There is no pat answer to that question, but we think the coach's statement, "I knew I could build a good program there," says a lot. Frustrations and temporary failures of one kind or another will follow you wherever you go in coaching because, like you, the people you're dealing with are only human. The time to look for greener coaching pastures is when you see no evidence of current progress where you are and no potential for future progress in terms of administrative, or player, parent, and community support for your program. If neither of those areas offers hope for improvement despite your best efforts, you're wasting your time and coaching talents at that school.

Of the two, we think player, parental, and community support is more critical to your success than administrative support. Not to minimize the need for administrative support, but we've known many soccer coaches at the high school level who have persevered and achieved success despite administrative relationships ranging from lukewarm to antagonistic or hostile toward soccer. In every such case that we know of, it was the players, their parents, grandparents, boosters, and others in the community whose loyalty and enthusiastic support at the high school level made staying worthwhile.

Developing a Soccer Booster Club

Ideally, your soccer boosters are not part of a general booster club that supports all of the athletic teams in your school. It's a matter of simple economics and effort: The farther removed from your control the money is, the lower the percentage of it your team will receive; and if you and your soccer supporters are adept at fund-raising (as you should be), you'll be raising money for teams other than your own if the proceeds go into one large pot, to be divided among all of the teams according to whatever formula exists.

Of course, those points may be moot if your school or athletic policies rule out separate booster clubs; if that's the case, work within the system while you're gaining support to change the system. It's not easy to do, especially in a small school where support is likely to be fragmented (e.g., by parents' having children involved in several sports). It's difficult in larger schools, too, but having a booster club for your soccer team offers advantages that are too great to be overlooked, and should figure prominently in your long-range plans.

The most obvious function of a booster club is raising money—in our case, about $7,000 to $10,000 per year for our high school soccer teams. Our boosters produce (and sell advertising for) our soccer game programs, which generate annual profits of up to $3,000 for our teams. But boosters are—or should be—much more than fund-raisers. Boosters can be used to run concession stands, sell tickets, host team cookouts or postgame meals, help to organize awards banquets and the like—and, perhaps most important of all, boosters can serve as a vital link between your program and contacts in the business community who can provide other services for your team and program.

What boosters cannot do—should not be permitted to do—is make coaching decisions or run your program. The same caveat applies to principals, athletic directors, or boosters: If you let them run your program, eventually they'll run you out of your program.

Seeking Sponsorships

One of the biggest advantages of having a booster club is that if, like most schools, your high school places limits on how many fund-raisers per year a team can have, the boosters can circumvent the process by doing things like selling sponsorships. Our soccer boosters are not at all shy about asking local businesses for sponsorship dollars to purchase new uniforms or warmups, or services such as free team and individual photos for our game programs. In return, we hang their banners around our stadium for home games and, in the case of warmups, traveling bags, and so on, we let them have their business logo affixed. (Regarding the latter, check with your a. d. and principal before doing this, since your school system may have rules restricting or prohibiting advertising in such a manner. The worst they can say is no. They shouldn't complain, though, since you're relieving the athletic department of the cost of those items by having them purchased independently.)[1]

With athletic expenses rising with every passing year, you and your boosters or supporters should apply yourselves rigorously to an in-depth exploration of business sponsorships in your community. You aren't likely to be permitted to rename your team the "Davis Funeral Home High School Soccer Team" to satisfy a sponsor—but you'll be surprised at what you can do with a determined effort toward securing sponsorships! We know of one coach who, when he needed a soccer field house for his varsity team, persuaded a local home builder to donate the materials, equipment, and labor to build it *at no cost to the school*, by promising to name the facility for the builder and his wife. You may not be so fortunate—but then again, you might. You'll never know unless you ask.

Gaining the Support of Medical Personnel

Most high schools enlist the assistance of a local physician to administer player physical examinations and attend home games as well. If your team is covered in this respect, so much the better; if not, talk to the parents, boosters, and supporters about which, if any, local physicians are ex-soccer players. That was the route we took, and it worked splendidly for us.

---

[1] In our state, school teams are permitted to put one business logo no larger than 2″ × 3″ on one sleeve of the players' jerseys as a means of rewarding a local business or industry for its financial support without the advertising overkill of, say, a NASCAR driver's racing gear.

Virtually all ex-athletes retain a measure of affection for their sport that lasts far beyond their playing days; possibly because soccer has for so long been regarded as an alien presence in the United States by the masses of sports fans who follow football, basketball, and baseball with almost religious fervor, ex-soccer players tend to be very concerned about the future of their sport and eager to promote its progress. Our team trainer, a physical therapist and ex-soccer player who is still passionately devoted to the game, has attended all of our home and away games for the past twelve years; he and his staff offer free rehab treatment for injured players throughout the year. Our team chiropractor, another ex-player, donates his services free to our players on a year-round basis because he respects our commitment to the sport he loves. Our team physician is the father of one of our varsity players.

Courting Media Coverage

No matter how successful your program becomes, you'll never outgrow the need for comprehensive media coverage on a continuing basis. The best way to attract the attention of the local media is to win so much that they cannot possibly overlook your team; unfortunately, this is possible only when your team is capable of winning consistently. Still, there are other ways to cultivate positive media coverage while you're building your team and program. One way is to understand the needs of the various media and place yourself at their disposal *when they need you*. Sports writers and reporters work on tight deadlines; you can enhance your status with them by endeavoring to make their jobs as easy as possible (e.g., by not being late for interviews, and by granting them access to your daily practices and your players; providing game summaries, stat sheets, and updated player profiles for them to use or keep on file; and alerting them to upcoming games and newsworthy team events and activities). You can invite the media to attend your pre- or in-season cookouts and your post-season awards banquets—or, better still, invite them to speak at your banquets. You can award an annual "Soccer Media Award" to deserving sportswriters or reporters. And if your local coverage is less extensive than you think it ought to be, you can and should wage an ongoing, positive campaign for increased coverage without resorting to constant complaining or griping. Media representatives don't like whiners any more than referees do.

In some cases, there may not be any soccer coverage to speak of in the local media; if that's the case, you can perform the task yourself by writing your own articles for the local newspaper or preparing weekly audiocassettes or videotapes for local radio or television use. Such an approach, although time-consuming, has the added advantage of always casting your team in a highly favorable light. If you lack the time or technical skills to perform those tasks yourself, you may be able to enlist the assistance of faculty members or students to help you. (If you do, be sure to recognize and reward their work for you and the team at your awards banquet.)

In considering media coverage, remember that your school newspaper can be a valuable recruiting tool, since it is read by the same people you're trying to recruit for your varsity teams. We know of one coach a number of years ago who, because his high school didn't have a school newspaper, started one himself and served as faculty advisor in order to ensure that his soccer program received coverage throughout the school year.

If all of the tasks and responsibilities in this section appear somewhat daunting or overwhelming, it is because building a successful soccer program is an all-encompassing,

365-days-a-year job. You'll get out of your coaching precisely what you put into it—no more, and certainly no less. The amount of work you have to do by yourself is likely to be prodigious initially, but it will decrease as your program grows and more and more people want to become involved in it.

The single factor that most clearly separates the coaches who eventually will be successful in their coaching from those who will fall by the wayside is willingness to assume as many essential tasks and responsibilities as necessary to promote program growth. At this point, we suggest that you go back and reread the introductory section on successful programs, which by now should hold new meaning for you in terms of how you approach your coaching and what you hope to achieve. Then, go on to read the rest of this chapter to find out what personal and professional qualities will be most instrumental in your quest to become, not necessarily the greatest soccer coach in history, but the very best coach you can be. That is, after all, what successful coaching is all about.

TEN QUALITIES YOU NEED TO BE A SUCCESSFUL COACH

1. Leadership Ability

Leadership begins with a delightfully simple either/or proposition: Either a program—or a team within a program—will improve, however slowly, or else it will stagnate and go downhill. Which way it goes will be determined by the amount and quality of leadership the team or program receives from the person responsible for its progress.

It's always nice to have effective team leadership from players who are willing to exert a positive influence on their teammates; still, regardless of whether such players can be found on the team, it's also important for everyone concerned to understand that *leadership begins with the coach*.

Leadership is achieved and maintained through a combination of *communication* and *motivation*. Taking them in reverse order, motivation consists of finding ways to persuade young athletes to do to the best of their ability those things that they need to be doing, and communication consists of finding ways to ensure that your players understand what you want them to know or to do. For now, we'll point out that, like public speaking, the ability to communicate, motivate, and lead others is a learned trait, not a God-given talent.

There's nothing wrong with making mistakes while trying to communicate and motivate; serious problems arise only if you assume that ongoing motivation and communication are unnecessary.

2. An Organized Approach to Your Coaching

Coaching is, in a very real sense, problem solving. You have to be organized to identify your problem areas with any precision, and you have to be organized to solve them. Two keys to solving your problems, then, are devoting time to studying them objectively, and writing down everything that's important so you won't forget it.

Consider: If *you* spend your free time thinking about your coaching problems and how to solve them and *we* spend our free time playing golf or tennis, which of us is more likely to solve our problems?

Or consider: If *you* take time to prepare daily practice schedules outlining precisely what you hope to accomplish and *we* play it by ear and (a) do whatever occurs to us spontaneously or (b) scrimmage throughout every practice session because "we're just not organized," which of us is more likely to solve our problems and teach our players what they need to know?

Organization is a form of motivation; it gives structure and meaning to your daily practices, and serves as a daily reminder to your players that what they're doing is part of a plan designed to make your team and your program successful.

3. The Ability and Desire to Teach

Unless you're foolish enough to assume that players will learn to execute ballhandling, dribbling, passing, receiving, shooting, and defensive skills on their own without being taught, you'll want to apply yourself rigorously to the task of teaching skills and correcting mistakes.

Regardless of the age or experiential level you're coaching at, you should function under the twin principles that *the need for learning is universal and constant*, and *when you stop learning, you stop improving*. The same applies to teaching, of course.

Chapter 5 offers a brief look at certain principles of effective teaching, and presents an abundance of tips and progressions for teaching the basic skills of soccer.

4. An Understanding of the Game and How It's Played

You don't have to be the World's Greatest Authority on soccer to coach the game effectively—but you do have to develop a basic and consistent philosophy of how it should be played. And it's undeniably true that *the more you know about the game, its rules, fundamental skills, systems of play, and strategies, the better coach you're likely to be*. Chapter 4 outlines the basics of the game, its rules and playing procedures, and Chapters 7 and 8 investigate the various playing systems and stragegies associated with soccer.

5. Open-mindedness

There are two ways to approach the task of organizing your team offense and defense. One way is to choose a playing style and fit your players into it; the other is to choose a playing style that fits your players. The difference between the two approaches is broader than it may appear at first glance.

The former, fitting your players into a given style of play, is most likely to be beneficial (a) when your players are highly skilled, experienced, and versatile enough to make it work for them, or (b) when you have been at your school long enough to develop a feeder program in which players at lower levels already understand your system by the time they reach the varsity level. It is least likely to be beneficial when it's the only style of play that the coach understands, since it may fail to take into account team or individual weaknesses that will hinder its effectiveness.

The latter approach to organizing a team offense and defense—adapting a style of play to the players and their skills—is especially important with teams and players of limited skills or experience. Try as you might, you won't fit size 18 feet into size 7-1/2 shoes; getting unskilled players to master a complicated playing style that exceeds their abilities is equally useless.

Open-mindedness refers to a coach's—or a player's—willingness to learn. In the coach's case, that can mean, among other things, learning about new or different playing styles and systems in order to ensure compatibility between players and playing styles, or finding new drills to challenge your players and keep daily practices from becoming stale. As more than one coach has noted, it's what you learn *after* you know it all that counts.

6. A Love for the Game and Coaching

The writer James M. Barrie had a lovely notion that fits coaching nicely: "It's not work unless you'd rather be doing something else." Striving for excellence in your coaching is a given if you want to be successful—but building a team or program from the ground up, or turning around a losing program, is a challenge that will demand every ounce of dedication you can summon if you hope to survive the experience to fight another day. We know; we've been there. While the experience was invaluable in terms of what we learned about handling teams, it was also incredibly demanding and frustrating. Without a deeply ingrained love for the game and coaching, a coach is unlikely to survive for more than a couple of years after he or she discovers that the road to glory is actually a mountain to be climbed.

7. Determination

We've said it before, and we'll say it again: *We're glad that coaching isn't easy;* if it were, laziness would be a virtue and you couldn't hope to catch up with or surpass other teams or programs by outworking them.

We're not geniuses—far from it. Building a soccer program from scratch took *five long years* before we had our first winning season. At any time during that period, it would have been easy for us to throw in the towel and admit that we weren't up to the task of building a winning program at the school. It is *not fun* being a doormat for the teams you play.

Now, however, having finished second in the state two years running and having been rated as high as seventh in the nation by *USA Today* in the process, we see coaches in our region starting new programs of their own; having been there ourselves and knowing the hardships they face, we wonder: Will they have the determination to carry them through the building process? Or will they, like those coaches who enter the profession expecting primrose paths rather than rock gardens, quietly fade from the scene—not with a bang but a whimper?

We suspect that determination ultimately derives from a fear of failure. And since you aren't a failure until you admit that you are, it follows that the difference between successful and unsuccessful coaches lies in the former's absolute refusal to accept defeats or obstacles as anything but temporary deterrents on the road to success.

We can't give you determination—that virtue comes from *within*, not from without—but we can tell you that, if you are determined to succeed in your coaching regardless of the price to be paid, you *will* be successful.

8. Patience

TV quiz show host Monty Hall once said that it took him twenty years to become an overnight success. We know what he meant. In the past few months, a number of young coaches have asked us how we built our program; it was the same question *we* asked the successful veteran coaches in our area when we were starting out. And our reply has been the same one we received, way back when: "The same way *you're* going to build your program. Slowly. And with patience."

Don't misunderstand us; patience doesn't mean accepting one's situation as hopeless or irreversible; it simply refers to accepting that you and the people around you are doing the best you can under the circumstances, if that is in fact the case.

Patience is especially important in teaching skills. Inexperienced players usually are blown away the first time we show them Franz von Balkom's ballhandling tape (see Appendix A), never having suspected that soccer involved such complex and intricate footwork patterns. They are highly skeptical when we tell them, "*That's* what you're going to learn to do," until later, on the practice field, we explain that they won't be expected to learn it all at once. "*Here's* what you're going to learn today," we say, and we proceed to take a single footwork skill and break it down into manageable segments for concentrated drill and practice.

Patience is a virtue; however, it does not follow that impatience is always undesirable. We have little or no patience with players who don't want to *listen*, to *learn*, or to *practice* the skills they must master in order to become effective soccer players. And we have no patience at all with players who habitually miss daily practices or arrive late for practice, forget their uniforms or equipment, violate team rules, expect special treatment above and beyond that afforded their teammates, or are disloyal to their coaches or teammates. Life is too short, and our practice time too valuable, to be wasted on players who simply don't care what the team is trying to accomplish.

9. A Sense of "Fun"

The coach's initial address to his boys' varsity team seldom varies by more than a few words: "I don't know whether you know it or not," he tells them, "but I'm stark, raving crazy. And if you're not crazy, too, you won't make it on this team, because we're *all* crazy." The newest and youngest players glance uneasily around the room at their teammates, several of whom are nodding in agreement, and they wonder: *What have I gotten myself into?*

"That's right, *you're* crazy, too," the coach goes on. "You'd have to be crazy to be willing to spend 2-1/2 hours every day, rain or shine, running marathons up and down a soccer field and sweating like a pig when you could be flipping burgers at Hamburger Heaven to pay for the gas, insurance, and monthly payments on a flashy set of wheels to impress the women." (Laughter. It's an old, familiar line to the veterans, but it's always good for a laugh.)

"Okay, we're crazy," he says, "but that doesn't mean we have to be miserable, too. We're gonna work so hard this year that your sweat glands are gonna dry up—well, maybe not *quite* that hard, but that's the kind of effort it's gonna take for us to be the kind of team we know we can be. But I want you to understand that, if we ever reach the point where you get bored or dread coming to practice, it's *your* fault, too, and not just mine.

"I'm gonna try very hard to make our drills and practices fun whenever I can, but to do that I need you to tell me when I'm not succeeding and we're getting into a rut. My door is always open, and I'm always willing to listen if you're willing to tell me how we can do things better. I may ask you from time to time how you like certain drills or whether you think they're effective; if you care about the team, you'll give me an honest answer. Hey, you can't insult me; I've been insulted by *experts!*"

The coach passes out ice cream bars among the players and team managers. "I was gonna bring the brownies my daughter baked this morning," he says in conclusion, "but she dropped one on the floor and cracked the linoleum." (The story changes from one year to the next; last year he told them that he made the brownies himself, but he gave one to his dog and "it swelled up like a blowfish.")

Now, you tell us: If *you* were a player on that team, what kinds of expectations do you think you might bring to tomorrow's practice? The coach is, in fact, a marvelously gifted teacher of soccer whose kids are always fundamentally sound. He simply feels that the best way to keep his players sharp and on their toes at daily practices is to occasionally vary the routine in ways that leave the players wondering what's coming next and wanting to come back for more. Then, ask yourself: Would it be worth it to occasionally add a small dose of the unexpected to my daily practices somewhere between warmups and hitting the showers?

We don't mean to imply that your daily practices should be filled with zany antics or silliness—far from it. It isn't necessary to wear a tuxedo or flippers and scuba diving gear to practice to get your players' attention—but it *is* occasionally necessary to find ways to get their attention without yelling at them. It's so easy to get into a rut of doing the same things over and over—after all, learning usually results from repetition of movement or footwork patterns until they become habitual—that players always welcome a break in the familiar routines. New drills can be fun; so can competitive drills, scrimmaging, and an occasional activity such as keepaway, dribble tag, or soccer golf.

10. A Supportive Family, Spouse, or Significant Other

This isn't so much a coaching quality as it is an absolute necessity if you're married or emotionally committed to one person. So let's talk about how you're likely to spend your time in an average week during the season.

About 42-1/2 hours per week—or possibly more, and certainly no less—will be devoted to your responsibilities as a teacher. Assuming that you play two matches that week, one on the road and the other at home, you can pencil in, say, another 9–11 hours of team-related responsibilities on those days. Daily practices on the other three days will add another 10-1/2 hours, preparing game plans and practice schedules can run as high as 3–5 hours, and various responsibilities such as field maintenance and checking arrangements for home and away games can easily consume 3–5 hours or more per week. Throw in 3 hours on Saturdays for your coaching and refereeing clinics, 6 hours a week working with your local club teams or refereeing other games, and 4 hours for scouting an upcoming opponent on your "free" night, and you have devoted a total of somewhere between 81 and 87 hours that week to your professional responsibilities. And if you're the sort of person who occasionally needs sleep, you can toss in another 42–48 hours in which to snore your life away.

Of the 168 hours in that week, then, you're likely to devote as many as 135 of them to activities that do not involve your family or loved ones. That doesn't leave you much time for being with them or enjoying them—in all, about one day in every seven-day period. One coach's wife said she was confident that, if she died tomorrow, her husband would find a way to preserve her until the season was over and he had time to give her a nice funeral.

It's even tougher when you factor children into the equation. They grow up so quickly that, in retrospect, they seem to change from newborns to toddlers to teens to young parents with children of their own in a succession of eye blinks. Every coach entering the profession will face the decision of which takes precedence—professional or personal responsibilities; which you choose is entirely up to you, and there is no "right" or "wrong" way to proceed except, as we noted, in retrospect—and in the necessity of your loved ones' being able to adapt to your constant absence in pursuit of professional goals.

We'll say this and leave the subject alone: A supportive family, spouse or loved one is as wonderful—and rare—as a flawless diamond, and should be regarded as such. If you're lucky enough to possess such jewels—as we have been in our combined 36 years of coaching—we hope you'll recognize it and treat your time together, however fleeting, as moments to cherish rather than as merely random points along the moving hands of time.

Chapter 2

SURVIVING THE FIRST YEAR

Do the best you can with what you have, where you are.

—Teddy Roosevelt

The more difficult the victory, the greater the happiness in winning.

—Pele

If you're just starting out in coaching, we wish you many years of great success and championships, undefeated seasons, and Coach of the Year honors. However, we also wish you one season—no more than that (and early in your coaching career)—in which nothing seems to go right except your players when the ball goes left. We say that facetiously, but surviving the challenges of a losing season can be a powerful impetus for learning what you need to know about coaching. It stops there, though; the lessons to be derived from losing can all be learned in a single season.

One lesson to be learned from losing is *humility*. It's nice, of course, to enter an established situation in which the players already possess soccer skills worthy of *Ronaldo* clones and your most pressing task is distributing playing time equitably among your many all-star candidates. The temptation always exists, however, to overlook the fact that those players are the product of someone else's work, not yours. Beyond that, if you win big initially, you won't know until later where your coaching weaknesses lie, and your professional growth may be put on hold until your current players graduate. Until you've undergone the experience of trying to extract gallons of performance from pint jars of talent, you may not feel inclined to subject yourself and your team to the sort of intense scrutiny that turning around a losing season or an unsuccessful program demands.

So that's where we'll begin—by assuming that either (a) you're building a program from the ground up, or (b) you've inherited a program in which recent teams have done very poorly in terms of winning often enough for the players to have developed a winning attitude.

UNDERSTANDING WINNING AND LOSING

That soccer games are played to be won is indisputable; if it were otherwise, we wouldn't keep score. Nevertheless, the derisive claim of some critics that team sports are bad for children because, for every winner there must also be a loser, doesn't hold water unless you assume (as they do) that the final score is all that matters. We've always preferred Ben Sweetland's contention that "success is a journey, not a destination." We've had *many* games over the years—and you have, too, if you're a veteran coach—that we've won but felt as if we'd lost because we played poorly against an inferior opponent, and as many other games that we lost on the scoreboard but won in our hearts because we played well against a superior opponent. It's a matter of attitude and expectations.

Unfortunately, a direct correlation exists between winning regularly and building or maintaining a winning attitude. (We define "winning attitude" as *willingness to give 100 percent physically and mentally for as long as necessary in games and daily practices in order to accomplish team goals.*) Unless their thinking is redirected toward other goals, players who lose consistently eventually tend to regard losing as an inevitable outcome rather than as a steppingstone toward future success.

Every team and every player wants to win every game, of course—but not every team and player is equally committed to doing what it takes to win. When players adopt a losing attitude, they will give 100 percent in any given game only for as long as they think they have a chance to win. When they decide that a game is lost, you can bet the house and car that they're absolutely right because, from that moment on, they aren't playing to win, or even to compete, but just to finish the game. And the worst part of it is, *that's not their decision to make, it's yours.* The only decision your players have a right to make is whether to put on the uniform and take the field; after that, it's up to you (and not them) to decide how the game will be played, both individually and as a team. Accepting that fact and attempting to play up to your expectations regardless of the score, time remaining, or other circumstances is what a "winning attitude" is all about.

The way out of the downward spiral of expectations of failure leading to reduced efforts to succeed is to perform a major attitude adjustment on everyone involved. As any psychologist or psychiatrist will tell you, attitude adjustment is nothing more than replacing one set of goals and values with another—in this case, exchanging *their* negative goals and values for *your* positive ones.

CHANGING ATTITUDES

Generally speaking, politicians are elected to office because they promise the voters something better than they had. Whether they always deliver on those promises is another story; what concerns us is the process involved: *communication.*

Every good politician—and every good coach, as well—is at heart a salesperson; in our case, we're selling the virtues of hard work, dedication, and sacrifice as worthy and necessary steps toward the achievement of something that will ultimately be of great value to everyone involved. We're selling a vision of personal and team achievement, and a plan for achieving that vision somewhere down the line. Since you can't sell things to people who won't listen to your sales pitch, it stands to reason that your first and most important objective in communicating your dream and your plan is to find people who will believe what you tell them.

It's not that players who have negative attitudes don't want to believe you when you describe your long-range plans in glowing, highly positive terms; it is, rather, that, having grown accustomed to losing—and having discovered that its effect on their lives is neither fatal nor entirely unacceptable to them—they may not be willing to accept the rest of your plan (i.e., the part about its requiring them to work harder than they're used to working).

On a long-range basis, nothing generates winning attitudes as effectively as winning consistently. In a losing situation, attitudes will gradually improve as you work with your feeder program to develop players who possess the skills—and the desire—to excel and win consistently at progressively higher competitive levels. But what about this year's team? What, if anything, can you do if your current players' work ethic and commitment to excellence and winning are not highly developed? Well, if all you have is lemons, make lemonade. We have identified a four-step process for turning around losing attitudes: surrounding yourself with believers, teaching players how to win, devising achievable short-range goals, and extending your players' comfort zones.

1. Surrounding Yourself with Believers

The "survival" aspect of this book starts right here, with your inheriting a team of poorly skilled, mentally undisciplined athletes who probably think they're working just as hard in daily practices as this year's eventual state champs. They're wrong, of course, as they'll find out the first time you put them through the sort of rigorous practice session that superior teams go through every day. Some of the players may quit, and others who don't quit may remain, but with their basic negativity intact. They'll be the complainers, gripers, loafers, backbiters, and malcontents who will make life far more miserable for you that first year than losing games could ever do. You'll never reach them, because you're the perfect person for them to blame for their own shortcomings. That's why coaches say things like "You graduate your problems" and "It takes three to five years to turn around a program." After all, you can't just throw players off the team because they don't like you, no matter how much you might want to.

You can hope that the rest of your team that first year will comprise a small but solid core of believers who share your vision and accept your plan for realizing it. It is around *those* players that you'll build your team, the same way that Jesus built His church around only a dozen believers—the twelve disciples. Sometimes, even small armies can change the world. Those players' loyalty to you and commitment to the goals you set for your team will be worth their weight in gold to you that first year.

If their hard work, support, and faith in you mean anything to you, *tell* them so at least once a day. In the same way that your "Crabby Appletons (Rotten to the Core)" will spread their poison among their friends regarding your evil, brutish nature, the players who believe in you will do a far better job of advertising among *their* friends the good things you stand for than you could ever do on your own.

If forced to choose in a firmly established losing situation between good athletes with bad attitudes and mediocre athletes with good attitudes, we'll go with the latter every time. We call the kids with positive attitudes and good work ethics *undertakers:* They're the last ones who'll let you down.

2. Teaching Your Players How to Win

What??!!! You mean there are players who don't know how to win? You've gotta be kidding, don't you? Well . . . no, we aren't. In a losing program the players, like everyone else, understand that the winning team is the one that outscores the other team. They also understand that someone has to step up and make the plays that either win games or keep from losing them. What they *don't* understand is the level of physical and mental effort necessary to make winning possible; and they *don't* want to be the ones who take the risks that lead to victory or defeat. Such players don't understand concepts such as "elevating your game" or "taking it to the next level"; they tend to play at one comfortable level or pace regardless of the situation, and ultimately they rely on the opponents' playing at that level, too.[1]

There are three stages in the transformation of a team that loses consistently into one that wins consistently. Each stage follows the previous one so predictably that it is extremely unlikely for a team to progress rapidly from stage one to stage three. The first stage is *finding ways to keep from getting blown out of games;* the second stage is *finding ways to win the close games; and* the third stage is *winning games consistently and convincingly.* The easiest path through each stage is to avoid talking about winning altogether, but to focus instead on the quality of the players' and team's performance.

It's axiomatic in all coaching that, *before you can win a game, you have to not lose it.* In a severely negative situation, you may figuratively find your players fashioning white flags of surrender during the playing of the national anthem. If that's the case, your coaching task is to devise a game plan that can keep your games relatively close via conservative tactics;[2] your players' task is to play hard enough to give your game plan a chance to succeed, not necessarily in winning games but at least in showing evidence that the team is improving and advancing toward becoming the kind of team that everyone wants it to be.

When players reach the stage where most of their games are close, they have to learn how to win them. This involves not just playing hard but also being able to handle pressure in crucial situations by focusing on the task at hand. Because it's difficult for unskilled players to divide their concentration between the ball, the opponent who is marking them, their teammates, and their relative field positions at the same time, this stage represents a major, but formidable and (normally) agonizingly slow, step up the competitive ladder.

By the time a team reaches the third stage—winning most of the close games and conducting their own blowouts the rest of the time—the bulk of your nuts-and-bolts coaching is done and you can devote most of your time to fine-tuning the parts. This stage, then, is your reward for all the hard work you've done to turn things around. You don't have to teach the players how to win, because they already understand the level of effort that separates the consistent winners from the rest of the pack. Your biggest problem at this point is likely to be overconfidence, or players' forgetting that it is *they* who are responsible for winning and not the opponents who are responsible for losing. Overconfidence explains how lesser teams occasionally are able

---

[1] Coaches, too, can fall prey to such thinking if they sit around wishing they had talented players like Coach So-and-So. Well, wishing is fine but, like complaining, it doesn't get anything done. As a coach told us, "It's my daddy's fault that I ain't wealthy. He was too lazy to go out and earn a million dollars so I could inherit it."

[2] See the section titled "System Priorities" in Chapter 7.

to score major upsets over sleeping giants. You shouldn't have much trouble in this regard if you focus on the players' responsibilities, and the quality and intensity of their performances, rather than simply talking about winning.

3. Pursuing Achievable Short-Range Goals

Here, in a nutshell, is how coaches turn negative attitudes into positive attitudes: First, you sell your players on the merits of your dream, and tell them how playing on your team will enrich their lives. Second, you get them in shape and teach them how to play the game the way you want it played. Third, because your methods and plan are based on sound coaching principles, the team eventually wins a few games that previous teams would have lost. And fourth, having discovered that winning is both a viable possibility and a heckuva lot more fun than losing, your players apply themselves vigorously to the task of preparing to win; as a result, they find themselves winning with increasing frequency and shrugging off defeats that previously would have been devastating to team morale.

There's only one thing wrong with that scenario—the word *eventually*. Those words that read so nicely on paper won't amount to a hill of beans if your team loses its first four games and the players start grumbling among themselves. "He said things were going to be different this year, but they aren't. We're still losing." "Dad's right; Coach doesn't know what he's talking about. This team will never be any good!" "Hey, it's not my fault; I'm doing my job!"

So let's take a quick peek at our team's future and recent past via our handy crystal ball.

This time, it appears, we're lucky: The crystal ball tells us that, five years from now, our team will be in the region championship game. It also tells us that this year's team will lose its first four games. And then, taking a quick peek back in time, we see that the team we've inherited has won only five of its last 42 games, including one win last season.

Under such dismal conditions, we need not waste time wondering how our team will improve so quickly as to make the region playoffs in only five years; after all, crystal balls don't lie. For now, our most pressing concern is how to keep the team together when it appears that everything is falling apart.

As children, we enjoyed searching for the hidden objects in puzzle book cartoons. The solution to dealing with mounting losses while trying to transform negative attitudes into positive attitudes during that difficult first year is, like those hidden-object searches, surprisingly simple once you know where to look: It consists of *not allowing winning or losing to be the criterion by which your team's status or progress is judged*. Focus instead on areas of individual and team improvement.

Yeah, the skeptic may think, that sounds nice but it doesn't work that way. In real life, the kids will start grumbling, making excuses and blaming each other—or me—for those losses, and team unity will collapse like a house of cards! But hey, Coach, if you think that way, you're thinking just like the kids whose attitudes you're trying to change!

What we need to do here is, first of all, establish the ground rules governing team attitudes at the earliest possible moment in our coaching:

> Only the coaches will decide who is playing well and who is playing poorly. You don't know enough yet about what we want from you and the team to decide whether you or anyone else is doing as well as you should be doing. Your job is to

play the game the way we want you to play it, and to support your teammates and coaches at all times. Whether we win or lose isn't important;[3] our goal is to teach you the skills that will make our team as good as it can be. Your role is to cooperate with us and your teammates. We want you to feel that you can count on us and your teammates to support you in good times and bad; for that to happen, though, you have to accept that the Team is more important than you, me, or any other player or coach, and act accordingly.

Then, like the magician who uses misdirection with one hand to conceal what his other hand is doing, we'll proceed in practice sessions and in games to divert our players' attention away from winning or losing and toward the accomplishment of whatever performance goals we set for them—both individually and as a team.

Unlike our long-range goals, our short-range goals will be both specific and achievable. Since our players do not yet possess the kinds of skills to achieve lofty goals, we'll have them pursue simple goals such as giving up fewer goals and/or shots on goal per game than last year, or improving our takeaway totals, time of possession, penetrations into our attacking third, assists, shots on goal, or whatever else our players may be able to accomplish.

Still . . . with four losses to start our season, we may need further "hard" evidence to prove to our players that they're making progress. We'll search our detailed game and cumulative season stats and compare them on a game-by-game basis (or against last year's game and season stats) until we find areas where major or minor improvements have occurred. It shouldn't be difficult, since last year's team lost thirteen games and we're using a conservative, ball control-oriented playing style that spreads the field and slows games down to a crawl. We'll find improvements wherever they exist; count on it. That's a major reason why we keep detailed game and season stats.

We'll also use "star charts" to show individual achievements: issuing stars to the players for takeaways, fast breaks, blocked shots, and various other offensive or defensive categories.[4] And to make it competitive, we'll announce that the player who has accumulated the most stars at season's end will be the team's MVP, and other trophies will go to the players with the most stars in whichever categories we designate for such recognition.

Incidentally, in analyzing the team's performances, there's nothing wrong with pointing out areas where the team or individual players showed no improvement, or even regressed—but you should be prepared to offer specific suggestions on how to improve their performances next time out. Don't dwell on the negatives, though; players who are used to failure don't need to be browbeaten or constantly reminded of their shortcomings. What they need is to be led, in short steps, through the process of learning from their mistakes and to be told how to avoid them in the future.

Defining roles. Every player on your team, whether a starter or the least-used substitute on the team, should have a specific role to play, and the duties and responsibilities of that role should be carefully explained in terms that the player fully understands prior to entering the game. We do this by virtue of our game plans. The more precisely you define your expectations for each player, the more likely they are to reach them, as long as you don't expect more than a given player has to offer. (For

---

[3] It does matter whether your team wins or loses—but do you really want to say that to your players?

[4] Note: We'll keep negative statistics, too, but we won't take away stars for subpar performances. We'll also give stars for team achievements, both to emphasize the team-oriented nature of our game and to ensure that every player receives stars. To personalize the process, we'll let the players themselves put their own stars on the chart.

example, your midfielders should know beforehand whether you want them to join the attack or stay back to support the attack and bolster the defense, and they should be notified promptly whenever you decide to change your strategy. After the game is a bit late to inform a player that you wanted him back on defense rather than joining the attack during the last five minutes of play.)

Creating a siege mentality. It's not so much creating an "us-against-the-world" mentality as it is exploiting a situation that already exists. After all, even players who haven't been losing consistently will understand that there are certain individuals and groups who enjoy seeing them lose. If your team is a habitual doormat for the teams you play, opponents who have been accustomed to easy wins in the past will expect this year's team to roll over and play dead for them, too, and they will bitterly resent your players' fighting back. Somewhere along the way to losing your first four games and bringing the team's two-year won-lost record to 1–17, many fickle, fair-weather fans will jump off your bandwagon, and game officials may subconsciously tend to give your opponents the benefit of the doubt in close calls based on their low estimation of your players' skills. In a losing situation, it may very well be true that the world at large expects your team to fail and treats you and your players accordingly.

If all that seems paranoid—well, it *is*, but losing and paranoid thinking go hand in hand.[5] The alternative to promoting this type of group mentality to keep your team together through periods of adversity and turmoil is to sit back silently and watch your players lose their will to compete, and thus fulfill other people's expectations for them. We think it's better to point out the truth to your players, namely, that *while there are people out there who, for whatever reason, think you're losers who will quit when the going gets tough, there are a few other people—and just a few, most of whom are here with you right now—whom you can count on for support and friendship through thick and thin. We're all in this together. Since there is no one else who can help us, we'll just have to help ourselves by helping each other.*

Is that negative? We don't think so. All we're doing is telling our players whom they can count on in troubled times. It's just one of many approaches a coach can use in searching for the glue that will bind his or her team together when the natural adhesive—winning—is in short supply.

Competitive scheduling. There is one other thing you may be able to use to make your players competitive; it's what we sometimes refer to as "creative scheduling."

Faced with truly awful prospects for winning often enough in your first season to change attitudes that way, if you accept your job early enough you may be able to do next year's scheduling and drop some of the tougher opponents from last year's schedule, replacing them with weaker opponents against whom you can compete on a roughly equal basis. It's not the sort of thing you'd consider doing with a better, more experienced team; still, it beats facing the prospect of another 1-13 season of drubbings by massively superior opponents.

There are basically two approaches to competitive scheduling. One is to retain your region opponents and traditional rivals and fill the rest of your schedule with weak nonregion teams. The other is to drop your region schedule altogether for a year or two in order to give your teams a chance to improve to the point where you can be competitive in a perennially strong region. The main differences between those

---

[5] "Just because you aren't paranoid doesn't mean that there aren't people out there who are out to get you."
—Anon.

approaches are that, if you play a nonregion schedule, you won't be allowed to participate in post-season tournament play; and a nonregion schedule consisting of weak teams probably will involve traveling greater distances to play your road games.

About scheduling: With all other things being equal, your first priority is scheduling the games you are required to play (e.g., subregion or region games); your second priority is scheduling whatever traditional rivalries exist; and your third priority is filling out the rest of your schedule. If you aren't interested in competitive scheduling—and you shouldn't be if your team is capable of winning upwards of, say, 40 percent of its games—you should bear in mind your priorities as described above, or you're likely to find yourself facing massive scheduling conflicts with the teams you have to play. See the sample schedule in Figure 2-1.

4. Extending Your Players' Comfort Zone

If you were to ask the players on our fictional team that has lost 37 of its last 42 games why they lose so much, they'd probably tell you that they don't have as many good players as the teams they play. While that's probably true, there's likely to be another villain lurking in the wings, namely, the universal myth shared by *all* players—winners and losers alike—that they're working just as hard as everyone else. We've never known a player to confess to having lazy work habits, except obliquely in comments such as "Games are okay, but I don't like to practice." Players who don't want to learn are mentally lazy, and players who give a half-fast effort when everyone else is going full speed are physically lazy.

When players lose consistently, they tend to forget what a total effort consists of. Because experience has taught them that they're going to lose most of the time regardless of whether they hustle or merely go through the motions of playing their games, they tend to decide—independently of their coach's wishes—that games in progress are lost long before the final whistle sounds. Why, after all, should they continue to work hard in a game that's already lost?

This is the most perplexing problem that you're likely to face in assuming leadership of a team that has lost its will to compete: If you drive the players too hard, they'll quit, but if you don't extend their willingness to accept pain and fatigue as normal parts of the game, they'll never learn what a winning effort is like. Overcoming this obstacle will be the most difficult task facing you that first year in a losing situation; surviving it will require every ounce of psychology and motivational skill you possess.

To turn things around, it is necessary to extend the players' *comfort zones* (i.e., the level of physical and mental intensity at which they are used to competing)—and that, in turn, means adjusting their work habits upward toward a more realistic understanding of what a total effort entails. Great teams are capable of playing comfortably and productively at *any* tempo or pace, with the players automatically adjusting the intensity of their play in a manner that is consistent with team needs at any given point in the game or daily practice. That's what is meant by the adage "When the going gets tough, the tough get going." It's a habitual—and *learned*—response to pressure situations.

Extending players' comfort zones should begin the first day of preseason practice. It is, after all, the first day of a new season that brings with it fresh hopes and expectations, and there are no bad attitudes yet because you haven't expected or demanded anything of anyone. We agree wholeheartedly with those coaches who

FIGURE 2–1
GRIFFIN HIGH SCHOOL SOCCER SCHEDULE

Day	Date	Opponent	Time	Location	Teams
Tue.,	Feb. 17	EAST COWETA*	5:30/7:00	Griffin	JVB/VB
Fri.,	Feb. 20	SHAW*	5:30/7:00	Columbus	VG/VB
Wed.,	Feb. 25	FAYETTE CO.*	5:30/7:30	Griffin	JVG/VG
Thu.,	Feb. 26	NEWNAN*	5:30/7:00	Newnan	JVG/JVB
Fri.,	Feb. 27	POPE	6:00/8:00	Pope	VG/VB
Mon.,	Mar. 2	LaGRANGE*	5:30/7:00	LaGrange	JVG/JVB
Tue.,	Mar. 3	CARVER*	6:00	Griffin	VB
	Mar. 5-7	NEWNAN CLASSIC TOURNAMENT			VG/VB
Tue.,	Mar. 10	NEWNAN*	5:00/7:00	Newnan	VG/VB
Thu.,	Mar. 12	LOVEJOY	5:30/7:00	Griffin	JVG/JVB
Fri.,	Mar. 13	LaGRANGE*	5:30/7:30	LaGrange	VG/VB
Mon.,	Mar. 16	GRIFFIN JV GIRLS' TOURNAMENT			
Thu.,	Mar. 19	McINTOSH	5:30/7:00	Griffin	JVG/JVB
Fri.,	Mar. 20	McINTOSH	6:00/8:00	McIntosh	VG/VB
Sat.,	Mar. 21	GRIFFIN JV GIRLS' TOURNAMENT FINALS			
Mon.,	Mar. 23	GRIFFIN JV BOYS' TOURNAMENT			
Tue.,	Mar 24	TROUP CO.*	5:30/7:00	Griffin	VG/VB
Fri.,	Mar. 27	PARKVIEW	6:00/8:00	Griffin	VG/VB
Sat.,	Mar. 28	GRIFFIN JV BOYS' TOURNAMENT FINALS			
Tue.,	Mar. 31	EAST COWETA*	5:30/7:00	E. Coweta	JVG/VG
Wed.,	Apr. 1	NEWNAN*	7:00	Griffin	JVB
Fri.,	Apr. 3	FAYETTE CO.	6:00/8:00	Griffin	JVB/VB
Fri.,	Apr. 3	WOODWARD ACAD.	5:30/7:00	Woodward	JVG/VG
Tue.,	Apr. 7	UPSON-LEE*	5:30/7:00	Griffin	JVG/VG
Thu.,	Apr. 9	UPSON-LEE*	5:30/7:00	Griffin	JVB/VB
Fri.,	Apr. 17	ST. PIUS X	5:30/7:30	St. Pius	VG/VB

Apr. 21-24   REGION PLAYOFFS
Apr. 28, May 1, 5, 9   STATE PLAYOFFS

  * = Subregion matches
JVG = Junior Varsity Girls (Head Coach: Terry Baxter)
JVB = Junior Varsity Boys (Head Coach: Jerry Fields)
VG = Varsity Girls (Head Coach: Shane Pulliam)
VB = Varsity Boys (Head Coach: George Danner
Strength Coach: Arthur Graves

believe that *the level of a team's intensity is set for the rest of the season on the very first day.* You'll never get a better effort from your players than you will on that first day of practice. Young legs are fresh, an attitude of expectancy is in the air, and players are curious about the new coach and eager to show him or her what they can do; what better time could there be to start molding positive attitudes toward commitment, sacrifice, and hard work?

Preliminary preparations. You should already have begun the process of preparing your players for what doubtless will be a severe shock to their minds and bodies. Many coaches send letters to their players or talk with them as a group prior to the onset of preseason practice, outlining what they—the players—might do to get themselves in shape for the first day of practice. We especially like the idea of meeting with the players—and possibly their parents, as well—to introduce yourself; go over team rules, procedures, and academic eligibility requirements; and explain your concept of the program's potential (your dream) and your plan for making membership on this year's team something that everyone associated with the team will benefit from (e.g., learning new skills and forming lasting friendships with teammates who genuinely care about them). You won't, of course, refer to winning or losing except in one very important regard.

Somewhere in the meeting, you'll want to mention something to this effect:

> In talking with other coaches at other schools, I've been told that, if I work you as hard as their teams are working, you'll quit. I think they're wrong, and I hope you think so, too. We're going to work and play very hard this year, and I can't tell you that it will always be easy or fun, but if you'll work with us and play your hardest from the very first day of practice I can promise you that you'll be proud of what we accomplish.

In saying this you are, of course, building a siege mentality—but you're also challenging your players to rise to your expectations rather than allowing them to set their own performance standards as previous teams have done. You are, in essence, preparing their minds for what their bodies must endure.

"We're all in this together." Some coaches like to issue practice jerseys inscribed with messages like "I Survived (the coach's) Preseason Practices" at the end of that phase of training, as a first step in building pride where none existed previously. We also like the approach of the coach who gave out jerseys inscribed "I'll Survive (the coach's) Preseason Practices and You Will Too" on the first day of practice as a first step in building determination. The coach told us, "The other way is cheaper, but I thought that, if I gave them out early, they'd want to keep them to show their teammates that they were tough enough to meet the challenge."

Pain is individual. President Clinton's "I feel your pain" messages were eloquent, but not rooted in fact. No one feels anyone else's pain. When muscles and minds that have not been properly conditioned for physical exertion produce pain and fatigue, players must be reminded that today's pain is tomorrow's gain, and that their teammates are experiencing exactly the same difficulties and playing through them. If you don't tell them otherwise, they will assume that no one else is hurting. It won't stop the hurting, but it can make it easier to bear.

"We're doing more than other teams." Part of being up front with your players consists of helping them to understand that *since we're behind the teams we play, the only way we can catch up with them is to work harder than they're working.* To exemplify this "extra effort" with a team of the sort that we've described, we might start out by assigning the players a mile of running before practice every day. To assure that they

don't complain about it (and to promote the idea, *We're all in this together*), we'll run the mile with them—every day.

Now, a mile a day to start your practices isn't much for players who will be running from 5 to 7 miles in every game, and it certainly won't account for more than a fraction of the running they'll do in the course of each daily practice session. Still, it's not the mile itself that matters as much as what it signifies—it's the kind of extra effort that is going to help us turn our program around. So we'll ask the players: "Do you think that (one of our opponents) is running an extra mile today?" Since they have no way of knowing what any other team is doing in its daily practices, we'll answer our question with another one: "Would *you* run an extra mile a day if you didn't have to in order to catch up with other teams?" The answer to the second question will be painfully obvious to your players whose previous idea of a second effort is turning off the snooze alarm.

Learning to hustle is like learning anything else: *The more you do it, the easier it gets.* We'll add numerous touches to our practices to emphasize hustling, such as the rule that *no one walks anywhere.* We'll give the players two minutes for water breaks, with penalties for those who aren't back in time (or rewards for those who are); after a day or two of this, most will be back with a minute to spare.

We'll discuss specific aspects of daily practices in Chapters 10 and 11; for now, we'll note that you have every right to expect your players to give 100 percent throughout every practice session and game; how much less than that you'll accept will determine how much less than that you'll accomplish. For the players, that translates physically into never giving up on any play, no matter how badly you've been beaten; if you'll give up on a play, you'll give up on a game. Mentally, it translates into listening, concentrating, and focusing. Both are forms of hustling, albeit vastly different—the same way that your players' hard work at practice and in games is vastly different from the hard work you do in preparing for daily practices and games.

Accentuate the positives. In drastically upping the ante via rigorously demanding drills and practice sessions, you're asking a lot from players who aren't used to that sort of treatment. Our philosophy is, *Do whatever it takes to get your players to do what they need to do.* Try to keep the negatives to a minimum by accentuating the positives—congratulating players whenever they make good plays; singling out individual players for praise when they hustle—and not always the same players; reminding everyone *every day* of how much we're accomplishing and how fortunate all of us are to have such good, loyal, hard-working players and coaches on our team; apologizing for how hard our practices are and thanking the players for their hard work on behalf of the team; and—most important of all—showing the players, through the example of our own hard work and commitment to the team, that their faith in us and what we say, do, and believe is not misplaced.

Your personal challenge and goal for a team of the sort we've described in this chapter should be, not merely to survive that terrible first year, but *to do so without losing a single player along the way*—not by lowering yourself to the previous team's standards but by slowly and carefully raising the current team's performance standards to new levels.

If you can do those things—keep your team together and playing hard under all conditions—you'll have a team that you and everyone else will be proud of regardless of the team's won-lost record. It won't be an easy task—but as you'll probably tell your players a thousand times over the course of the season, *nothing worthwhile in life comes easy.*

THE SECOND YEAR

Next year will be easier. The returning players will be more receptive to your leadership and coaching because they will know what to expect from you and understand what you expect from them. If you're lucky, most of your bad apples will have graduated, transferred, or decided not to play next year; the rest can be eliminated via preseason tryouts if they still resist your coaching or are openly or covertly hostile to you or their teammates.

Without the disruptive, divisive influence of negative team leaders, your true team leaders will emerge; their wholesome work ethic and positive attitude will have a highly beneficial impact on the new and younger players who are entering your program. With everyone pulling together in the same direction, there will be fewer distractions, and you'll find yourself and the team accomplishing more and enjoying your daily practices in ways that this year's team could not. With everyone working hard from the start, you'll find it easier to build on the players' current skill levels. (Not coincidentally, your players should be improved by the time preseason tryouts roll around, having had nine months to practice on their own the skills you taught them last year, and to apply them to rec league or club soccer games during the off-season.)

With all this going for you, you should be able to improve on this year's won-lost record next year, and thus further improve team morale and the players' determination to accomplish whatever goals you set for that team. Even if the wins don't come in abundance, though, the quality of your team's play should improve dramatically, and you should have no trouble keeping your players motivated—both individually and as a team.

Chapter 3

YOU AND YOUR TEAM

And now abideth faith, hope and love, these three;
but the greatest of these is love.

—I Corinthians 13:13

SHORTCUTS TO EXCELLENCE

As anyone who has coached before will tell you, *there are no shortcuts to excellence.* There are, however, shortcuts to the *pursuit of excellence.* They consist of *focusing on essential tasks* and *eliminating nonessentials.* The essentials are your long-range goals and the day-to-day steps (short-range goals) you take in striving to accomplish them. Nonessentials include the sorts of distractions produced by players who resist coaching or serve as a disruptive influence on their teammates.

If we harped on the subject of players' negative attitudes in the previous chapter, it was because those attitudes divide teams and promote disunity and disharmony, making focus difficult, if not impossible. There is room on a team for only one vision—the coach's. Any other view of the team or the program is nonessential and counterproductive to team goals. A united team is a focused team.

THE BENEFITS OF TEAM MEMBERSHIP

If a team is to accomplish what it sets out to accomplish, the players must be united in terms of where they're going and how they expect to get there. In accepting the coach's vision and plan as best for them and the team, players acknowledge the existence of a purpose that is higher and more worthy than they are; through recognizing that the *team* and not they themselves is that higher purpose, they learn to subordinate, or sacrifice, their own needs to those of the team—at least, that's the theory. The question *does* arise: *Why should any player want to regard the team as more important than himself or herself?* Because the team can provide benefits for the player that he or she cannot readily achieve or receive apart from the team.

And what might those benefits be? They vary from one player to another. Some players simply want to be seen in the team uniform to satisfy Mama or Daddy sitting in the stands, or else they like the self-esteem that comes from being associated with a varsity athletic team. Others enjoy the camaraderie and interaction with coaches and teammates, or else they want to be part of a winning team or a winning program. Some play for the simplest and most obvious of reasons: They love the game of soccer and relish the competitive challenges it affords them.

This brief listing doesn't begin to explain the myriad reasons why youngsters might prefer playing on your soccer team to everything else they might do in their spare time. For example, we've intentionally omitted what we think is the most important reason of all—*to be part of a relatively large group of people who regard them as special.*

THE FAMILY PLAN

Like the "Old Gray Mare," family life in the United States ain't what it used to be, and the changes have not improved the quality of our lives. Terms like *broken homes, single-parent families, working parents,* and *latchkey children* attest to the reduced effectiveness of modern family life. Without a parent around to monitor their free-time behavior, youngsters in ever-increasing numbers have turned to drugs, sex, crime, delinquent behavior, or gang membership—to relieve boredom, to find meaning in their lives, or to gain a sense of acceptance or security among their peers.

Being a member of your soccer team *can* and *will* be regarded by your players as one of the greatest and most valuable experiences in their lives regardless of whether the team wins championships or reaches more modest levels of accomplishment—if, that is, you take pains to create an environment that satisfies your players' need for stability and direction in their lives. In doing so, you will, of course, benefit your own coaching by building teams of closely knit individuals who will accomplish together what could not be accomplished separately.

More important, though, the relationships forged in such a manner will reach far beyond this year's team or players, making future recruiting tasks easier and forging lifelong friendships that your players will cherish long after their playing days are over. We know; we've seen it happen on our own teams and those of other coaches as well. Unless you've been a member of such a Team—we'll capitalize it throughout the rest of this chapter to denote its very special nature that sets it apart from other teams—you cannot possibly imagine how great its impact will be on everyone involved.

First Steps

Four characteristics distinguish a Team (i.e., a Family) from a team (i.e., a group of individuals): *acceptance, respect, loyalty,* and *love.*

In building a family atmosphere, you should expect and require your players to follow the golden rule—treating their Teammates as they themselves would like to be treated. *Acceptance* means acknowledging their right to be treated as equals. *Respect* entails players' recognizing that their Teammates' contributions, however minor they may be perceived to be, are important to the Team, and treating them with dignity—

as opposed to, say, ridiculing them or making fun of them. *Loyalty* involves supporting one's Teammates on and off the field and in good times and bad, and endeavoring to act responsibly in all situations as befitting a Team member. *Love* refers to being genuinely concerned about the well-being of one's Teammates. Love is the most powerful motivator at your disposal.

Your players should understand these four traits and the necessity of treating them, not merely as words, but as *a way of life*—and they should understand *from the very first minute of preseason practice* that (a) they will be required to adhere to your behavioral guidelines regarding the treatment of Teammates, (b) violators will be punished, and (c) there will be *no* exceptions made and *no* excuses accepted.

"All I'm asking," you might tell your players, "is that you put aside whatever biases or dislikes you may have and accept all of us as a part of your family. If you can't love us, you'd better at least plan to do a wonderful job of faking it, because my Number One goal for this Team is *to surround you with Teammates you can count on, and who care about you and consider you an important and very special part of their lives.* We can't do that if you reject us." This little speech is essentially the old "hereafter routine" in action: If you're not here after what we're here after, we'll be here after you're gone.

That's all you have to tell them—for now, at least. The reasons you're using this approach will become evident after you've had the players working together in formal practice sessions and playing together in informal social settings long enough to discover that their Teammates really *are* special. It's natural to regard people as special if they treat you as if you're special to them.

Your goal is, of course, for your players to feel grateful to their Teammates for caring about them and obligated not to let them down in any manner. When you reach that point, everything else (including wins and losses) will be minor in comparison and won't affect your Team at all.

It's important to note that, even on a Team whose players lack the skills or experience to win consistently, the Family approach is *always* an achievable goal—and it is guaranteed to produce positive attitudes no matter how good or bad the Team's won-lost record might be. If you keep your players focused on working together, improving their individual and Team skills, pursuing Team goals, and getting to know and love one another, they will have neither the time, energy, nor inclination to develop negative attitudes.

Building Togetherness

Your players will, of course, start getting to know one another via their interactions before, during, and after daily practices—but that's not enough. The apostle Paul wrote of "the communion of like minds"—bonds of fellowship uniting individuals toward a common goal—as the driving force behind the growth of the early Christian church; you want your players to develop the same single-mindedness of purpose in the pursuit of Team goals. Still, what we're looking for here is not merely our players' commitment to Team goals, but also their personal commitment to *one another and their coach(es).* Such commitments arise naturally in families via blood ties (although they may be severed by faulty relationships within dysfunctional families); they do not arise naturally in team sport settings.

It's one thing to create and enforce rules designed to make your players accept and respect one another; it's something else again to get them to genuinely like one another. Doing that requires that they spend time together getting to know one another in informal, social settings. The more time they spend together away from the soccer field, the more they will find to like about one another.

Following are some of the ways coaches bring their players together in social settings:[1]

Attending summer camps. We place this at the top of the list because it brings the players together 24 hours a day for as long as a week, working on soccer skills, playing games, and getting the sort of in-depth exposure to one another's personalities that cannot be duplicated elsewhere. The summer camp experience also helps them to feel relaxed with each other and develop the sort of intimacy based on shared experiences that distinguishes friends from classmates or acquaintances.

Sleepovers/pajama parties. You don't need beds, cots, sleeping bags, or even pillows, blankets, or spacious accommodations for this. The kids can bring their own sleeping gear and toothbrushes. All you need is enough food and drink for one meal, popcorn, a videotape or two that won't send their parents out to find a lawyer to sue you for contributing to the delinquency of a minor, and willingness to monitor the proceedings until the players start drifting off to sleep. Their late-night conversations about whatever it is that young people talk about will do more to bring your Team together than all the pregame pep talks you'll ever deliver.

Parent-player cookouts. Easily arranged, such informal get-togethers aren't really for the players as much as for the parents, giving them a chance to meet one another—and you—in an informal, noncompetitive setting. It also allows them to interact with the players and watch them interacting with one another, which is always enjoyable to do when they—the players—enjoy one another's company. It shows players and parents alike that you consider parents an important part of the Team.

Trips. Overnight (or weekend) camping trips. Fishing trips. Trips to the beach or an amusement park. Trips to wherever the players might want to go, or for whatever they might want to do. The activities themselves are nice enough, but the interactions that occur on the way to and from the site are valuable and can be informative, too. (For one thing, they can yield valuable clues as to who your team leaders might be.)

We don't know your players, of course, but we *do* know this: Their personalities may differ markedly, but they are basically good people who want to be liked by their coaches and Teammates, or else you wouldn't have them on your Team. In providing informal settings for them to get to know one another on a personal (as opposed to competitive) basis, you're simply allowing them to find out what you already know, that is, that *these* are people you can count on when the rest of the world is letting you down. In socializing together away from the soccer field, they learn that, when they drop the public masks they wear to keep the world at arm's length, they are still accepted by their Teammates, warts and all. Realizing that will come as a great and very pleasant surprise to them, since most teenagers are insecure and privately harbor grave doubts as to their worthiness to be accepted, respected, and loved by their peers.

---

[1] With rules and close supervision, of course. While smoking, drinking, and drug use are never acceptable in any context, Team or otherwise, we also prefer not to permit players to bring a date to any Team function except games. The presence of members of the opposite sex can create problems that none of us needs, so we simply announce that a given Team function is "for players only" or "for players and parents."

YOU AND YOUR PLAYERS

Everything we've said so far about how you expect your players to treat one another also applies to *you*, of course. If you don't love your players, you aren't the person they need to coach them. If you can't love them for their hard work and the sacrifices they make on the Team's behalf, you'll never reach them, and your Team will never become what it might have been. The days of coaches' regarding their players as "meat on the hoof" are long gone, and deservedly so. The depth of all Team relationships is always set by the head coach.

What, specifically, should your players expect from you? In addition to acceptance, love, and respect, first and foremost they have the right to *fair, equal, and consistent treatment* regardless of whether they are potential all-stars or perennial benchwarmers. This means eliminating double standards and enforcing your rules the same way for everyone—but it also means spreading your praise, compliments, and criticisms in equal doses among *all* of your players rather than reserving it for a select few players who please or displease you.

Your players also have the right to your being *honest* with them. The way we see it, you may as well tell it like it is, since they'll see through your dishonesty in a heartbeat; once you've lied to them you'll find it *very* hard to regain their trust. We tell our players, "Don't ask us questions about your skills level or how you rate on the Team unless you're prepared to accept the truth, because we aren't going to lie to you." It doesn't always make us popular with those parents who tend to regard Team needs and goals as minor compared to the joy of seeing a son or daughter out there playing—but in the long run it builds respect for us as coaches. Honesty *is* the best policy.

Your players have the right to expect you to function as the *Team's leader* at all times, the same way that parents function as family leaders. Being liked by your players may be important to you; frankly, we've always preferred being respected. Still, if you want to be liked you should pursue that goal only within the context of acting responsibly and professionally in a mature manner. Some players may "like" the idea of being asked to share a beer or two with you, but they won't respect you in the morning—or ever again. If your players can't *look up to you*, they'll *look down on you*.

Responsible leadership means more than that, however. It also means taking time to organize your daily practices, teach fundamental skills, correct players' mistakes, prepare for upcoming games, and generally run the Team in at least a semi-organized fashion. And it means helping your players with their personal problems, showing concern for their academic progress, and trying to ensure that their Team membership is such that they will look back on it in later years with pride and fond memories.

Finally, your players should expect you to *be yourself.* You may try to emulate or adopt other coaching methods you've seen, but it will work only if those methods fit your personality. The key here is *consistency;* you can be laid-back, intense, a worrier, an optimist, black, white, male, female, married, single, Jewish, Catholic, Baptist, or Muslim, and it won't matter to your players as long as the same *you* shows up every day for practice and games with the same set of expectations. You shouldn't feel that you have to be perfect or mistake-free in your coaching, as long as your errors result from having tried to do what's best for the Team. As one coach told his players, "We ain't perfect—none of us—and especially me. That's why God invented the words 'I'm sorry' and 'I'll do better next time.' And that's what I'll expect from you and what you can expect from me: to occasionally make mistakes, admit them and, hopefully, learn from them."

"Being yourself" does not, of course, extend to the use of cruelty, spitefulness, violence, pettiness, or other evidences of a flawed personality. It simply means "being the best *you* you know how to be"—which is, after all, what most of us are trying to do anyway.

MOTIVATION

Motivation in team sports is often associated in coaches' minds with slogans, pep talks, and inspirational speeches exhorting players to go out and "win one for the Gipper." True motivation is much more than that, though; it encompasses everything you do to ensure that your players work hard and do what they're supposed to be doing when, if left to their own devices, they might choose to do something else.

We've had coaches tell us, "It's impossible for anyone to motivate anyone else. All motivation comes from within the individual." It's true—but it's also a cop-out that gives coaches an excuse for not trying to motivate their players.

Yes, motivation is internal. But hustling and working hard are nothing more than habits, and players can exchange bad habits for good ones; they can also be persuaded to work hard when their natural inclination might be otherwise.

Ideally, every player will be self-motivated to strive toward excellence and the attainment of team goals. Because human nature dictates, however, that many (if not most) people will try to get by with a minimal rather than a maximal effort unless induced toward the latter, most coaches consider it necessary to find ways to motivate their underachievers.

Incentives

Motivation often involves the use of positive or negative incentives to produce desired behaviors or eliminate undesired behaviors. Both rewards and punishments are, or can be, valuable coaching tools; knowing which to use at any given time or with any given player depends on whether the player needs to be *pushed* (i.e., prodded by negative feedback or the threat of punishment) or *pulled* (i.e., encouraged by positive feedback or the promise of rewards). While unskilled players or players who lack confidence generally need (and respond more favorably to) encouragement, players who possess skills and confidence but lack a highly developed work ethic may require either or both types of motivation.

Rewards normally consist of such simple things as the coach's approval (e.g., a compliment, a pat on the back, or a smile); increased playing time in games or a position in the starting lineup; or an extra water break or avoidance of unpleasant tasks such as running wind sprints in daily practices. For self-motivated players, the greatest reward of all is the sense of satisfaction that derives from knowing that they've done their best in a winning effort. That's a high that no drug could ever produce. Whatever the case, to be effective the reward must be something that the player values enough to work hard to earn it.

That the need for punishment exists at all is due to the fact that everyone wants to be rewarded, but not everyone is always willing to pay the price involved. Some people simply want to be rewarded for others' hard work, and others may not care about the rewards. For example, most—but not all—players want their coaches' and Teammates' approval, and will work hard to get it and keep it. The threat of punishment, then, is an alternative inducement to work hard for players who do not respond favorably to positive incentives. Be advised, though, that creating a perpetual aura of fear in daily practices is unwise and counterproductive to team goals, and while the threat of punishment can motivate players to work hard and hustle, it cannot improve their ability to execute fundamental skills.

Space limitations prevent us from telling you everything you may need to know about motivation,[2] but even if you've never coached a day in your life, you'll devise your own effective incentives system if you adhere to two simple guidelines:

1. Treat your players the way you'd want them treated if they were your children and someone else were coaching them.

2. Never touch a player in anger.

The Best Motivation Program of All

The easiest and best way to assure the success of your motivational efforts is to build the sort of Team we've described in this chapter. If your players know that you and their Teammates love them, that alone will far exceed the persuasive power of any motivational speech you'll ever devise. Put yourself in their place: Knowing that your Teammates and coaches love you and are counting on you to do your best, how far would *you* go to keep from letting them down? How much is being accepted, respected, and loved by people who consider you part of their family worth to you? Why should it be any different for your players?

Under such circumstances, motivation will be the least of your worries, since practically everything you do or say will motivate your players to rise to your expectations. You can be as positive or negative as situations require, and you won't lose your players as long as they know that, when the dust settles, you'll still love them.

USING TEAM LEADERS

Leadership may be exercised by setting a good example for others to follow or by exerting the force of one's personality over others. The most effective form of team leadership combines those traits.

On a perennially weak team in which the players do not possess the physical skills or positive attitude necessary to pursue high performance standards, the most effective team leaders are, unfortunately, likely to be your most vocal critics. The situation will change with time as players' skills increase and new players with fresh attitudes and positive outlooks gradually replace the ones who find it easier to complain than to support you. As your team and program develop, you'll find increasing numbers of players exerting both types of positive leadership. Newcomers to the Team will admire and emulate the work ethic of your veteran players, some of whom by now will have become ardent supporters of your philosophy and coaching methods. Their value to you and the Team cannot possibly be overstated. They will, in

---

[2] For a more detailed analysis of motivation and team sports, see *Dr. Warren's Coaching and Motivation* (Englewood Cliffs, NJ: Prentice Hall, 1983).

effect, join you in creating the glue that binds the Team together. In physically and verbally reinforcing your positive values, they will motivate their Teammates every day toward accomplishing Team goals in a thousand little ways that you'll never see unless you're watching very, very closely.

How can such leadership be developed? Slowly. You don't want to force leadership roles on players who don't want them.

The first and most important trait you're looking for is unswerving loyalty to you and the Team. Beyond that, you want players who will serve as role models for what you want their Teammates to be or to become. They may or may not be your best players, but they should be positive, hard-working contributors to the Team's progress. Such players, when identified, are ideal candidates for Team captain(s).

Team Captains

We've always selected Team captains ourselves, on the grounds that the position is too important to be left to chance or the players' whims. If you prefer to let your players choose their own Team captain(s), by all means do so—but *not* if you're starting out in a hard-core losing situation, unless you're willing to risk the players' choosing captains who regard you as an evil person trying to make their lives miserable.

Before announcing Team captain selections, discuss the matter privately with the candidates. They must understand two things: (a) that, as far as you're concerned, being named Team captain is the highest honor that can be bestowed on a player; and (b) that the honor bears responsibility. The title *Team Captain* should signify that its bearers are extensions of the head coach.

And *that* is precisely what you should tell your players in announcing this year's Team captain selections: "Our Team captains have been empowered by us to make any and all decisions in daily practices and games that are not specifically reserved for the coaches." While that declaration may or may not carry much water in terms of actual responsibilities, it does get your point across, namely, that *these individuals have been singled out for special recognition and will at all times be treated with the respect that they've earned.*

Incidentally, we do the same thing with our Team managers, telling the players, "Their (the managers') responsibilities are different from yours, but they are just as important to the Team's success. Don't *ever* interfere with [the managers] when they're carrying out their duties and responsibilities." Again, we've overstated things here, but for the best of reasons. In addition to earning our managers' unflagging loyalty and devotion, it reinforces our message: *Everyone who contributes to the Team's success is important to us, and worthy of our respect and gratitude.*

Beyond naming Team captains, it is important to provide them with leadership opportunities. If you regard your Team as a family, you and your assistant coaches are the parents, your players are the children, and your Team captains are the older brothers and sisters who bear responsibilities for tending their younger brothers and sisters. We use our captains and other Team leaders to demonstrate individual skills techniques and work with players on an individual or small-group basis. In addition to having them direct daily and pregame warmups and stretching exercises, we often consult them regarding game strategies; it is, after all, their Team as well as ours, and we want them to feel a sense of proprietary concern for its progress. We've been known to stand aside in practice and let our captains direct drills and scrimmages— it's an excellent learning experience for everyone involved—and we *always* ask them to evaluate the effectiveness of new drills that we use in daily practice.

Senior Leadership

The old military slogan, "Rank Hath Its Privileges" (R.H.I.P.), applies here, but with one important alteration: Rank Hath Its *Obligations*. You should expect your seniors to be leaders and exert a positive influence on their Teammates. A senior who doesn't want to lead, whether by example or by force of personality, is one who isn't interested in contributing to the Team's progress and well-being. He or she is a problem waiting to happen, and one that you don't need or want.

We always hold a "Seniors Only" meeting at the beginning of preseason tryouts. At that meeting, we tell our seniors that, skills aside, we are going to expect more from them than we expect from their less experienced and younger underclass Teammates—better attitudes, and willingness to work hard and encourage their Teammates to do likewise. If that seems unfair to them—well, that's life. Younger Teammates tend to model their attitudes and behavior after those of their coaches and the seniors; a senior who will not exert positive leadership is, in essence, a wasted slot on the Team roster (or starting lineup, for that matter) that could better be filled by a younger player who will benefit more from the experience. It's nothing personal— just a matter of everyone doing what's best for the Team. It's not a matter of trying to get rid of seniors who haven't attained a high level of skills proficiency, either; we just want our seniors to understand our expectations for them.

This is likely to be a problem only when you're new to the school, since players you've coached previously will understand your expectations. Still, it doesn't hurt to remind your seniors that they will be expected to function as positive role models for their Teammates; the meeting itself will reinforce your belief that *the Team will go only so far as its senior leadership takes it.*

USING ASSISTANT COACHES

If you're lucky enough to have one or more assistant coaches, your goal should be to see how many ways you can find to put their talents, experience, and knowledge of the game to good use. Every task that your assistant coaches perform or help you with is a task that you won't have to do all by yourself—at least, not if you've trained them properly.

You should expect the same loyalty from your assistant coaches that you expect from your players. While it's unnecessary—and possibly undesirable as well—for your assistants to be carbon copies of you, it *is* important for them to support your Master Plan for developing the Team. They may not share your philosophy of how the game should be played or how the Team should be handled, but they nevertheless should give their full support to your efforts to take the Team in a desired direction. A disloyal or lazy assistant coach is of no more value to you than a disloyal or lazy player.

Assistant coaches can prove invaluable to you in these areas:[3] recruiting and squad selection; player conditioning and weight training; scouting; paperwork and administrative tasks; publicity and fund-raising; conducting seminars for local rec league coaches; preparing and evaluating daily practice schedules; serving as extra pairs of eyes in evaluating players' performances in daily practices and in games; analyzing

---

[3] We don't expect our assistant coaches to keep game stats (or videotape games or scrimmages) while we're coaching the team; solve player problems or deal with angry parents; or spend their own money on the Team's behalf unless they volunteer to do so.

game situations and devising appropriate strategies; and, of course, working with players on an individual and group basis in daily practices. Other areas of responsibility doubtless will occur to you as you study your situation and its overwhelming work demands.

One thing should be remembered, though: Your assistants are there to supplement your own hard work, not replace it. The example you set for your assistant coaches and players will determine how seriously they take their own responsibilities, so your assistant coaches should expect the following from you: a positive work ethic; loyalty and respect; effective leadership; unqualified support from you in executing the responsibilities of their job; recognition for the quality of their work on the Team's behalf and yours; willingness to share your knowledge of the game and your personal soccer coaching resources with them in order to shore up whatever gaps exist in their training or experience; and opportunities to exercise their own leadership of the Team in games as well as in practice sessions.

Regarding the latter, a coach once remarked that she was 2-2 in games in which she had let her assistant coaches make crucial strategy decisions. "I took the blame for the losses, of course," she said, "since it was my decision to let them find our way out of the trouble we were in. It was the right thing for me to do, though. You might even say that we came out winners in all four games because we won two of the games outright, and in the other two we got assistant coaches who were better and wiser coaches from the experience."

HANDLING PLAYER PROBLEMS AND PROBLEM PLAYERS

If you didn't already know it, counseling your players will be an important and ongoing part of your off-the-field coaching duties. Like it or not, their problems are *your* problems, too, since if left untreated those problems may adversely affect the Team's development or chemistry. Thus, we begin by offering a couple of suggestions and guidelines for dealing with players' personal problems.

Encourage Your Players to Come to You With Their Personal Problems

Let them know that what is important to them is also important to you, and that your office door will always be open to them when they need to talk to you. They should understand, though, that the soccer field is not the proper place to resolve their personal problems; on the practice field, they should be willing to set aside their problems and help *you* solve *your* problems (i.e., improving the Team or getting ready for the next game).

They should understand, too, that the needs of the Team always take precedence in any discussion of personal problems, and you will not support any position or decision that is not in the Team's best interests.

Be a Problem Solver. Tackle Problems Head-on

For us, at least, the easiest problems to solve involve disputes among players. They're easy to handle because our favorite slogan, "The Team Above All," offers immediate access to sensible solutions in a wonderfully direct either/or proposition: *Either you're 100 percent committed to the Team and every player on it, or you'll lose this dispute.*

Taking the players involved in the misunderstanding into our office, we'll start out by explaining another either/or proposition that they'll have no trouble comprehending: "Either the two of you will solve this problem to your mutual satisfaction and ours here in this office, *right now,* or we'll solve it for you in ways that you might not like." After letting them explain and discuss the problem for awhile—usually it involves one or more members of the opposite sex—we'll shift the discussion to the players themselves and their commitment to each other as Team members. We've done it so many times that it feels as if we're following a script.

"Do you love [the Teammate]?" we'll ask each of them in turn. We've never had anyone tell us no, since it would evoke the response, "Then why are you still on the Team?" and they aren't really interested in quitting the Team over what is essentially nothing more than a disagreement. (If it were more than that, they'd have quit when we offered them that alternative at the end of preseason tryouts.)

At that point, the light at the end of the tunnel becomes a searchlight. If they'll admit to loving each other, they'll find a way to iron out their differences and escape with their Team status intact and no damage done to their egos.

Of course, that doesn't cover the range of problems you'll encounter—far from it. But by applying the principle, The Team Above All, in all cases, you'll help your players to find solutions they can live with.

We once had a player come to us and say that he was being harassed by another student—a nonathlete—who was trying to pick a fight with him. He came to us, he said, because he didn't want to be punished for fighting. We told him to keep on avoiding trouble and ignore the boy. He said he'd been trying to do that, but the boy wouldn't leave him alone. We repeated our statement. "Don't fight. Don't talk to him. Try to act as if he doesn't exist."

Then we went to the other boy and told him we understood he was having trouble with one of our players. He nodded sullenly, expecting us to bawl him out or take him to the principal to protect our player. Instead, we told him we'd instructed our player not to bother him again or even speak to him, and we asked the boy to tell us if the player bothered him any more. He agreed to do so.

Finally, we told the boy that we expected him to leave the player alone, too, and that if he didn't comply we'd bring in the principal, the sheriff, or whoever it took to keep the peace between them. We ended our brief talk by reminding him to let us know if our player bothered him any more. He said he would.

Fortunately, there were no further incidents involving the two of them. Did we solve the problem by talking to the two boys, or did the problem resolve itself naturally? Who cares? The player believed that we'd solved it, and that was good enough for him.

In problems involving players and teachers, over the years we've tended to side with the teachers even when they were wrong because (a) the teacher is the authority figure in the classroom, and we always want our players to respect their elders and authority, and (b) the teacher controls the gradebook. It's like the old saying about bosses: "They may not always be right, but they are always the bosses." We once told a player, "Sometimes being on the Team means saying you're sorry when you'd rather not say anything at all. Say it for yourself, or say it for the Team, but *say it.*"

In discussing problem players, we'll point out as before that *Coaching and Motivation*[4] covers the topic in far greater depth than is possible here.

Although there are many ways that players can create problems for their coaches or Teammates, we're probably not far off the mark in lumping all such problems into one large group, that is *problems attributable to selfishness or disloyalty*. Players who place the Team's needs ahead of their own at all times seldom cause problems or get themselves into trouble.

Make Team Loyalty Your Top Priority

After nearly forty combined years of coaching, our greatest regret is not the losses over the years that might have been transformed into wins through more skillful coaching or a lucky break here and there, or championships we almost won but didn't, but rather the players we've coached who refused to believe that Team membership would change their lives. *These* were our "problem players"—players who never considered their coaches and Teammates important enough to receive their unqualified loyalty.

In dealing with problem players, you will, of course, try in every way possible to "save" them by attempting to correct improper behaviors, instill positive values, or adjust negative or selfish attitudes—if, that is, saving them is in the Team's best interests. You'll do well, though, to consider the wisdom revealed in the moral of humorist James Thurber's fable "The Bear Who Let It Alone": *You might as well fall flat on your face as lean over too far backward.*

After you have done your best to rehabilitate a troublemaker or bring an errant thinker back into the fold, the time may come when you have to give up, admit defeat, and cut the player loose to follow the path of his or her own choosing. It's not what you want to do, of course, but it may be what you have to do to preserve the Team. After all, if you allow one player to pursue individual goals that conflict with Team goals or violate Team rules, you may as well let all of them violate your rules, or you're creating an unhealthy double standard of rules enforcement that will lose your players' respect for the rules and for you.

Behaving badly is inexcusable. Your players know right from wrong, and no amount of alibiing will conceal that fact. They know, for example, that drug abuse is harmful and potentially dangerous, and they also know that their continued drug abuse will hurt the Team as well as themselves; why, then, might a player be willing to risk so much for a drug high? Because *the feeling induced by the drug is more important to the player than his or her commitment to the Team.* If that's the case—if the player cannot be persuaded to mend his or her ways—well, you have far more important uses for your time than to waste it trying to reach unreachable stars.

"A man cannot serve two masters," Jesus said—and it's true; to cite another either/or proposition, *either* the player will embrace the Team concept and consider its needs of paramount importance, *or* the Team doesn't need that player, no matter how highly skilled he or she may be. Overlook that fact, and eventually it will come back to haunt you. Sooner or later, the unrepentant problem player will let you and his or her Teammates down—usually, just when you need that player most.

---

[4] Prentice Hall, 1983 (ch. 16, "Motivating the Problem Athlete"). This book also has chapters devoted to handling superstar athletes and benchwarmers.

In closing, here's a thought regarding problem players from a coach we greatly admire: "I never kick a player off my team. If a player is a chronic rule-breaker or does something really bad to place her or the Team in a bad light, I'll make the penalties so severe that she may decide to quit the team rather than take the punishment. But, like the decision she made that got her into trouble in the first place, that's her choice to make and she can live with it.

"I just don't want her or her parents coming to me later and saying, 'It's *your* fault; *you* were the one who threw her off the Team.' That can't happen if it's *her* decision to quit the squad rather than *my* decision to let her go."

Part 2

PLAYING THE GAME

Life is but a game of football.

—Sir Walter Scott
English poet (1771–1832)

Chapter 4

DEVELOPING AN UNDERSTANDING OF THE GAME

Soccer is a complex structure of strategy, skill, and stamina, with elements of ballet, chess, and bar fights.[1]

THE PLAYING FIELD, OR PITCH

To coach and play soccer, you and your players should be thoroughly familiar with the field upon which the game is played (called a *pitch*). We spend considerable time teaching our young players about soccer pitches and their dimensions, lines, markings, and associated terminology; then we test their knowledge by having them draw a soccer pitch and label its parts. We think it's important because, over the course of their playing days, those youngsters are going to be spending hundreds, or even thousands, of hours practicing and playing on soccer pitches. It's their workplace—and ours, too—and all of us must be familiar with every facet of that workplace. The sooner familiarity is achieved, the easier all subsequent instruction and coaching becomes.

Figure 4-1 shows a pitch with its areas and lines labeled; we've also included a reproducible (unlabeled) diagram of a pitch in Appendix C so you can test your own players' knowledge.

Although dimensions vary from one playing site to another, all of them fall within limits prescribed by the Federation Internationale de Football Association (FIFA), the sport's worldwide governing body. Soccer pitches may vary from 100 to 130 yards in length and 50 to 100 yards in width.

The best dimensions for high school players are, we feel, 120 yards by 75–80 yards. While a regulation high school football field measuring 120 yards by 53.3 yards may be adequate for middle- or even junior-high schoolers, it is too long for elementary-age players and far too narrow and confining for older players who need greater maneuvering room and passing space. When high school games are played on football fields, the results are balls constantly flying out of bounds, countless throw-ins, and a lot of dead time that is frankly boring for spectators and frustrating for players.

---

[1] _____. "Soccer carries its own faithful." *Griffin Daily News* (June 20, 1998), p. 3B.

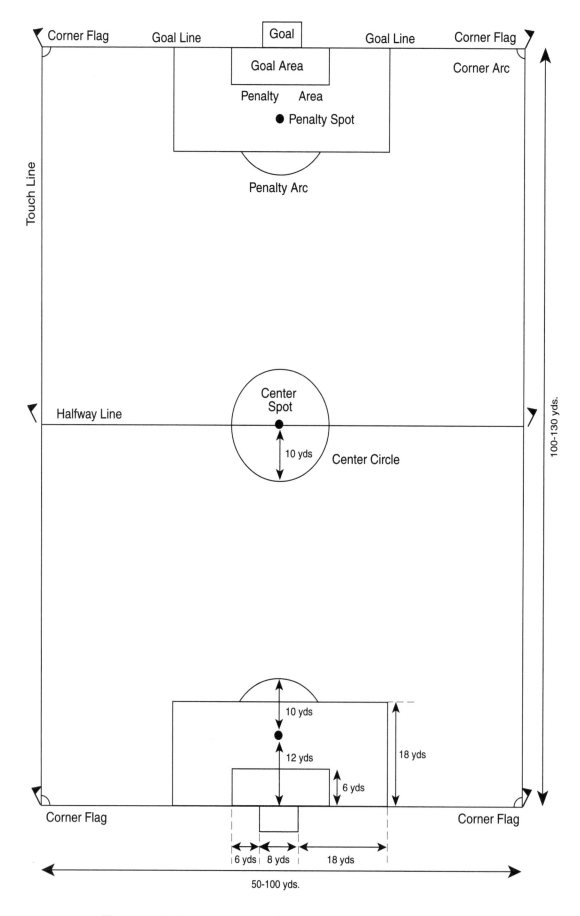

FIGURE 4–1. Soccer Pitch: Dimensions, Lines, and Flags

The good news here is that, as Bob Dylan observed back in the 1960s, "the times, they are a-changin'." Soccer is, at long last, finally gaining popular acceptance in this country. You can see its growth in popularity, not just in the thousands of club-level teams and rec leagues springing up everywhere year by year, or in the growing number of high schools across the nation that are adding girls' and boys' soccer teams to their athletic programs, but in the fact that many towns and cities are installing soccer pitches—*real* soccer fields, not football fields with running tracks around them.

Layout of the Pitch

The soccer pitch is enclosed by four boundary lines: two *touchlines* (sidelines) and two *goal lines* extending the length and width of the field, respectively. These pairs of parallel lines form the large rectangle within which play occurs. As with baseball, tennis, and volleyball, the boundary lines of a soccer pitch are considered part of the field of play; the ball is not out of bounds until it moves beyond the touchline or goal line.

The *halfway* or *midfield line* extends across the center of the pitch, dividing it into two equal halves. The halfway line separates the attacking and defending zones.

The *center circle* bisects the halfway line in the middle of the pitch, with a radius of ten yards from the *center spot*. Kickoffs are taken from the center spot to start each half of the game and to resume play after goals.

The goals at either end of the field are eight yards wide and eight feet high, with nets attached to catch the ball after goals are scored. The size of the goals is, like the rest of the field, scaled down for younger players; your state association will provide information regarding all such field and goal modifications upon request.

The *goal area*—commonly referred to as "the goal box," "the Box," or "the Six"—is a relatively small, rectangular area measuring 20 yards wide by 6 yards deep in front of the goal. Since the goal posts are eight yards apart, the goal area extends an additional six yards on either side of the goal. Goal kicks are taken from anywhere within this 20 yard by 6 yard area.

The rectangular *penalty area* measures 44 yards wide and 18 yards deep from the goal line. This area, which encloses the smaller *goal area*, is sometimes called "the Eighteen"; a defensive infraction occurring in the Eighteen and involving any of the nine major offenses (see p. 52) results in a direct free kick from the *penalty mark* located 12 yards from the center of the goal line, directly in front of the goal.

The *penalty arc* lies just outside the penalty area and behind the penalty mark; its purpose is to ensure that no one but the attacker and goalkeeper is within 10 yards of the ball in any direction when a penalty kick is taken. The attacker can move outside the arc for extra running room in approaching the ball.

The *corner arcs* are small semicircles, one yard in diameter, located in each of the four corners of the field. They define the areas from which corner kicks are taken.

In each of the four corners of the field stands a flag that is at least 5 feet tall.[2] The purpose of the flags is to aid the referee and linesmen in determining whether balls directed toward the corners went out of bounds over the touchline (resulting in a throw-in) or the goal line (resulting in a corner kick or goal kick, depending on which team last touched the ball). The flags are not removed for corner kicks.

---

[2] The height of the flagpole is an important safety factor. A short pole can impale a player who is unlucky enough to fall on it. Broken poles should be replaced or mended immediately, not used in their broken state.

RULES AND PLAYING PROCEDURES

The basic rules of soccer are the same wherever the game is played. While worldwide soccer is administered by FIFA and its various affiliated national associations, however, American high school and club soccer is governed at the state and local levels, with rules varying slightly from those of FIFA in certain minor respects (e.g., length of games, substitution limits). At the public high school level, all 50 state high school associations are members of (and play under rules sanctioned by) the National Federation of State High School Associations (NFSHSA).

Thus, while FIFA sets the length of international soccer matches at two 45-minute halves, NFSHSA uses two 40-minute halves for high school games, and club-level soccer in Georgia features halves of 45 minutes for 17- to 19-year-olds, 40 minutes for 15- to 16-year-olds, 35 minutes for 13- to 14-year-olds, 30 minutes for 11- to 12-year-olds, and 25 minutes or less for younger players, at the discretion of local governing bodies. Other states set their own club-level time limits for matches.

Regarding substitutions, FIFA permits a maximum of five substitute players on a team's roster and three substitutions per team to be made during a match, and players who are replaced may not reenter the game. In the United States, where soccer officials are and have been doing everything in their power to broaden participation at all levels of play, these rules have been dramatically relaxed, at least, from the high school level downward. Under NFSHSA rules, players may be substituted as freely and as often as their coach desires, as long as the substitutions are made during stoppages in play (i.e., after goals, between periods, during injury timeouts or issuance of yellow [caution] or red [disqualification] cards, or before a throw-in, corner kick, or goal kick). Other specifics of the rules regarding length of games, substitutions, and other modifications for high school or club play may be drawn from their respective rulebooks, both of which are readily available through state governing bodies. Rules regarding player eligibility at the high school level are contained in a separate handbook that is issued to coaches annually by state high school associations.

These cosmetic changes do not affect the validity of our opening statement: The rules that govern the sport of soccer are the same wherever it is played. Soccer is, like hockey (and unlike American football, basketball, baseball, or volleyball), a game of virtually continuous action. Once the game is started via the opening kickoff, there are no timeouts, and the clock stops only when a team scores,[3] time expires at the end of either half, injuries occur on the field, or unavoidable delays arise (e.g., a dog running out on the field or the ball is found to be losing air). The referee may also add time to the clock whenever a team is deemed to have wasted time after play has been whistled to a stop.

Scoring

The object of the game of soccer is to win by scoring more goals than your opponent does. To count as a goal scored, the entire ball must cross the goal line under the crossbar and between the goal posts.

---

[3] At the high school level, that is. The clock does not stop after scores at the club level.

The various governing bodies in soccer have their own formats for resolving games that are tied at the end of regulation play. Generally, however, in most regular league games throughout the world, draws at the end of regulation play are not resolved.

Kickoffs

A pregame coin toss decides which team kicks off and which goal each team will defend, with the winner of the toss choosing the ball or end of the field and the loser making the other choice. When the ball is placed down for kickoff, all players must be on their own half of the field and no one is allowed in the center circle except members of the kicking team.

Unlike American football, in soccer the kicking team kicks off to itself; the kick must travel forward, and a goal can be scored directly from the kickoff. The ball is in play when it travels its circumference (i.e., 27–28 inches), after which any player from either team is free to enter the center circle or cross the halfway line. The player who kicks off cannot touch the ball again until someone else has touched it.

After halftime, the teams change ends of the field. The kickoff to start play in the second half goes to the team that did not kick off to start the game.

Resuming Play After Stoppages

Play is not always continuous in soccer, but it *is* continuous until the referee's whistle signals that play is halted. When play stops, it is resumed in one of five ways: by a *drop ball*, a *throw-in*, a *goal kick*, a *corner kick*, or a *free kick*.

Drop Ball. When neither the referee nor linesmen know which team caused the ball to go out of bounds—or when play is temporarily halted for reasons such as the ball losing air or an infant wandering onto the playing field—the referee resumes play by dropping the ball between the players somewhat in the manner of a faceoff in hockey, except that any number of players may be involved rather than just two.

Throw-Ins. When a team last touches the ball before it crosses the touchline and goes out of bounds, the other team is awarded a throw-in at that spot to resume play. The player making the throw-in must stand behind the touchline, holding the ball above and behind his head with two hands, and facing the field of play. He must make the throw either with both feet flat on the ground or with his front foot flat and the toe of his other foot dragging the ground (to generate greater force as he throws). He cannot lift either foot in the air or jump in making the throw-in, nor can he throw the ball one-handed. Then, having thrown the ball, he cannot touch it again until someone else has touched it.

Goal Kicks. When the offensive team last touches the ball before it crosses the goal line and goes out of bounds, the defensive team is given a goal kick. Although the goalkeeper is usually chosen to make goal kicks, anyone on her team may do so. The ball is placed on the ground anywhere within the goal area. No one from the opposing team may enter the penalty area until the ball leaves that area. If the ball is double-kicked—or if it does not clear the penalty area—it is rekicked.

Corner Kicks. When the defensive team last touches the ball before it goes out of bounds across the goal line, the offensive team puts the ball in play via a corner kick taken from the corner arc nearest to where the ball went out. No player from the defensive team is allowed within 10 yards of the ball until it is kicked. The ball is in play when it travels its circumference, and the kicker may not touch it again until someone else touches or plays it. Goals may be scored directly from corner kicks without any other player's having touched the ball.

Free Kicks. There are two types of free kicks, *indirect* and *direct*, the differences being that (a) whereas indirect free kicks result from unintentional violations of the rules (e.g., offside), direct free kicks are awarded for major (intentional) infractions; and (b) while someone else besides the kicker must touch the ball before a goal can be scored off an indirect kick, the kicker himself (or herself) can shoot and score off a direct kick.

Indirect free kicks. An indirect free kick is awarded to a team when an opposing player commits a minor infraction. Offsides is one such infraction; others include dangerous play, such as executing high kicks or low headers; charging into an opponent with the shoulder when neither player is playing the ball (called an "off-the-ball incident"); intentionally obstructing an opponent when not playing the ball; charging into the goalkeeper when he is not holding the ball; the goalkeeper's taking more than four steps with the ball before throwing or kicking it; and technical offenses such as the same player's kicking the ball twice in executing a free kick.

Players may be cautioned, or "yellow-carded," for such acts as persistent minor violations; entering or intentionally leaving the field of play without the referee's having signaled for her to do so; arguing with the referee; or otherwise indulging in unladylike or ungentlemanly behavior. Such infractions give the opposing team an indirect free kick at the spot of the foul.

Players may be "red-carded" and ejected from the game for violent conduct, for using profane or abusive language, or for being yellow-carded a second time. A player who has been disqualified may not be replaced by a substitute; instead, that team must play one player short for the rest of the game.

At the high school level, coaches may be yellow- or red-carded for improper conduct of the sort described above; additionally, it is entirely within the referee's discretion to order hostile or abusive fans from the premises or face having their team disqualified and the game awarded to the opponents by forfeit.

In soccer, the referee reigns supreme, and woe be unto the coach, player, or fan who fails to grasp that fact. You may be the king or queen of your castle at home, Coach, but on the soccer pitch the referee's word is law. If you or any of your players insist on getting in the last word where referees are concerned, that word is likely to be *Good-bye.*

When an indirect free kick is awarded, no opposing player is allowed within 10 yards of the ball until it is kicked,[4] and a goal cannot be scored until someone else has touched the ball.

Direct free kicks. Direct free kicks result from any of nine major rules infractions: kicking an opponent; tripping an opponent; jumping at an opponent; charging violently or dangerously into an opponent; striking or spitting at an opponent; holding an opponent; pushing an opponent; charging into an opponent from behind; or

---

[4] Except when the kicking team elects to execute a fast free kick, whether indirect or direct. The 10-yards-away rule is in effect only when the kicking team requests it.

deliberately using any part of the hands or arms to control the ball. In all cases but one (see below), direct kicks on goal are taken from the spot of the foul. No opposing player may be within 10 yards of the ball until it is kicked.

The exception to the above involves *penalty kicks*. As previously noted, when a major foul is committed inside the penalty area, the offended team receives a free, 1-v-1 kick from the penalty spot 12 yards from the goal, and no one but the penalty taker and goalkeeper is permitted inside the penalty area until the ball is kicked.[5]

Penalty Kicks. Involving just two players—an attacker and the opposing goalkeeper—penalty kicks rank among soccer's most exciting and challenging confrontations. The two players stand 12 yards apart, with everyone else watching from beyond the penalty box and its arc; the keeper can position herself anywhere along the goal line between the posts and under the crossbar,[6] and the attacker cannot kick the ball in any direction except toward the goal. The attacker also cannot kick the ball for a second time until someone else touches or plays it.

If the keeper deflects the ball out of bounds, the offensive team is given a corner kick; if the ball is deflected into the field of play, it is considered a live ball, and the kicker or anyone else within range of the ball can collect it and shoot on goal; and if the penalty kick rebounds off the crossbar or a goal post, the kicker may not touch the ball again until someone else has touched or played it.(The penalty: an indirect free kick for the opponents from the spot of the infraction.)

Offside. In basketball, there's a strategy known as "snowbirding" in which, while the other nine players are playing at one end of the court, the tenth player stays under his own basket at the other end of the court, waiting for his teammates to get the ball back and pass it to him for an easy score. That can't happen in soccer, because of a sometimes-confusing rule known as *offside*. The offside rule is intended to keep soccer games from degenerating into endless successions of long passes and 1-v-1 confrontations near the goals of either team. Scores of 80–76 or higher may be the norm in basketball, but they are *not* the norm in soccer.

Basically, the offside rule states that, when a player is ahead of the ball in the opponents' half of the field, at least one defender other than the goalkeeper must be closer to the goal line than he is when the ball is passed to him. However, simply being ahead of the ball with only the goalkeeper between an attacker and the goal does not in itself constitute being offside, since it becomes an unfair advantage only when the attacker receives the ball from a teammate. *Offside is determined by where the player was when the ball was passed to her, not by where she was when she received the ball* (Figures 4-2 and 4-3).

Offside cannot be called when a player receives a teammate's throw-in, goal kick, or corner kick.

All of this surely appears somewhat confusing to someone new to soccer; after all, FIFA's *Laws of the Game* devotes 24 pages to analyzing the offside rule and its applications. So let's try it again from a slightly different perspective.

---

[5] When the offensive team commits an infraction inside the opponents' penalty box, the defense is awarded a direct free kick at the spot of the foul.

---

[6] In high school soccer, the keeper cannot move her feet until the ball is kicked; under FIFA rules, she can take one step in any direction before the ball is kicked.

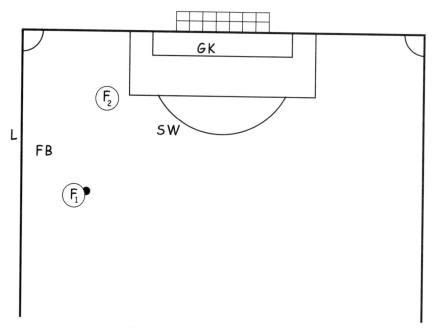

FIGURE 4–2. Not Offsides

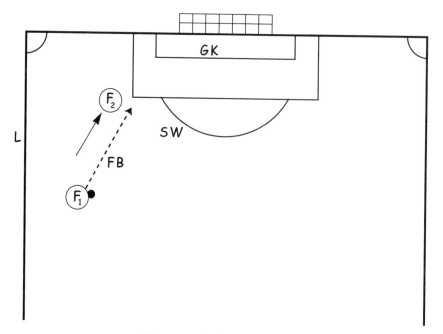

FIGURE 4–3. Offsides

You're the attacker with the ball, and *I'm* the defender who is marking (guarding) you. If you already have the ball in my half of the field, offside is not a problem as long as you keep it; if you can dribble by me and shoot on goal, 1-v-1 with the goalkeeper, hey, that's *my* tough luck, not yours! Score one for the good guys.

The situation is radically different, however, when you're in my defensive end of the field and one of your teammates decides to pass the ball ahead to you. If, when the ball is passed, you're closer to my goal than I am, and no other defender except the goalkeeper is closer to the goal than you are, you're offside. At least a 2-v-1 initial defensive advantage must exist (i.e., the keeper and I must be closer to our goal than you are) when the ball is passed to you, if you are not to be considered offside.[7]

After the ball is passed, however (or while it's traveling forward), you can run past me, collect the pass and go 1-v-1 with the goalkeeper, as shown in Figure 4-3; if you do, well, chalk up another one for the good guys. You weren't offside when the ball was passed. I should have played better defense.

The offside rule and its many applications offer ample evidence of why it's important for you and your players to understand the *Laws of the Game* as thoroughly as possible. If your players don't know the rules—and if they don't possess the field awareness necessary to recognize when they're offside—the rules themselves will function as a twelfth player on the field working against your team.

Think of it this way: Every time one of your players is offside, your team loses ball possession and possibly a scoring opportunity as well, since you can't score when the other team has the ball. Throw away enough scoring opportunities, and you wind up losing games that you should have won.

Someone wiser than we are noted that "an ounce of prevention is worth a pound of cure." Understanding the rules of the game is the ounce of prevention that you and your players need if your team is to achieve its potential and prevent winnable games from slipping away via avoidable errors. You won't ever completely eliminate preventable mistakes such as offsides violations, but the closer you come toward that goal, the better your team will perform.

THE PLAYERS

A full team consists of eleven players: a goalkeeper (hereafter referred to as the *keeper)* and ten field players. The ten field players may be aligned in a number of ways, one of which is shown in Figure 4-4. While everyone but the keeper plays offense and defense, the other players are customarily regarded as defenders, midfielders, or attackers.

The players whose primary responsibilities are defensive in nature include the *keeper, sweeper, fullbacks,* and *stopper,* all of whom must be quick, strong, alert, aggressive, and fundamentally sound if you hope to control opponents defensively.

As will be seen in Chapter 7, the midfield area is crucial to team strategy. It is here, in the middle third of the field, where offensive and defensive advantages are most likely to arise; thus, the team that controls midfield is likely to extend that control to the attacking and/or defensive thirds as well. Your *midfielders* are the team's workhorses; they must be versatile performers, skilled in passing and attacking as well as in playing defense.

---

[7] "Closer to the goal" means just that; you're not offside if the pass is made while we're running side by side.

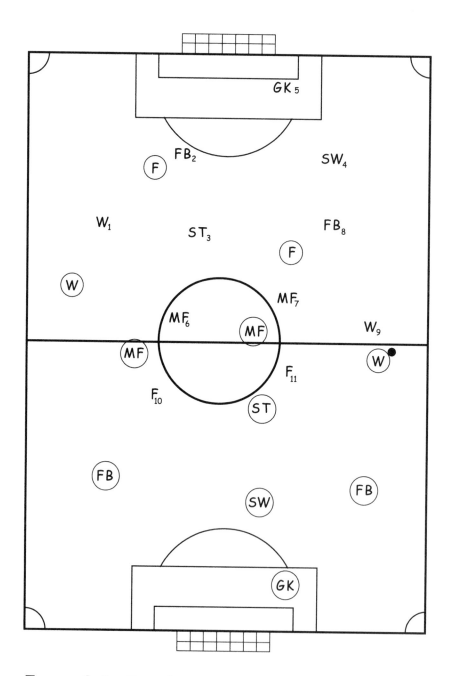

FIGURE 4–4. Typical Man-to-Man Defensive Alignment, Ball Near Touchline at Midfield

The *wingers* and *forwards* are primarily attackers (i.e., offensive players). Wingers attack offensively along the touchlines, spreading the defense and creating space for the attack. The primary job of the forwards is to lead the attack and score goals.

The Goalkeeper

Keepers wear uniforms of a different color from that of their teammates. Their primary responsibility is to keep the ball from crossing the goal line, their secondary role that of directing the defense. Of the 22 players on the pitch, the keepers are the only ones who always have a full view of the entire field of play. They also are the only players who are legally permitted to use their arms and hands to catch, deflect, or pass the ball; however, such usage is restricted to the penalty area.

Since the keeper—GK_5 in Figure 4-4—represents the last line of defense short of surrendering a goal, it follows that he seldom ventures far from the Six, or goal area. Keepers normally stand just in front of the goal line, midway between the goal posts, and move parallel to the goal line with the movement of the ball. We call this movement toward the ball side of the pitch *reducing the shooting angle*. It involves surrendering a certain amount of open goal space on weak side (i.e., the side of the pitch away from the ball) in order to intensify coverage on the ball side, where a shot on goal is most likely to be aimed (Figure 4-5).

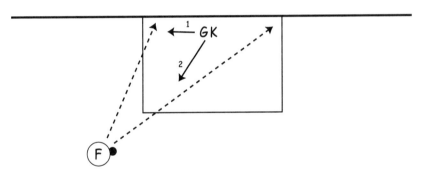

FIGURE 4–5. Keeper Moving to Reduce Shooting Angles

If there were no defender in the goal area, the forward in Figure 4-5 would aim her shot at the center of the goal to give it the greatest possible margin of error. With the keeper stationed midway between the goalposts, however, the forward will, in all likelihood, aim for the lower left-hand corner of the goal because it's closer than the other side. Knowing this, the keeper will move toward the ball side of the goal—not all the way, of course, since that would leave the entire right side of the goal unguarded, but enough to increase her chances of catching or deflecting the closer shot.

The "1" and "2" shown in Figure 4-5 indicate the relative positions an inexperienced and veteran keeper might assume to defense a shot on goal as shown, the beginner (1) moving along the goal line and the veteran (2) moving out from the goal line as well as toward the ball side. The veteran's outward movement serves to further reduce the shooter's effective angle on goal if she decides to take the longer shot.

Sometimes the keeper may even leave the goal area entirely to retrieve a free ball or challenge an unmarked attacker. Doing so can entail great risk, though, since if the attacker gets to the ball first—or if he foils the keeper's attempt to contain him—there is no one left defending the goal.

Having blocked or caught a shot on goal (called *making a save*), retrieved a loose ball, or otherwise collected the ball in play, the keeper may elect to use one or both hands to throw it or roll it to a teammate, or else she may kick it away. She may take as many as four steps before throwing it or kicking it away. What she *cannot* do is keep the ball in her possession indefinitely. If she fails to release the ball within six seconds, she is charged with *wasting time*, and the opponents are given an indirect free kick from the point of infraction.[8]

The Sweeper

If the keeper is the defensive team's last line of defense, the sweeper—SW_4 in Figure 4-4—is the next-to-the-last line of defense; he is the defender who covers the ball side of the penalty area between the keeper and the ball. The sweeper is essentially playing zone defense regardless of what the rest of the team is playing; his primary responsibilities are to organize and direct the team defense, mark any unmarked attacker who threatens the defense, and stop any dribbler who breaks through the defense and attacks the goal area.

Offensively, the sweeper normally functions as a supporting player, especially in relaying the ball from one attacker to another or in maintaining ball possession while the offense is reorganized after the initial attack has stalled or broken down.

Fullbacks

Fullbacks — FB_2 and FB_8 in Figure 4-4 — mark forwards in man-to-man defense. In zone defense, the fullbacks must avoid being maneuvered into the center of the pitch, or else the defensive flanks along the touchlines will be open to attack.

Fullbacks defend and attack along the wings, staying wide to extend the opponents' defense across the field. They may also serve as "safety valves" in maintaining ball possession when protecting a lead, or when the attack has stalled and the players need time and space to realign themselves for a fresh attack.

The Stopper

If Pele or Diego Maradona were still playing and in his prime, you'd probably assign a stopper — ST_3 in Figure 4-4 — or else a midfielder, to mark him. Marking quick, aggressive attackers who have more moves and fakes than a purse snatcher on a busy street is by no means easy, but it *is* challenging, and highly satisfying when done successfully. Playing in the middle, your stoppers must be adept at heading the ball out of danger.

We want our stoppers to believe that every potential goal they deny opponents' star forwards is the equivalent of a goal scored for our team. It's not, of course, but we want our stoppers to play with urgency and abandon, since nothing less than a total effort is likely to contain a highly skilled attacker.

---

[8] Unless the keeper was inside the Six, in which case the ball is placed on the 6-yard line in front of the goal.

Midfielders

Playing primarily in the middle third of the field, the midfielders—MF_6 and MF_7 in Figure 4-4 — serve as the vital link between defense and offense. Defensively, the midfielders function as second stoppers, marking midfielders or weak side attackers. Offensively, central midfielders are ideally situated for the task of moving the ball upfield and making penetrating passes to wings or forwards in the attacking third of the field.

Wingers

Primarily offensive players, the wingers —W_1 and W_9 in Figure 4-4 — should be capable of running the touchlines and maneuvering into position for shots on goal or combination passing sequences with teammates in 2-v-1 situations.

Your wingers should be skilled dribblers and passers, especially when it comes to executing accurate crossing passes. Regarding the former, it's generally easier for the wingers to advance the ball by dribbling along the touchlines than it is for the forwards to try to dribble through the heart of the defense in the middle of the field. Regarding the latter, the wingers should be able to "see" the field while dribbling in order to spot openings in the defense or find teammates breaking free of their markers, or to know when to cross the ball to the other side of the pitch to catch the defenders off guard.

Forwards (also called *Strikers*)

Functioning as the team's premier ballhandlers and/or shooters, the forwards—F_{10} and F_{11} in Figure 4-4 — are the heart and soul of the attacking unit. Their primary function is to create and exploit offensive advantages—and to *score*. Forwards should be, as coach Jake Gaither described his football players, "a-gile, mo-bile, and hos-tile"; that is, they must be quick, aggressive, willing to take chances, and capable of outmaneuvering their markers and pressing attacking advantages at high speed under intense defensive pressure. Besides being skilled at passing, dribbling, and executing shots on goal with either foot from all angles, forwards should be adept at heading the ball and making one-touch collections on the run in order to maintain attacking advantages. They should be able to pressure opponents defensively after losing the ball, whether to recapture it or to slow the opponents' attack and give their teammates time to retreat and organize the team defense.

The best forwards play with confidence that borders on arrogance; they want the ball regardless of the situation, and they take charge at crunch time when the game is on the line, the clock is running out, and their team is one goal behind. When nothing but a successful shot on goal will do, every team needs a forward who wants to create the scoring opportunity and expects to make the shot.

In concluding this chapter, we should note that unlike, say, American football, the positions in soccer are highly flexible. With the exception of the two keepers, every player on the field is likely to play two or more offensive and/or defensive positions during a match. These changes are not announced; they simply occur naturally as the game unfolds.

For example, if an outside fullback (wingback) in a 5-3-2 defense is out of position to join the attack when her team regains possession of the ball, someone else—

possibly a midfielder who is in position to do so—will take her place running the touchline. Later, perhaps, they may revert to their former positions—or, as is equally likely depending on their versatility, one or both of them may have occasion to swap positions with other players.

The most important thing to remember is that *soccer is a game of opportunities to be taken advantage of or wasted*. It is both impractical and imprudent for the attacking team to slow down and wait for a given player to catch up with the lead attackers when the defense is disorganized and unsure of how to mark the attackers. Only when the initial attack has been blunted should the players even begin to consider reverting to their former positions.

The same holds true regarding defense: If, in man-to-man defense, two players are forced to alter their marking responsibilities, they will stay with their new marks for as long as the other team has the ball, changing back to their original marks the next time the opponents have the ball.

Chapter 5

SOCCER FUNDAMENTALS

*My father saw me kicking with my right foot as a boy,
and he . . . taught me to kick with my left foot, too, so I could kick
from any position in any direction, very quick! To kick with great power
depends on leg muscles, but you must also practice how to use that power
best with the nicest placement of the foot on the ball. The impact position is
most important. I believed in this and I began to kick against the wall,
to practice with both legs, kicking and rebounding, hour after hour.
Right foot, left foot, until I got the same power in both legs.*

—Pele

TEACHING SOCCER SKILLS

No one is born with soccer-playing or -coaching skills. While some players possess greater athletic ability than others (e.g., greater quickness, balance, or agility), those advantages are important only when soccer's fundamental skills have been mastered. Quickness and anticipation can get you in position to make the play, but they can't make the play for you.

As in most sports, many of the basic skills of soccer are unnatural; they must be learned through rigorous instruction, drill, and practice, as Pele noted. For example, the "natural" way to kick objects is with the *toe*, not the side of the foot; however, controlling the speed, direction, and loft of the ball in passing, shooting, or dribbling requires the flat surface afforded by the side of the foot or the instep (which in turn requires a significantly different kicking motion than toe-kicking).

As coaches, we already know that, of course; are we then justified in assuming that players know it when they come to us for the first time? Should we assume that they will execute those skills—or any others—properly if we neglect to teach them? Can players with natural ability reach their potential without instruction and drill in the fundamentals? Of course not.

> *The ideal condition*
> *Would be, I admit, that men should be right by instinct;*
> *But since we all are likely to go astray,*
> *The reasonable thing is to learn from those who can teach.*

—Sophocles
Antigone (c. 442 B.C.)

If you're just starting out in coaching, you should begin from a single premise. Over the long haul, this premise will determine how effective your coaching will be:

All good coaching is teaching.

The two all-important aspects of teaching are *communicating* and *using repetitive drills to make skills execution habitual.*

Communicating consists of finding ways to get players to understand what they need to know in order to play effectively. Sometimes it involves demonstration and explanation of new skills; sometimes it involves correcting mistakes. In all cases, it requires patience and willingness to try, try again if at first your players don't succeed in learning what you're trying to teach them.

Learning is unpredictable; it occurs at its own pace, and you never know in advance when it is going to occur. The best any coach can do is create conditions favorable for learning in daily practices, be a teacher rather than a spectator, and constantly look for new ways to show and tell players how to execute the fundamental skills of soccer.

Soccer is a game of habits. Its high-speed nature and constant movement require that players make split-second decisions while executing fundamental skills. Correct execution of skills requires constant practice and repetition. Within that context, teaching consists of communicating concepts of proper form, and using drills and activities involving specific skills repeated over and over until players no longer have to think about how those skills are supposed to be performed.

Four Principles of Teaching and Learning

1. *You can't teach people who aren't listening.* You should require that all action and conversation cease and all heads turn your way whenever you're talking to the team or coaching an individual player in a team context. (This is especially important in coaching young children of elementary age, whose attention spans are measured in milliseconds. We find ourselves constantly telling them, "Give me your eyes.") Otherwise, you'll find yourself repeating things that need not have been said but once if your players had been listening. You should expect your players to concentrate, not just on what they're doing, but on what you're saying as well.

2. *You can't teach people who don't want to learn.* In fact, you shouldn't even have them on your team. It's something to think about when selecting your squad in preseason tryouts.

   The converse of the above statement is equally important: *You should never give up on a player who wants to learn.* The desire to learn is what makes learning possible.

3. *Practicing the fundamentals should precede competitive drills.* It's difficult to compete when you're unable to perform the skills necessary for competing.

4. *The more organized your practice is, the more you'll accomplish.* Organization is a habit—a learned trait—not a God-given talent. We've never known a really effective coach who wasn't organized. Planning your daily practices—and writing them down so you'll remember what you want to accomplish—gives structure to your practice sessions. Knowing beforehand what areas you want to cover and how you plan to approach them gives you confidence starting out; it also gives your players confidence that you know what you're doing, where the team is heading, and how you plan to get it there.

Hints for Effective Teaching

1. *Don't assume that players understand what you're talking about just because they don't ask questions.* Maybe they're just shy and afraid to speak up; or maybe they don't want to look stupid for not knowing what they think everyone else understands.

   If you want to know whether your players understand you, ask them questions about the subject under discussion. You should always encourage your players to ask questions whenever they don't understand something, no matter how trivial or insignificant it may appear to them. If you create a team atmosphere in which *no* question is silly or unimportant—except, of course, the one that goes, "How much longer do we have to practice?—and if you treat players' questions with the respect they deserve, you're likely to find them speaking up more and more frequently because they want to learn and have no fear of your displeasure or their teammates' disapproval when they don't understand. Answering questions is never a waste of time. The hard part is getting your players to ask them.

2. *Teach new skills and strategies in small doses.* Always consider the K.I.S.S. principle: *Keep It Simple, Stupid.* Use specific drills to teach specific skills. Break down team techniques and strategies into their component parts and practice each part separately before putting it all together. Start where they are right now, and don't try to teach more at any given time than the players are prepared to handle.

   There are two corollaries to the notion of teaching in small doses: *Don't try to teach everything at once*—and *don't expect your instruction to provide instant success.*

   Regarding the former, we recommend limiting your teaching to one or two new skills or strategies in a single practice session, using the remainder of your practice time to work in areas that you have covered previously.

   Trying to touch all the bases in every daily practice can be frustrating for players, especially for those whose inexperience limits what they can absorb at any given time. A shotgun approach to instruction may seem necessary or desirable when there is so very much for players to learn and so little time for them to learn it in; still, highlighting one or two different areas in every daily practice and using a variety of drills to practice those skills and supplement your instruction serves to keep players focused within narrow limits. It also helps to improve their concentration and increases the chances of their achieving successes, however slight, in what they're doing. Broadly focused practices are all right for experienced and highly skilled players—but even then, new skills or patterns should be introduced in such a manner as to inspire players to master them rather than frustrating them because they cannot master a given skill instantly. Frustration impairs players' ability to concentrate, and thus increases the odds that they will fail in subsequent attempts.

Regarding the latter point, that instant success is unlikely in your teaching, keep this in mind: *Instruction does not build soccer skills; it introduces or modifies them.* Skills are built through a three-step process: repetition, repetition, and repetition. One you have introduced a given skill through whatever demonstration and explanation (show and tell) techniques you employ, your next goal is to have your players rehearse the skill under close monitoring, with mistakes being corrected as they arise, until the players are capable of performing the skill correctly and consistently without having to think about it. The quality of your drills will influence the rate at which they master skills, of course, but time is also a prime factor in speed of learning. Encourage your players to practice at home and on their own time the skills and drills you use at your daily practices; it's the only known shortcut to success in teaching and learning soccer skills.

3. *When in doubt, go back to the basics.* All aspects of team play, no matter how simple or complex, are based on successful execution of fundamental skills. When a given aspect of your team's play isn't working, go back and work on the individual skills involved. Time spent working on basic skills is never wasted time.

4. *Use every available resource in teaching skills.* If you've never played soccer, and you aren't comfortable with the idea of demonstrating proper form in skills execution, maybe you can find someone local—perhaps a high school varsity player or an experienced adult—to help out. There are a number of very good fundamentals videos available (see Appendix A), and we've known coaches to collect soccer photos from magazines to create montage posters depicting various skills. We've lent books and videos to players from our professional library, and encouraged young players to check out books from the local and school libraries as well.

Young players who are still in the early stages of their development as soccer players should understand from the start that there is a right way and a wrong way to execute the fundamentals; the development of their playing skills requires that they see those skills demonstrated correctly by someone using proper form. As King Solomon wisely noted, "Train up a child in the way he should go, and when he is old he will not depart from it." (Proverbs 22:6)

Game films and videos are excellent teaching tools; they can be used to demonstrate skills and correct mistakes. They offer the advantage of showing players what they are doing—as opposed to what they may *think* they're doing—which is important for players who are too inexperienced to have developed a kinesthetic sense of their own bodies in motion. Along these same lines, videotaping individual players (or the team as a whole, for that matter) in practice can pinpoint strengths and weaknesses of which players may be unaware.

5. *Teach new skills or strategies early in practice while players are physically and mentally fresh.*

6. *Have your players practice the basic skills stationary before performing them in motion.* The usual progression is stationary, walking, trotting, running. More than occasional inability to perform a skill properly at a given speed indicates that the skill has not yet been mastered. Have the player drop back to the next slower speed.

   The same rule of thumb applies to individual and group drills. The progression is individual, pairs, groups of three or more players, and team drills. When such drills break down regularly, go back to the next smaller grouping.

   For team offensive pattern drills, the progression should be (1) walking through the pattern without opposition; (2) walking through the pattern against passive (unaggressive) marking; (3) trotting through the pattern against passive marking; (4) running the pattern against passive marking; and (5) running the pattern at game speed against active (aggressive) marking. In all cases, the drill sequences should conclude with the attackers taking shots on goal.

7. *Try to make daily practices enjoyable.* "I like to see players smiling through the sweat and tears," as one coach put it. Admittedly, this is sometimes easier said than done; still, it should be considered a desirable goal since the alternative is players' dreading coming to practice every day. (*Note:* We aren't saying that practice should always be fun in the sense of a casual atmosphere, or allowing players to indulge in horseplay, because enjoyment also derives from accomplishing goals, mastering skills, and participating in competitive drills and activities.)

   There are a number of ways to make practices enjoyable, one of which is to vary the drills and activities from one day to the next, thus avoiding the sort of sameness that leads to boredom. Another method that we've used is to ask our players how they liked a particular drill that we're trying out. (Bear in mind, though—human nature dictates that people often dislike anything new that fails to produce instant success.) Some coaches gradually reduce the length of their practices as the season wears on, going from as long as 2-1/2 hours in early season to as short as 45 minutes as tournament time draws near. Some coaches occasionally give their team a day off from daily practice, and some also give their starters an additional day off in late season, both as a reward to those players for their hard work and to give the coaches one full practice session to focus all of their attention on the rest of the team.

   We've interrupted our practices for such offbeat activities as having an ice cream break, letting the players eat popcorn while watching game films, dragging out the P.E. volleyball standards and a beach ball to play soccer volleyball, or playing soccer golf with safety cones as the "holes" on the day before an important region playoff game—*anything* to keep the kids wondering (rather than dreading) what comes next.

   The best way of all, though—and the method that underlies much of what we do in daily practice once our players have at least partially mastered the basic skills—is to make drills and activities competitive and game-related wherever possible. Our kids are highly competitive—as all athletes should be—and they enjoy the challenge of competing in drills or scrimmaging sessions. If we play our starters as a unit, we like to put them at a disadvantage, whether by giving the other unit additional players, reducing the number of attackers they can have, or anything else we can think of to make them work harder. The better they are, the greater the obstacles we present them with. Highly skilled players love challenges; they also get bored without them.

8. *Be a learner as well as a teacher.* You don't have to know all there is to know about soccer to be a good coach—but you *do* have to know at least as much about it as your players do, and preferably more. You don't need professional playing experience in order to teach soccer fundamentals effectively—but you *do* need to understand concepts of proper form as applied to passing, shooting, heading, dribbling, tackling, and receiving the ball. If you don't understand what constitutes proper form in playing skills, you won't know when your players are developing bad habits that will limit their effectiveness. Unless you recognize their mistakes as such, you won't know how to correct them. Doing things correctly doesn't always win games, but you can bet your next two paychecks that doing things wrong will lose games.

9. *Learn the* Laws of the Game—*and teach them to your players.* One of the many aspects of soccer we've always liked is that, unlike some other sports (e.g., basketball) there is only one set of rules governing the game. Regardless of whether you're coaching a team in Abilene or Abu Dhabi, an Olympic team or a group of 6-year-olds who couldn't tell you whether the ball is round or square, the rules are the same for everyone.

   Developed by the Federation Internationale de Football Association (FIFA), the *Laws of the Game* of soccer vary between sexes or age groups only in terms of the dimensions of the ball and playing field, duration of periods of play, and number of substitutions allowed. Beyond that, the game is the same regardless of who is playing it, or where. Is any excuse, therefore, justifiable for any coach's or player's failing to understand the rules?

   Upon agreeing to coach a team, the first step that any soccer coach should take is to acquire a current FIFA rulebook and read it from cover to cover until the rules are thoroughly familiar and understood. The second thing the coach should do is explain the rules to his or her players. Failing to take those two preliminary steps is as serious an oversight as attempting to run a business without understanding the federal, state, and local laws pertaining to operating a business. Yet, over the years, we've seen many coaches, players, and fans react to referees' calls as if the rules governing offside had just been added to the rulebook last week.

   Do yourself and your players a favor: Even if you've read the rules before, go back and read them again. Purchase a new rulebook every year, and study whatever changes have occurred since last year. If your players are old enough to read and understand the rules, have them read the *Laws of the Game,* too—or at least take the time to explain the rules to them in a manner that they can understand.[1]

---

[1] The catalogs listed in Appendix A offer USSA-approved videotapes covering the rules of soccer.

Inasmuch as you—and your players, as well—intend to devote a large portion of your time to practicing and playing soccer, you owe it to everyone concerned to see that you—and they—understand the rules by which the game is played.

SOCCER'S BASIC SKILLS

Soccer's fundamental skills are *passing; shooting; heading; dribbling; receiving; tackling;* and *goalkeeping.*

Passing

Professional golfers have a saying that places golf's fundamentals in their proper perspective: *You drive for show and putt for dough.* Soccer's equivalent to that adage could well be, *You dribble for show and pass to win.* Dribbling is important, undeniably so, but it is the ability to make quick, accurate passes to open teammates (or to open areas of the pitch to which teammates are making a run) that leads to the majority of scores (Figure 5-1). Without good passing and collecting (receiving), all you have is kick ball. It is far easier to defend a team that dribbles well than one that passes well. In the former case, all you have to do is control the dribbler; in the latter case, you have to control everyone.

FIGURE 5–1. Passing

The ability to make quick and accurate passes with either foot or the head is a skill that requires many hours of concentrated practice. Like the interaction between a quarterback and his receivers in football, passing and receiving the ball in soccer require a high degree of timing, accuracy, pacing, power, and deceptive moves that can only be mastered through constant practice. The result of such mastery is players who, through familiarity with one another's playing habits, always seem to be in the right place at the right time to make or receive passes. The ability to pass well places great pressure on defenses, since on-the-ball defenders cannot rely on their teammates' helping out lest they surrender a quick pass to an attacking teammate.

The Basic Passes. While the inside or outside of the foot, the instep, the heel, or even the head may be used in passing the ball, greatest accuracy is achieved when using the inside of the foot—the "meat of the feet"—to make short- to medium-length passes. The most common such pass is the *push pass,* so called because the player pushes the ball away from his body (Figures 5-1a and 5-1b).

FIGURE 5–1a. Push Pass *(see a - b)*

FIGURE 5–1b

In performing the push pass, the kicker's nonkicking foot should be planted 6–8 inches away from, and to the side of, the ball, toes pointed in the direction of the pass. As the kicking foot begins its downward movement, the player turns his foot sideways, locking his ankle and aiming for the middle of the ball. The kicking movement consists of a pendulumlike leg sweep through the ball that continues in follow-through, with the kicker facing in the direction in which he intends to pass.

Push passes should always be kept low and directed toward the receiver's feet, or toward open space. As with all of the passes described in this chapter, players should, through constant practice, be able to execute push passes accurately with either foot.

The outside of the foot is used in making push passes when a player is not squared up to the ball and thus is unable to push the ball laterally across his body. In executing an outside push pass—which, incidentally, is a difficult pass for beginners to master—the player uses her right foot to flick the ball toward a teammate on her right in a give-and-go situation. ("Give-and-go" refers to the attacking technique of passing to a teammate and running past the defender to receive a quick return pass, as shown in Figure 5-7.) Figures 5-2a and 5-2b show a player making an outside push pass.

FIGURE 5–2a. Outside Push Pass *(see a - b)*

FIGURE 5–2b

For long passes, such as clearing the ball from the defending third of the field or passing from one side of the field to the other (called *crossing the ball*), the instep, or shoelace area of the foot, is used to provide greater power; passing or shooting the ball in such a manner is known as *driving the ball* (Figures 5-3a through 5-3d).

Power in kicking comes from a combination of coordination, timing, and follow-through. A long stride and solid base (for balance) by the nonkicking, "plant" foot[2]

FIGURE 5–3a. Driving the Ball *(see a - d)*

FIGURE 5–3b

---

[2] Sometimes referred to as the "target foot" because, when planted prior to kicking, it is pointed at the target, that is, in the desired direction of the kick.

FIGURE 5–3c

FIGURE 5–3d

permits full use of the powerful thigh muscles in generating force in an easy, natural manner. Flexing the knee fully in the backswing portion of the kick allows the lower leg to "whip" into the ball, adding speed to the force generated by the thighs. Full extension of the kicking leg in follow-through assures that maximum force is applied throughout the kick. We illustrate these principles for beginners by having them assume a stiff-legged, "Frankenstein" stance in kicking for distance or power; they learn very quickly that that method won't work, and that the only ways to maximize the power of their kicks are to (a) use a stride that is neither uncomfortably long nor abbreviated by stutter-stepping in their run-up to the ball, (b) flex their knees fully in the preparation phase, and (c) kick through the ball and beyond. To whatever extent any of those factors is lacking, they will be off balance and generate less force in driving the ball. We tell our players, "You don't have to weigh 250 pounds to kick with power; all you need is to *do it right*."

Controlling the Loft and Bend of Passes. The height to which a soccer ball rises when passed or shot is determined in large part by where the player's foot (or head) contacts the ball. As can be seen in Figures 5-4a and 5-4b, the three contact points that govern the amount of loft that the ball achieves in flight are the midline and the areas above and below the midline. If contact is made at or above the midline, a low pass will result; if the foot strikes the ball below the midline, the ball will rise higher in the air.

FIGURE 5–4a. Contact Points and Loft *(see a - b)*

FIGURE 5–4b

In making long crossing or clearing passes, players should position the plant foot 6–8 inches behind and to one side of the ball, pointing toward the target. Their arms should be extended as necessary to maintain their balance on one leg throughout the kick. The toes of the kicking foot should be extended and that foot kept rigid throughout the kick, making almost a straight line with the shin of that leg. The ball should be struck below the midline, causing it to rise higher and stay in the air longer than in most other forms of passing. Failing to keep the kicking foot extended rigidly, toes down, throughout the kick will result in a pass that is weak and off target. Leaning backward slightly at the moment of contact allows a fuller follow-through—and therefore greater kicking power—with the kicking leg. (*Note:* Be careful in your teaching not to overemphasize the importance of backward lean. Leaning backward prior to making contact with the ball may result in topping the ball, that is, kicking a high-bouncing grounder with neither power nor distance.)

Unless told, players are usually unaware that where the foot contacts the ball determines its loft. Demonstrating the effects of the various contact points on loft is easy to do, and is easily understood by the players.

When the ball is struck on either side of its center, the resultant spin imparted to the ball will cause it to bend, or curve, in the opposite direction (Figures 5-5a and 5-5b). For example, striking it on the right side with the instep or inside of the right foot will cause the ball's arc to bend in flight from right to left. Such passes, known familiarly as *banana passes*, are usually long passes, and intended to clear or cross the ball. Bending is unnecessary in short passes, where directness and quickness are greater priorities.

FIGURE 5–5a. Contact Points and Bend

FIGURE 5–5b. Contact Points and Bend

© 1999 by Parker Publishing Company, Inc.

Other Passes. The *chip*, or *lofted*, pass is kicked over the head of one or more opponents. (In shooting on goal, it is used to arc the ball over the keeper's head.) Loft is achieved in the chip pass by striking the ball well below the midline.

To execute short chip passes, the player's plant foot should be directly beside or slightly behind the ball, and the knee of the kicking leg should be fully flexed. Unlike power passing, in chip passing the kicking foot is not extended, toes down; instead, that foot remains parallel to the ground when contact occurs. In the downswing, the kicking leg straightens and the toes slide under the ball far below the midline, causing the ball to roll up onto the instep and rise quickly with little or no follow-through involved (Figures 5-6a through 5-6c).

Although legs and feet (rather than arms and hands) are used in executing the chip pass, the motion is similar to the chip shot in golf; both techniques emphasize swinging *down* on the ball to produce loft, and reducing follow-through to impart controlled backspin to the ball.

For longer lofted passes of more than about twenty yards, the nonkicking foot is set farther from the ball, and the kicking foot is turned sideways, toes outward, and held rigid. The lower part of the ball is struck underneath using the inside of the instep; holding back on the follow-through imparts backspin, reducing power somewhat but offering greater control of the ball.

Useful in passing, clearing, and shooting, *half-volleying* is a skill that every soccer player should possess. Like its tennis counterpart, half-volleying is a quick-striking technique in which the ball is struck as it hits the ground and rebounds upward. Either the instep or the inside of the foot may be used in half-volleying, the former for power and the latter for accuracy.

FIGURE 5–6a. Chip, or Lofted, Pass *(see a - c)*

FIGURE 5–6b

FIGURE 5–6c

In the initial stages of practicing half-volleying, players should begin by pairing up, holding the ball in their hands and dropping it to execute their kicks. Then, still stationary, their partners can toss the ball toward their feet for practice kicking the ball off the rebound. Only when players have achieved a semblance of mastery of the basic techniques involved should they go on to moving drills involving half-volleying.

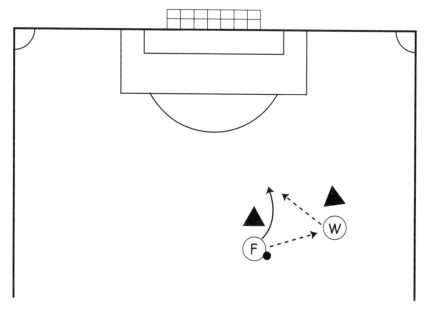

FIGURE 5–7. Wall, or One-Two, Pass

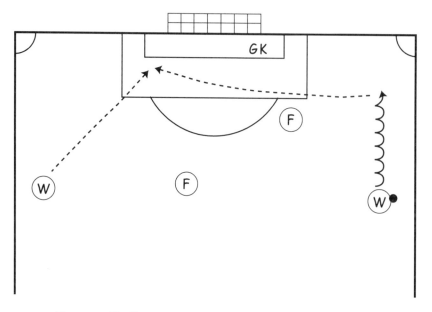

FIGURE 5–8. Cross, or Switch, Pass to Far Post

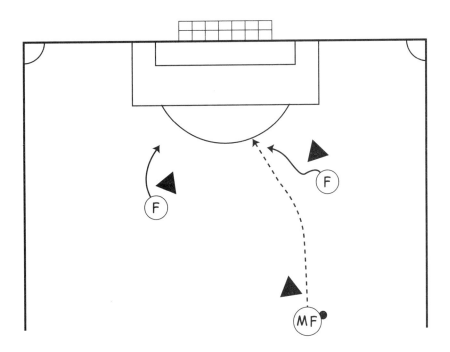

FIGURE 5–9. Through, or Penetrating, Pass

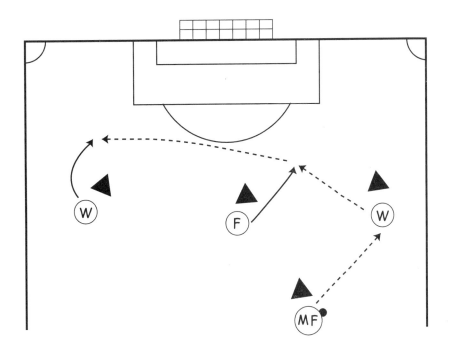

FIGURE 5–10. Typical Combination Passing Sequence

The *wall, cross,* and *through* passes are tactical plays that incorporate other, previously described passing skills.

Figure 5-7 shows a typical give-and-go attacking sequence. In this particular sequence, the winger (W) acts as a wall redirecting the ball back to the forward (F) who initiated the give-and-go. The winger's quick return pass—which is actually a push pass made with either the inside or the outside of the foot—is tactically referred to as a *wall pass,* or *one-two pass.*

The *cross,* or *switch,* pass is used in changing fields (Figure 5-8). Our players signal such switches by calling out "Switch!" in order to warn their teammates of the upcoming change in ball side of the field. Basically, cross passes are power passes made with the instep of the kicking foot; they may be executed as either banana passes or chip passes.

The *through,* or *penetrating,* pass is sometimes referred to as the "killer pass" because it is often used to set up 1-v-1 confrontations between an attacker and the keeper; however, the term *through pass* can refer to any pass made between or over two defenders to an onrushing attacker (Figure 5-9).

The essence of attacking at soccer's highest levels of play involves sequences of combination passes—short, low, safe passes intended to maintain ball possession as the attackers advance toward the opponents' goal. As shown in Figure 5-10, such sequences generally involve two-player give-and-go sequences, with the players and ball locations changing as the ball moves upfield.

Teaching Progression: *Passing.* The teaching progression for any or all of the various passes starts with stationary passing: players pairing up and standing about 10 yards apart to pass the ball back and forth with their partners. Since all passing drills are also receiving drills, players should also practice collecting the ball with the instep, inside, and outside of the receiving foot—practicing with either foot, of course—and receiving the ball with their chests and thighs, too, since not every pass directed at them in game situations will be aimed at their feet. The final step in stationary passing is one-touch passing, or passing the ball without trapping it.

Since soccer is not a stationary game like chess or horseshoes, players should graduate to moving drills as soon as they exhibit accuracy in passing and receiving. Some of the better passing and collecting drills we've seen and used are described in Chapter 6.

Shooting

Soccer is a difficult and complicated game to play and to coach. For coaches, the difficulty lies in formulating offensive and defensive strategies that will synchronize the movements of eleven players into a unified team effort throughout every second of every game. For players, the complication lies in the presence of 22 players on the field at one time, all of whom take up space and therefore tend to limit the effective maneuvering room available to any given player at any given time. Although large in terms of square footage, the pitch can be exceedingly small when 11 of those players are actively engaged in trying to take the ball away from you.

There are, however, two closely related aspects of basic soccer strategy that are easily understood by players and coaches alike at any level of play: *If you don't shoot, you can't score,* and *if you don't score, you can't win.* Your team may play defense as tenaciously as the Russian army fighting off Hitler's troops at Stalingrad in the winter of '42—but if your players can't put the ball in the net at least occasionally, you can't win. The team that scores the most goals wins the game; it's as simple as that.

There is only one way to score in soccer—by kicking or heading the ball over the goal line. Penalty kicks aside, there are two ways to set up scores in live-ball situations—by maneuvering past a defender on the dribble to set up a shot on goal, or by receiving a pass in an area where a shot on goal is feasible.

To be consistently successful at shooting, players must have an aggressive, confident attitude toward their shot-making. Both of those qualities derive in turn from the development of proper form in executing shots on goal. The more supervised shooting practice players receive—and the more they practice shooting on their own time outside formal practice—the sooner they will develop the skills and confidence necessary to become accurate shooters.

We tell our attackers that shooting is like rocket science: They can and should "reach for the stars" in their hopes, dreams, and aspirations—but unless they take the time to develop the skills necessary to get them where they want to go, they'll never really get off the ground at all.

In terms of technique, shooting is exactly the same as passing. In fact, shooting *is* passing, except that the attacker is delivering the ball toward the goal rather than toward a teammate or an open area of the field. In that sense, then, shooting is easier than passing because the goal is 8 yards wide and it never moves. (Lest we appear overly simplistic here, we should point out that it's not easy to maneuver the ball into high-percentage scoring areas because such areas are precisely where collapsing defenses and defenders congregate most heavily.)

All your players need to know about shooting at this point is that the skills they practice in passing drills are exactly the same skills they'll use in shooting. Since any shot in a player's repertoire—push shot, drive shot, chip shot, volley, half-volley, or header—can be used to score, all should be practiced daily with either foot (except the header, of course), and from a variety of angles on goal.

As with passing, shooting involves the integration of many separate elements into one skill, including timing, aim, and power of the kick; the mechanics of the plant, swing, and follow-through; and whatever deceptive moves one employs to get the ball past the keeper or other defenders. There are times when a driving shot is required, and other times when a chip shot or just a simple push shot past the keeper will do. Since the defenders aren't likely to stand around idly while the attacker decides which shot to use or where to aim it, the only way to teach players to make such split-second decisions correctly is to include game simulation shooting drills as an integral part of every practice workout. For many coaches (including us), every individual and team offensive drill ultimately becomes a shooting drill.

Players should be aware that, in most cases, the most difficult shot to defend against is a low, hard shot driven toward a corner of the goal (Figures 5-11a through 5-11c). Low is generally regarded as preferable unless the keeper is out of position because, as one coach explained, "The keeper's arms are located in the upper part of his body, away from his feet." One way to practice low-goal shooting is to stretch a tape or rope across the goal, halfway up the goal posts, and count as goals only those shots that cross the goal line below the rope.

In executing low, line-drive shots, the player's kicking foot must contact the ball on the laces, toes down, above the midline; kicking at or below the midline usually results in shots sailing over the crossbar and out of bounds. The other imperative in

FIGURE 5–11a. Driving the Ball Low Past the Keeper *(see a - c)*

FIGURE 5–11b

FIGURE 5–11c

this type of shot is to keep follow-through to a minimum. Follow-through creates loft, which may be fine for long, desperation shots that arc over the keeper's head but is undesirable in shots taken from anywhere near the goal.

Beyond that, there is old-time baseball player Wee Willie Keeler's famous advice: "Hit 'em where they ain't." Any shot, no matter how hard it is delivered, is likely to be caught or deflected if it is aimed directly at the keeper.

To recap the basics of kicking as they apply to shooting: The inside or outside of the foot is used to nudge the ball gently past a keeper who is out of position. The instep, or top of the foot, is used to apply power to a shot. Maximum power is achieved by using the full instep; bending (curving) the ball on a long shot on goal is achieved by using the inside or outside part of the instep.

Volleying. Although difficult to master, volleying is nevertheless an important technique in every player's repertoire. To execute a volley, whether shooting or passing, the player steps into the path of the ball while it is airborne. Keeping his eyes on the ball and his head erect, he leans into the ball, meeting it in the air and kicking through the center of the ball with his instep, and following through in the direction of the kick to drive the ball toward the goal (Figures 5-12a through 5-12c).

In teaching this shot, as in all others (and in passing, as well), we tell our players, "Keep your eyes focused on the ball and your mind focused on the spot where you want to make contact." In the same sense that hitters in baseball "look" the ball onto their bats and fielders look the ball into their gloves, soccer players should look the ball onto the kicking foot, regardless of the type of kick they are using.

Half-volleying. As applied to going for goal, opportunities for half-volleying usually come directly off a teammate's pass. In half-volleying, instead of trapping the ball, the player times his kick to coincide with the bounce, striking the ball as it begins to rise and driving it hard and low toward a corner of the goal (Figure 5-13).

FIGURE 5–12a. Volley Shot
(see a - c)

FIGURE 5–12b. Volley Shot
(see a - c)

FIGURE 5–13. Half-Volley Shot

FIGURE 5–12c

Heading

Heading is a variation of volleying in which the ball is struck with the forehead rather than a foot. The main uses of heading include clearing the ball out of danger, passing to a teammate, and shooting.

Whether because of difficulties involved in teaching heading skills, players' reluctance to practice heading, or the safety risks involved (e.g., biting the tongue, strained neck muscles, headaches), heading is one of soccer's most neglected skills, particularly at the lower levels of play. This is an unfortunate oversight that delays players' development, since heading is an important skill for every player to learn.[3] Proper instruction can minimize whatever risks exist:

❏ Constantly remind young players that *real soccer players never let their tongues hang out while hitting headers.*

❏ Use a beach ball, volleyball, or soccer ball trainer (a softer version of the regular soccer ball) in your heading drills to help young players overcome their fear of the ball.

❏ Teach your players to keep their necks stiff and *meet* the ball in heading.

Woodpeckers, Rattlesnakes, and Headers. In teaching the mechanics of heading, it may prove helpful for players to consider the woodpecker or the rattlesnake. Woodpeckers don't wait for trees to come to them, nor do rattlesnakes wait for their prey to run onto their fangs. Both animals initiate the action in a forceful manner.

The first step in correctly executing a header is to get into the ball's path. Keeping his eyes focused on the ball (and his tongue inside his mouth), the player's first movement as the ball approaches him is to arch his upper body backward like a cobra preparing to strike (Figure 5-14a). When the ball is about 12 inches away, he swings his upper torso forward and, with his neck rigid and unbending, uses his upper body momentum to drive his forehead through the ball, still watching it as it leaves his forehead (Figure 5-14b). As a coach we know tells her players, "Push your eyes through the ball. Throw your shoulders into the ball. And keep your hands up like a boxer."

FIGURE 5–14a. Heading

---

3 In the 1998 World Cup finals, France's stunning 3–0 upset of Brazil featured *two* goals off headers by playmaker Zinedine Zidame.

FIGURE 5–14b. Heading

The player should hit the ball from underneath to execute a defensive header (i.e., clearing the ball), and hit it "over the top" in attacking or shooting on goal, in the latter case to keep the ball low and prevent it from sailing over the crossbar.

Teaching Progression: Heading. A good way to start off your heading practice with young players is to have them hold the ball 6–10 inches from their foreheads and, without moving their heads, bounce the ball off their foreheads and catch it in their hands. This simple drill is intended to acquaint them with the "feel" of the ball on their foreheads.

Still holding the ball 6–10 inches from their foreheads, in the next drill they arch away from the ball and swing their upper torsos, heads, and necks forward to strike the ball with their foreheads, keeping their necks rigid and watching the ball throughout. Since this drill introduces proper mechanics as well as extending the players' "feel" of the ball, you should closely monitor such things as the contact point (i.e., where the players' foreheads contact the ball), eyes watching the ball, and keeping the neck stiff.

The next practice phase involves the players' sitting on the ground with their feet spread for balance. The ball is tossed toward their foreheads. They strike through the ball to head it back to the tosser, using a rocking motion of their upper bodies (Figures 5-15a through 5-15c). Then they do the same thing *from their knees,* adding follow-through and catching themselves on their hands in landing (Figures 5-16a through 5-16d).

The frog position (i.e., players squatting on all fours) is used for practicing *diving headers,* in which the ball is tossed slightly to one side or the other and struck while the player's body is airborne (Figures 5-17a through 5-17c).

FIGURE 5–15a. Sitting Header *(see a - c)*

FIGURE 5–15b

FIGURE 5–15c

FIGURE 5–16a. Kneeling Header *(see a - d)*

FIGURE 5–16b

FIGURE 5–16c

FIGURE 5–16d

FIGURE 5–17a. Diving Header *(see a - c)*

FIGURE 5–17b

FIGURE 17–c. Diving Header

In the *standing header,* players' preparations include watching the flight of the ball, arching their backs, bending their knees, raising their heels off the ground, and driving their foreheads through the ball in the direction they want it to go (Figures 5-18a through 5-18c).

The next step in the teaching progression is the *jumping header,* the most difficult of all the heading skills. In practicing jump heading, the ball is tossed high enough to make the player leap to strike it, arching *her* back to provide added power (Figures 5-19a through 5-19c).

Once they have practiced these skills without opposition, the last steps are to add, first passive, and then aggressive, defense.

FIGURE 5–18a. Standing Header *(see a - c)*

FIGURE **18–b**

FIGURE **18–c**

FIGURE 5–19a. Jumping Header
(see a - c)

FIGURE 5–19c

FIGURE 5–19b

Dribbling

If you were to ask your players what they consider the most "fun" part of soccer, most of them probably would place scoring at the top of the list, followed by dribbling.

Soccer is basically a game of 1-v-1 (one-versus-one) confrontations, and dribbling is the most basic form of 1-v-1 confrontation. Dribbling is (or can be, at least) a highly creative and versatile attacking weapon, incorporating start-and-stop moves, changes of pace and direction, and feinting moves that give on-the-ball defenders fits (Figure 5-20).

FIGURE 5–20.
Dribbling in Close Quarters

Dribbling is essentially an individual rather than a team skill. Many of the young players who come to us, while possessing the quickness, balance, and agility to become proficient dribblers rather quickly, have what might be called a "backyard" mentality regarding team offense, that is, *When I get the ball, it's my turn to dribble.* Our task is to teach them that dribbling is a tool, not an end in itself. All dribbling should be purposeful, and directed toward specific goals such as beating the on-the-ball defender, setting up a shot on goal or a pass to a teammate, or maintaining ball possession.

FIGURE 5–20a. Dribbling

Dribbling Techniques and Teaching Tips. Dribbling is nothing more than using a series of short, soft taps—not with the toes—to control the ball and guide it as the dribbler moves upfield (Figure 5-20a). Although your ultimate goal is players who can dribble under control with either foot at any speed, players should start out by walking while dribbling, being careful to nudge the ball forward, not kick it ahead, and to practice with either foot.[4] Most dribbling is done with the inside or outside of the foot near the toes. The instep, or laces area of the foot, is used when the dribbler has long distances to cover at high speed.

A full progression for teaching players to dribble while walking might include: 1. Walking in a straight line, dribbling right-footed; 2. Walking in a straight line, dribbling left-footed; 3. Walking in a straight line, alternating feet with every dribble; and 4. Walking and weaving through lines of cones.

When players can do that, they should substitute trotting for walking—then *running*, *sprinting*, and, finally, advanced techniques such as *changing speeds* and practicing *feints* (e.g., *single-* and *double-scissor* moves). In the single-scissor move, the dribbler, hoping to draw his defender out of position, steps hard past the ball in one direction, plants on that foot and turns and leans the other way, nudging the ball in that direction with his other foot to begin a run past the retreating defender. The double-scissor feint repeats those movements as *two* foot-fakes to maneuver past the defender in the same direction in which the dribbler was going originally.

Receiving the Ball

Because it isn't as exciting or crowd-pleasing, receiving doesn't always rank as high on players' preference list of things they'd like to spend their spare time working on as we coaches might like. Preferences aside, however, receiving is a crucial part of individual and team offense and defense; it is also a deceptively complex skill involving anticipation, reaction, timing, spatial awareness, depth perception, and coordination. It is imperative to a team's chances of winning games (or remaining competitive in them) that, having received a teammate's pass, intercepted an opponent's pass, or taken the ball away by tackling, players be able to bring a ball under control quickly in order to maintain ball possession and press whatever attacking advantage exists. Your goal in practicing collecting skills is to develop players who can receive the ball, control it, and either pass it to a teammate, dribble, or shoot in one smooth, fluid movement. Your players will have no trouble understanding this "three-in-one" concept if you refer to it as *control, pass,* and *move.* Through awareness of field position and their teammates' whereabouts, the very best soccer players know what they're going to do with the ball before they receive it.

Such ball control is not easily attained; it is, however, easily practiced, since every passing drill you use is also a receiving drill. Part of every daily practice session should be devoted to players' receiving balls on the ground, in the air, and from goal kicks, punts, and corner kicks. Training should include collecting with the feet, thighs, and chest.

The two most important aspects of receiving are (a) keeping the ball in front of you, and (b) preventing the ball from rebounding away from your body.

---

[4] To help them develop a "feel" for the ball, some coaches have their players practice barefooted in the initial stages of dribbling instruction and drills.

Having positioned himself to collect the ball, the receiver adjusts his body to give slightly with impact, creating a cushion to soften the ball's impact. This isn't always easy to do, since the ball doesn't always arrive at a desirable angle, and decisions on how the ball will be received must be instantaneous; still, failure to properly cushion the ball will result in the receiver's having to chase it down to regain control, and few teams and players can afford such lapses in timing more often than occasionally.

Collecting Techniques. The inside of the foot, and not the sole, is used to receive hard, low passes, whether the ball is airborne or on the ground (Figure 5-21). Regarding the latter, if the player's sole misses the ball, he will neither stop it nor control it.

FIGURE 5–21. Collecting with the Inside of the Foot

The key to success in inside-of-the-foot collecting is weight transfer and "leading with the knee"—keeping the collecting knee high, bringing it over the ball so that a mis-hit that rebounds upward will stay on the player's lower leg. Moving his collecting foot into the ball's path, toes out and ankles rigidly locked, the player allows his leg to give slightly at contact, absorbing the ball's momentum and causing it to drop harmlessly to the ground. The player will then smother any bounce with his sole, a technique called *walking onto the ball.*

The *instep*, or "laces," is used to bring down balls in flight, especially high, arcing kicks such as punts, or clearing or crossing passes. Laces trapping is difficult for beginners, and even for intermediate players, because the control surface is greatly reduced over that afforded by the inside of the foot.

To collect the ball with his instep, the player lifts his knee toward the ball, toes extended, and, at contact, pulls his foot down with the ball on his laces, slowing its momentum and allowing it to drop rather than plunge to the ground (Figures 5-22a through 5-22d).

FIGURE 5-22a. Collecting with the Instep *(see a - d)*

FIGURE 5-22c

FIGURE 5-22b

FIGURE 5–23a. Collecting with the Chest *(see a - c)*

FIGURE 5–22d

FIGURE 5–23b

FIGURE 5–23c. Collecting with the Chest

FIGURE 5–24. Collecting with the Thigh

    Ideally, of course, the ball should be collected with the feet; when the ball is in the air, however, the receiver may elect to play the ball off his chest (Figures 5-23a – 5-23c), softening the impact by leaning backward or away from the ball as contact occurs; or, in receiving a low line drive, he may use an uplifted thigh to stop the ball, as shown in Figure 5-24. In all cases, the player will collect the ball with his foot after it falls to the ground.

    Teaching Progression: *Receiving.* In practicing receiving, start with stationary players using the insides and outsides of their feet, and their insteps, to collect balls rolled underhanded to them by their partners standing 10 yards away. As their skills improve, they can begin to move around to collect their partners' underhand throws or chip passes, working on their timing and developing a sense of the ball's path when it is not directed straight at them. Anticipation is important in learning not to over-run the ball.

Players should also be stationary initially when receiving airborne balls. They should practice collecting soft, floating chip passes and harder drive passes, working their way up through a progression consisting of the inside (and outside) of the foot, instep, thigh, and chest. When they are practicing at such close range, you don't want partners trying to take each other's heads off with line drives; players should be expected (and warned) to use good judgment in this regard.

From there, the teaching progression should extend to the more complex collecting skills—running into chipped balls (with partners 30 yards apart), using the various body parts in collecting the ball; running to collect hard-driven balls, using various angles and distances; and receiving balls while under pressure from an opponent, first with passive (loose) pressure and then with aggressive pressure and both players going for the ball.

In working on advanced collecting skills, players should be taught to look around before the ball reaches them. They must know what to do with the ball before they get it. Then, having quickly surveyed the field and decided how to play the ball, they should focus on it to the exclusion of everything else.

Cushioning is the next imperative: developing a soft touch to gain control of the ball quickly, thereby avoiding unnecessary bounces.

Finally, having gained control of the ball quickly and efficiently, they should be in a position to pass or dribble with minimal wasted time. Their goal should be to control and advance the ball in one fluid movement that takes no more than one second off the game clock. Until ball control is achieved quickly on a regular basis with a variety of traps, they haven't really mastered the art of receiving at all.

Receiving is not an easy skill to master; it requires many hours of concentrated practice that should begin immediately. Part of every daily practice workout should be devoted to practicing the various methods of receiving the ball, and players should be encouraged to practice those skills on their own as well. Receiving isn't the sort of activity that shows up in the game stats or brings crowds to their feet with shouts of approval—but it's the kind of skill that every superior player takes considerable pride in, and it is unquestionably one of the defining skills that teams who win consistently possess and teams who lose consistently fail to execute as often as they need to in order to win games.

Tackling

Tackling in soccer is radically different from the sort of tackling that is associated with American football, in which defenders grab ballcarriers and throw them to the ground. In soccer, tackling is nothing more than a defensive maneuver intended to take the ball away from an opposing player (Figures 5-25a and 5-25b); it is, in fact, the only way to obtain the ball from an opponent unless the ball goes out of bounds. Unintentional body contact occurs, but the arms and hands may not be used for pushing or to gain an unfair advantage; only one foot may be used in tackling the ball; and foul play is not allowed.

FIGURE 5–25a. Taking the Ball Away

FIGURE 5–25b. A Sliding Tackle

While taking the ball away from the opponents is always desirable, diving in to get it is inadvisable except in certain cases. Skilled attackers may use all sorts of dribbling feints to lure a defender into committing herself so they can get by her. Defenders must be coached not to go for the fakes, but to keep their eyes on the ball and wait for the right time to tackle. Tactical sense, timing, and patience are essential ingredients of successful tackling.

There are four basic types of tackling: the *block*, the *poke*, the *slide*, and the *shoulder charge* (which isn't really a tackle, but rather a way of maneuvering an opponent away from the ball or the path of the ball).

The Block Tackle. As shown in Figure 5-25c, the defender blocks the ball with the inside of his foot as the attacker kicks it. The defender should drive through the ball rather than merely blocking it; if he succeeds, he may be able to capture the ball. Even if he fails to take the ball away, making contact with the ball should stall the dribbler's progress and reduce his team's attacking advantage accordingly.

FIGURE 5–25c. The Block Tackle

FIGURE 5–26. The Poke Tackle

The Poke Tackle. This tackle is often used when the dribbler is using his body to shield the ball from the defender, or when the defender is trailing the ball (Figure 5-26). In executing a poke tackle, the defender reaches out with his toe and pokes the ball away from the dribbler. Poke tackles can be executed from the rear or the side of the dribbler; they are usually made near the touch line.

FIGURE 5–27a. The Sliding Tackle *(see a - c)*

FIGURE 5–27b

FIGURE 5–27c

The Sliding Tackle. This tackle is an extended—and riskier—version of the poke tackle. Instead of reaching out with his toe to nudge the ball away from the dribbler, the defender slides into the ball, staying low and kicking the ball away (Figures 5-27a through 5-27c). The tackler's feet must stay near the ground, with one foot extended toward the ball; the other, nontackling leg should be tucked under, in the manner of a baseball player sliding into second base. The slide can be executed from the front, side, or rear; the rear slide is the most difficult to do without being called for tripping.

Tripping is, in fact, always a possibility where sliding tackles are concerned; it adds to the other risks involved in tackling, carrying with it the possibility of injuring the dribbler—or of being red-carded and disqualified from the game. To avoid tripping his opponent, the defender must keep his legs on the ground throughout the tackle.

Sliding tackles should be used sparingly, and only when absolutely necessary. It is, after all, difficult to play soccer effectively while you're lying on the ground—and unless the defender does a good job of concealing his intent until just before he slides, the dribbler may suddenly pull up short or change direction while the defender is hitting the ground, leaving him tackling nothing but air.

FIGURE 5–28. The Shoulder Charge

The Shoulder Charge. This technique involves a defender's using his shoulder (but not his arms or hands) to maneuver a player away from the ball or its path when both of them are within playing distance of it (Figure 5-28). This is the only situation in soccer in which players can deliberately make body contact with an opponent.

Coaching Tips: Tackling and Defense

1. Find a soft area to teach tackling—preferably somewhere wet for sliding.

2. Always have players walk through the various tackles before attempting them at higher speeds.

3. Impress upon your players the importance of using proper technique in tackling. Failure to properly execute tackling skills can result in injury to the dribbler and a red card for the tackler.

4. Players should work to improve their timing in tackling to within rather precise limits: If they go for the ball too soon, they'll miss it—and if they are too late, they risk being hit with a tripping call.

   When is the right time for tackling the ball? Perhaps these guidelines will help:

   a. Tackle any time you have a good angle on the ball.

   b. Intercept the ball before your opponent receives it.

   c. Tackle at the moment she receives the ball (i.e., before she gains complete control of it).

   d. Tackle immediately after he receives the ball. (His attention may be focused on the ball rather than on you.)

   e. Tackle before the dribbler reaches the penalty area. (Shoulder-to-shoulder tackles are often effective here.)

   f. Tackle when the opponents have more attackers than your team has defenders available to stop them.

   g. Tackle when getting the ball back is of paramount importance (e.g., when your team is behind late in the game and you cannot afford to let the opponents run out the clock).

   When, conversely, is the wrong time for tackling? When your team is comfortably ahead and you don't need to take chances. When you have the dribbler contained or under control and your teammates are back in position on defense. Or when you can't reach the ball without tripping the dribbler.

5. The playing distance between defender and attacker is an important factor; if the defender is too close, the dribbler may get by him; too far away, and the dribbler can pass the ball.

6. Defenders should be taught to always watch the ball—not the dribbler or her foot-feints.

You can't motivate players to make their shots on goal—but you can motivate your players to move constantly on offense. Equally important, you can motivate them to work hard on defense. Passing, shooting, heading, and dribbling skills are acquired slowly through patient, repetitive drill and practice; defense, on the other hand, is an attitude, not a skill. *Any player, regardless of his or her offensive skills, can become a proficient defensive player by hustling and working hard to improve his or her marking skills.*

Goalkeeping

Perhaps we should start by addressing the notion that the keeper is different from the rest of the field players, and thus should be coached and developed differently.

Yes, the rules of the game treat keepers differently, requiring that they wear a uniform that contrasts in color with that of their teammates. *No*, keepers don't normally run up and down the field chasing the ball the way the other players do. *Yes*, keepers are unique in that they are allowed to use their hands to catch and throw the ball. Any coach who overlooks the keepers' kicking skills, however, is missing a critical phase of those players' development.

A recent rule change—the "dropback rule" requiring that keepers use their bodies or feet, but *not* their arms or hands, in handling the ball when it has been dropped back to them by their teammates—underscores the necessity of developing goalkeepers' total game. It has forced keepers to be more creative in handling the ball.

Stance. The keeper's "ready" stance in defending the goal area may be described in either positive or negative terms. Positively, it is the equivalent of basketball's "triple-threat" stance: feet spread, knees bent, tail down, back straight, head and shoulders up. Negatively, it entails *not* standing up in a relaxed posture with feet together and knees locked, and *not* leaning forward at the waist. In either case, proper stance entails keeping a low center of gravity to improve quickness and agility, and a broad base with the keeper's back straight to maximize balance (Figure 5-29).

Lateral movement within that stance is best achieved by keeping the feet close to the ground, the knees bent and spread, and moving via a series of quick, sliding steps of 6–8 inches with each foot while facing the ball. Keepers should never allow their feet to cross or their knees to come together when moving laterally; turning and running to protect an area of the goal should be resorted to only when a shot on an unprotected area of the goal is imminent.

Defending the Goal. The keeper's first priority is always to keep the ball from crossing the goal line; to do so, he moves along the goal line with the movement of the ball, keeping himself between the ball and the goal and attempting to bisect the attacker's shooting angle. How far he stations himself in front of the goal line depends on his experience level as well as where the ball is. Whenever possible, he should use his hands to catch the ball; if he cannot catch it, he should try to deflect it over the crossbar or to one side of the goal, even if he has to dive to knock the ball away (Figures 5-30a through 5-30c).

FIGURE 5–29. Goalkeeper's Stance

FIGURE 5–30a. The Keeper Protecting His Goal
(Diving to catch or deflect a shot) *(see a - c)*

FIGURE 5–30b

FIGURE 5–30c

Such catches and deflections, called *saves,* are the most visible aspect of goal-keepers' play; they are not all that the keeper does. Because he sees the entire pitch ahead of him, the keeper is perfectly suited to direct the defense by warning his team-mates when gaps arise in the coverage or attackers move into unprotected areas. Communication is the key to defensive control; an effective keeper will also warn her teammates away from a ball she is collecting, and she will immediately initiate the offensive attack when she collects the ball in any manner.

Drills. Shooting drills should be an integral part of every daily practice; such drills are, of course, goalkeeping drills as well. We also include our keepers in our ball-handling, dribbling, passing, and receiving drills—not just to keep them occupied but also because we think that such practice is never wasted.

If you want your keepers to maintain a low, broad-based ready stance while sta-tionary or moving laterally, you can use *step-slide drills* to get them used to it. Keeping the knees spread apart and bent for more than a few seconds at a time can be painful and tiring unless the keeper is used to it—but it's also critical in terms of getting fast starts, moving laterally, or making quick changes in direction. A coiled stance enables the keeper to literally "spring" into action when his goal is threatened.

In step-sliding, the keepers begin by assuming the proper stance and chanting the litany of its execution: *feet spread, knees bent, tail down, back straight, head and shoulders up.* Then, without standing up, they begin step-sliding in a given direction—stepping with one foot, sliding with the other—keeping their knees apart and taking small steps. Finally, having gone, say, 15 feet within that stance, they reverse directions and go back the other way, stepping with the original sliding foot and sliding with the stepping foot. Emphasis throughout should be on maintaining an exaggerated, knees-wide, tail-down stance, since a tall, narrow stance will not strengthen the muscles involved.

Step-sliding is not the sort of drill that will endear you to your goalkeepers, since it is in fact quite a strenuous activity; but it *will* prepare them to maximize their game performances when the action is hot and heavy and nothing less than a maximum effort can save the day.

Chapter 6

SOCCER DRILLS

Only those who have the patience to do simple things
perfectly will acquire the skill to do difficult things easily.

—Johann von Schiller
German poet

If you're satisfied with your players' playing kickball, all you have to do is teach them the rules of the game, divide them into two teams at practice, and scrimmage. You can even keep yourself in playing shape by playing along with them. But if you want more than that—for example, if you want your players to learn how to execute soccer's skills properly—you're going to have to teach them.

That's where drills come in. Drills provide a perfect format for teaching and practicing soccer skills.

THE IMPORTANCE OF DRILLS

Two aspects of drills render them an ideal vehicle for teaching. First, individual drill segments are of relatively brief duration, so you can target specific skills or areas for improvement; and second, the repetition of specific, isolated movements builds skills and permits correction of mistakes in ways that scrimmaging cannot accomplish nearly as efficiently or effectively.

Drills cannot exactly replicate game conditions—but you cannot effectively teach or practice new skills under game conditions, either. Drills emphasize mental and physical skills that can be applied to game situations; many of the most effective drills are those that simulate game conditions in small doses.

Drills, then, are for teaching and learning through repetition; scrimmaging is for practicing what has been taught and learned.

There's more, though. Unlike, say, baseball and American football, soccer was developed elsewhere in the world and is far more important on a worldwide basis than those sports. For example, children in Europe and South America are taught practically from birth that the proper way to propel a ball is to *kick* it, not throw it, hit it with a bat, or carry it while running. Such knowledge gives those children a tremendous head start in learning to play soccer over American children whose background in team sports—and their parents' as well—is likely to be oriented more closely to baseball, basketball, or football than to soccer. In sports, familiarity doesn't breed contempt, it breeds the desire to play that sport.

What all of this means is that, because the concepts and skills of soccer are unfamiliar to many children in the United States, *we have to make the game fun for them from the very beginning of their participation, or else they'll quit playing before they develop the skills necessary to enjoy the sport for its own sake.* The same can be said of any team sport, of course, but with soccer we haven't yet reached the point of acceptance where moms and dads across the nation routinely put a soccer ball in the newborn's crib.

Learning isn't always fun; we know that, and so do you. But it can be even more of a drudgery when the skills involved are almost completely at odds with what seems to be the natural way to play the game (i.e., with the hands rather than the feet, or kicking the ball with the toe rather than the instep or inside of the foot). That's why, in earlier chapters, we've emphasized the necessity of *making soccer practice fun for the players.* If we expect our players to run three to five miles or more in the course of our daily practices, or to practice at home the skills we teach them, we'd better find ways to make that running and practicing fun, or they'll start looking for less rigorous and demanding ways to fill their leisure hours than working to improve their soccer skills.

That's why, too, you'll find many of the drills in this chapter described in terms of "fun," "exciting," or "enjoyable." Having fun isn't our goal, *learning* is—or, to be more precise, *making learning fun.* If you can do that, whether via these drills that offer a representative sampling of what we do in our daily practices or via other drills gathered from any of the fine soccer drills books, magazines, or videotapes listed in Appendix A, you'll never have a problem motivating your players to come to practice, to be on time, to play hard, or to learn.

CONDITIONING

I go to the Bahamas every winter to get in shape for the season.
run 15 miles every day. Sure, I get fed up and say, "What am I doing?" but
if you want to score goals and play well you can't just lie on the couch and
say "I'll wait until tomorrow."

—Giorgio Chinaglia

Stretching Exercises

Having come along in the Dark Ages of physical conditioning theory and practice, we weren't always ardent advocates of stretching exercises, but we are now. Putting it simply, the more limber and flexible players are, the less susceptible they will be to pulled muscles—especially in cooler climates or cold weather. It's a mistake to assume, as we once did, that, because players are in shape to run three to five miles every day, they don't need to do stretching exercises at the beginning of practice or prior to games—or prior to calisthenics or weight training, for that matter. At least

10-15 minutes or more per workout session should be devoted to this all-important ounce of prevention.

As for specific exercises, we strongly recommend that you consult a track coach, athletic trainer, or physical therapist in your school or community. That's what we did a number of years ago, and we've never regretted it. Since we adopted a vigorous, track-style bending and stretching regimen as part of our daily practices, our players' non-contact-initiated muscle injuries have become as rare as Edsels and honest politicians.

Jogging

Purely as a loosening-up activity, we have our players jog three laps around our practice field at the beginning of daily practice, each player with a ball and dribbling as he goes. It's no big deal, just a standard part of our practice sessions that helps to prepare the players for what lies ahead.

Running

Whether due to the nature of the game or the fact that many players are involved in competitive soccer year-round, soccer players are quite possibly the most well-conditioned athletes in team sports. There is, however, no single, definitive answer to the question, *How much running do my players need?*—except this: *They need cardiovascular endurance sufficient to carry them through games without running out of gas in the latter stages.*

While we coaches cannot be expected to always enjoy a surplus of highly skilled players on our teams, we can and should be expected to get our players in shape to run and play hard throughout games. Except for players who are coming back from injury or illness, it is *always* the coach's fault when players are not properly conditioned to play at full speed for as long as might be required of them.

Some coaches use little or no endurance running *per se* in their daily practice sessions, reasoning that any endurance running their players need will arise naturally during workouts via game-related drills and scrimmaging. One such coach, whose practice time is limited, insists that endurance running that doesn't relate directly to game situations or improving soccer skills is wasted time. Other coaches, whose situations are different, incorporate running activities such as the Indian Run or wind sprints into their daily routines. While either or both approaches may be correct, you should not automatically assume that your players are in game shape when they come to you, even if they play soccer year-round. Too, we think it's a mistake to assume that drills and scrimmages will keep your players in shape without additional running; you must be absolutely sure that they will not fade in the latter stages of games.

If you send out letters to team prospects during the summer, be sure to advise them to be ready to go hard from the first day of preseason tryouts. Specifically, you might recommend that, prior to the start of practice, they work out on their own on a daily basis, running, say, ten 25-yard sprints, seven 50-yard sprints, seven 75-yard sprints, and three 100-yard sprints, jogging back to the starting point for the first three and walking back in the 100s. The serious candidates will do it because they know it will help them to get ready for the upcoming season.

The Indian Run

A running activity called the Indian Run (also known as Progressive Laps) is a good way to improve your players' endurance. In this activity, the players run laps around the practice field, single file, for a specified length of time. (You might start out at ten minutes three times a week, adding three minutes every week for seven weeks.) All of the players jog except the last player in line, who sprints to the front of the line before slowing down. As quickly as one player sprints, the player behind him becomes the new last player in line and begins his sprint, and so on.

We like the Indian Run because, although it involves a lot of hard running, it also involves easy running and is therefore easily justifiable to the players. (Would they rather run wind sprints?)

There are other ways besides timed runs to improve endurance. Rather than running continuously for a predetermined amount of time as in the Indian Run, the players could (a) run for *distance* (e.g., running 1–2 miles at the beginning or end of practice) or (b) run for *time and distance* (e.g., running a mile in, say, 6-1/2 minutes or less); however, the former may consume more time than is practical, and the latter is so physically demanding that few coaches use this technique more often than once a week in preseason practice—or at all once the season has begun.

A familiar problem associated with pure endurance running is overcoming many players' natural resistance to running that is not directly related to soccer. The best way we've found to deal with this problem is to train with the players—if, that is, you have no serious physical limitations other than simply being out of shape that would prohibit such participation. It is, after all, difficult for players to grumble about the running, calisthenics, weight training, and so on, that they're being forced to do when the coach is right there sweating alongside them. Distance runs are ideal for the coach's participation, as is the Indian Run if you're a regular jogger. Running for time and distance is not for the faint of heart unless you're in very good running shape.

However you do it, working out with your players is good for team morale; beyond its inspirational and motivational value, it reinforces your message that *we're all in this together,* and it offers solid evidence that you're working just as hard as the players are.

Other Conditioning Activities

During the season, we have calisthenics twice a week. Since most of our players play soccer year-round, we avoid extensive leg work. Our calisthenics consist of

➡ Pushups (regular)

➡ Elevated pushups, feet (on 12″ boxes)

➡ Elevated pushups, hands (on 12″ boxes)   } 3 sets of 10

➡ Reverse pushups (stomach facing upward, knees locked, hips up)

➡ Situps (crunches)

➡ Calf raises (lying on back)   } 3 sets of 25

We also use two other station activities besides the Indian Run in what we call our "complex run." They consist of *running the stadium stairs* (a) one step at a time and (b) two steps at a time, and *jumping onto (and down from) exercise boxes* that measure 16″, 20″, and 24″ in height, in succession. These activities enhance our players' explosive leg strength in ways that running cannot do.

Weight Training. We don't work with weights during the varsity season, and we don't recommend strenuous weight training for youngsters below age 16. Passing a physician-administered physical examination should be a prerequisite for *any* player's participating in any sort of weight training program.

The weight training program we use is described in Appendix S, and a reproducible training log is in Appendix T.

BALLHANDLING DRILLS

Ballhandling is dribbling with finesse, or touch; as such, it is unquestionably the most difficult attacking skill to master. While anyone can learn rather quickly to kick the ball and run to catch up with it, or to kick the ball in the general direction of the goal, it takes years of practice to master the art of protecting the ball or outmaneuvering a defensive player in close-quarter 1-v-1 situations (see Figure 6-1).

FIGURE 6-1. Beginning a Move

Ballhandling footwork is complex and far different from the footwork skills associated with other sports. That's why, when children begin playing soccer for you, you should immediately start teaching them basic footwork patterns, and devote at least 15 minutes a day to footwork drills and dribbling. The ability to apply touch to the ball clearly separates the real soccer players from the pretenders. No one—not even the pros—ever outgrows the need to practice fast footwork and ballhandling.

The basis for most of our footwork, dribbling, and feinting drills and practice is Frans van Balkom's excellent instructional videotape series, *Soccer on the Attack*.[1] Its "Fast Footwork" segment is the best of its kind we've seen, and we do not hesitate to recommend it to anyone who is coaching soccer at any level. We use van Balkom's fast footwork skills as a regular part of our daily warmup routine.[2]

In teaching ballhandling skills, we select ten players and teach them one skill apiece, and then have them teach their teammates, one skill at a time. This is, of course, a lengthy process with only 15 minutes a day devoted to ballhandling/footwork drills, but it has worked quite well for us over the years, and it will work equally well for you if you don't try to teach too much too soon. Start teaching ballhandling and fast footwork skills at the earliest possible moment in your players' development. Mountains are climbed, not with giant leaps upward, but with small, plodding steps.

Eventually, when your players have learned the rudiments of fast footwork, you'll be able to get in all ten skills in a 10-minute time allotment; with every player assigned a ball, they should get in about 500 touches on the ball per player before you go on to something else.

Ball Juggling

Unlike fast footwork drills, ball juggling is not specifically game-related. It is, however, a challenging, enjoyable activity that demands concentration and develops self-confidence by helping players to develop a feel for the ball on the insteps of their feet.

As the term itself suggests, ball juggling consists of keeping the ball aloft via a series of soft, controlled taps with either foot. Many coaches begin their ball juggling sequences with the players seated on the ground, thus emphasizing from the start that the ball must be *tapped*, not kicked. (A beach ball or soft soccer training ball may be used with young players.) A flat platform for contacting the ball is created by pointing the toes of the kicking foot outward. Players toss the ball up and out gently toward the kicking foot, tap it upward with the instep or inside of the foot, and catch it. As they progress and develop a rhythm with the ball, they will try to keep the ball alive without catching it. They should, of course, practice with both feet.

In practicing from a standing position, the player simply drops the ball to the instep and tries to get, say, five consecutive touches with either foot, without the ball's touching the ground. With improvement, you can switch from counting touches to setting time limits for their ball juggling. You can also have timed competitions to see who can juggle the ball the longest.

Moving upward, you should also have them practice thigh juggling and head juggling, the latter being far more difficult to master. In head juggling, the player tilts his head back and hits the ball with a gentle, upward stabbing motion through the ball, contacting it with his upper forehead, and then moving to stay under the ball.

---

[1] van Balkom, Frans. *Soccer on the Attack: A Comprehensive Look at Attack Skills*. St. Louis: Budweiser-Busch Creative Services Corporation, 1986. Part 1, "Fast Footwork and Feinting"; Part 2, "Dribbling"; and Part 3, "Shooting and Heading."

[2] Those ten skills are: 1. The Foundation; 2. Side-to-Side Push Forward; 3. Pulling the "V"; 4. Step On; 5. Roll Behind the Leg; 6. Step Over; 7. Alternate Push Out/Pull Back; 8. Side Roll; 9. Full Sole Roll; and 10. The Garrincha.

From there, the players can add a partner and take turns juggling and passing lightly back and forth, juggle in small groups of three to five players, or juggle while moving.

Coaching Tips—Ball Juggling

1. Keep eyes on ball.

2. Make a flat platform surface for the ball.

3. Tap the ball gently. ("Control the ball, don't let it control you.")

4. Balance. (Place your weight on the balls of your feet. Start out jogging in place between taps; as you improve, try to move around while juggling.)

DRIBBLING DRILLS

To control their dribble, players should keep the ball close to their feet and practice touching with the inside, outside, and instep of either foot. In the initial phases of dribbling practice, players should practice, first, dribbling in a straight line and at a slow pace, and then changing the speed and direction of the dribble in a confined area, without opposition.

Dribble Slalom

The players use designated parts of either foot while dribbling in and out of a series of cones. Have them start at a walking pace or trot and progress to higher speeds as control is achieved.

Dribble Tag

Everyone has a ball in a 20 yard × 20 yard grid. The person who is "It" attempts to tag someone else within the grid without losing control of the ball. No one can leave the grid to avoid being tagged. Tagging back, or tagging the person who tagged you, is not allowed. Tags don't count if "It" loses control of the ball.

An excellent activity for practicing changing directions and speeds while dribbling, Dribble Tag requires players to keep their heads up and watch the player who is chasing them as they make evasive movements. The game will also show you which of your players have the greatest—and poorest—acceleration; it works best when limited to five minutes or less.

Kickaway

In Kickaway (also called "Hot Dog" or "Hot Man"), everyone has his own ball within a 20 yard x 20 yard grid. The coach selects two "Hot Dogs," or players whose task is to maintain possession of the ball while trying to kick balls away from other players. As in Dribble Tag, no one may leave the grid, and kickaways don't count if a Hot Dog loses control of his dribble. When eliminated from the game, players practice ball juggling outside the grid until everyone is eliminated, at which point a new game can begin with new Hot Dogs. (*Hint: Don't* use your weakest dribblers as the Hot Dogs if you want the game to conclude before midnight. One way to avoid this problem is to use the last two players left in the game as the Hot Dogs in the next game.)

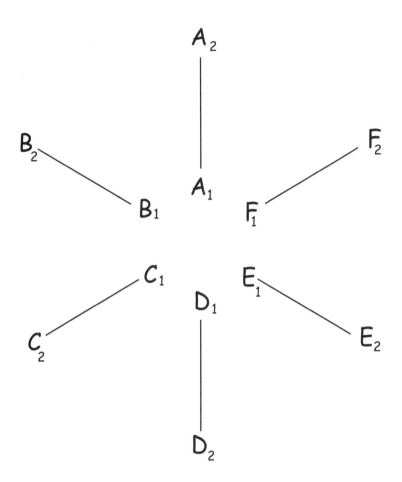

FIGURE 6–2. Double-Circle Drill Format

1-v-1 Offensive Moves

In applying offensive moves to 1-v-1 drill sequences, we use a double-circle format (Figure 6-2) with players of roughly equal ability paired up. A 20 yard × 20 yard grid will accommodate six to eight pairs of players, so you may need more than one grid to ensure that each attacker has adequate space to perform.

Sequences begin with the defenders on the outside passing to their partners (attackers). Initially, the attackers advance toward the stationary defenders to make their moves, after which the two players trade places and repeat the process. Later, the defenders may be instructed to walk toward the attackers, or even trot when the attackers are proficient enough to handle the reduced time to prepare their moves.

The receiver collects the ball and, when the spacing between attacker and defender is right,[3] executes whichever move she is working on. To ensure that the advantage remains with the attacker while the move is being learned, you might stipulate that defenders must move one speed slower than attackers: If the attacker is trotting, the defender walks, and if the attacker is walking through the move, the defender must remain stationary until the move is completed.

In addition to the "Dribbling" section of van Balkom's *Soccer on the Attack* videotape series, which features such moves as the single and double scissors and single and double Matthews among its fourteen dribbling skills, we also practice some of the attacking moves shown in the Wiel Coerver instructional videotape series, *Coerver Fundamental Series*.[4] In addition to other instructional videotapes listed in Appendix A, Coerver offers a nationwide network of summer camps, where children of all ages and both sexes can learn to play soccer in the manner popularized by the former Dutch star.

FIGURE 6–3. Protecting the Ball

Coaching Tips—Dribbling

1. Players should be taught to keep the ball close to their feet when dribbling, a skill called *close control*. Close control permits players to change the speed or direction of their dribble quickly, incorporate feints into their dribbling, avoid tacklers, or shield the ball from an opponent.[5]

---

[3] See the following section on dribbling tips, no. 4.

---

[4] Ames, IA: Championship Books and Video Productions, 1986.

---

[5] The difference between *shielding*, which is legal, and *obstruction*, which is illegal, lies in the attacker's proximity to the ball. If the attacker is close enough to the ball to play it (i.e., 2–4 feet away), it's shielding; if that distance stretches to, say, 6 feet and the attacker still attempts to block off his defender without playing the ball, it's obstruction. Although the fans in the stands don't always recognize such distinctions, good referees and coaches understand the difference between the two.

2. Stress an "eyes up" approach to dribbling. The dribbler's vision should be focused on the field situation, not on the ball, which should appear in the lower periphery of the dribbler's vision. There are, of course, times when players absolutely *must* look at the ball—but even then they should be able to divide their attention between the ball and the defender. The more players practice changing directions and speeds without looking directly at the ball, the less they will have to rely on direct vision of the ball in pressure situations.

   We tell our players, *When you're watching the ball, you're in a world of your own, just you and the ball—but unless you're taking a penalty kick there are 21 other players out there to consider. Eleven of them are opponents, all of whom who would like to take the ball away from you; the others are your teammates, several of whom are likely to be in position for you to pass the ball to them. But you can't do that if you don't know where they are or where they're going.*

3. Teach your players to avoid speed-dribbling over long distances. The quickest way to advance the ball over long distances is to pass it.

4. Perhaps the most common dribbling feint is to dip a shoulder as if going that way and—when the defender steps or leans in that direction—go the other way. For such a feint (or any other) to succeed, (a) it must be realistic and (b) the attacker must be close enough to the defender to finish the move while the defender is off-balance, but far enough away that the defender cannot tackle the ball. While precise distances between attacker and defender will vary according to the attacker's ballhandling skills, speed, and ability to execute realistic feints, effective feinting distances seldom exceed 6 feet.

   Regardless, while executing feints the dribbler should watch the defender's hips and plant (lead) foot to see if she is off-balance or leaning one way or the other. Then, having beaten her defender, the dribbler should look up to see which of her teammates is open. A quick give-and-go pass at this point will virtually ensure that the beaten defender will not recover and catch up with the play.

   Van Balkom's *Soccer on the Attack* videotapes offer superb instruction in ten feinting moves: 1. Let It Be; 2. Come Off; 3. Kick Up Knee; 4. Step Over; 5. Cruyff; 6. Pull Behind; 7. Feint Kick; 8. The "V"; 9. Roll in Front; and 10. The Cap. They're not very imaginative titles, we suppose, but learning some or all of them will greatly increase your players' attacking skills, as our three seniors in this year's GHSA State All-Star Soccer Game will attest.

PASSING/RECEIVING DRILLS

Having covered the basic structure of the most elementary forms of passing/receiving drills in Chapter 5, we'll start here with the assumption that you're already familiar with such activities as *stationary passing between partners* (using the familiar two-circle format shown in Figure 6-2).

Specific passing styles aside, there are three techniques for passing the ball that must be attended to: passing off the dribble; two-touch passing (i.e., collecting a pass before passing); and one-touch passing, or passing with first contact with the ball. Of the three, one-touch passing is the most difficult to execute accurately, and therefore requires the most work.

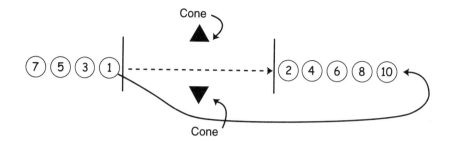

FIGURE 6–4. Target Passing Drill

Target Passing

Target passing is a basic two-line passing drill, in which players take turns passing to teammates through two cones arranged 3 yards apart, after which they go to the back of that line to await their next turn (Figure 6-4). You can start the players out at, say, 10 yards apart and gradually increase the distance between passers and receivers. Since their natural tendency is to advance toward the ball prior to receiving it, you can use cones or spray-painted lines to keep them apart. Players always run to their right—the receiver's left—after passing.

Golf

Each player has his or her own ball in this challenging and highly enjoyable activity. Use the largest possible area within your practice facility in arranging nine cones to simulate a Par-3 golf course. Stagger the distances between cones to make some holes easier than others, add a few obstacles such as pop-up goals and rebound nets here and there to increase the challenge, group the players in foursomes, explain the rules, and let them go.[6] That's all there is to it, unless you want to give each foursome paper and a pencil to record their scores for each hole (i.e., how many kicks it takes them to hit that particular cone). After playing 9 or 18 holes, the winners are the players with the lowest score in each foursome.

To avoid a backlog of players standing around waiting to get started, you might want to stagger the starting locations around the course rather than having everyone start at the first tee. (The "tee area" for each hole should be designated in advance, whether by using field marking paint or cones located, say, 3 yards to the left of the previous hole's cone. However and wherever you designate your tee areas, everyone should "tee off" from the same place for that hole.)

Technically, Golf might properly be considered a shooting drill; we consider it a passing drill because of the extraordinary precision and delicacy of touch required to hit the cones.

---

[6] To avoid their favoring one foot over the other, have them alternate kicking feet on each hole (not each kick).

© 1999 by Parker Publishing Company, Inc.

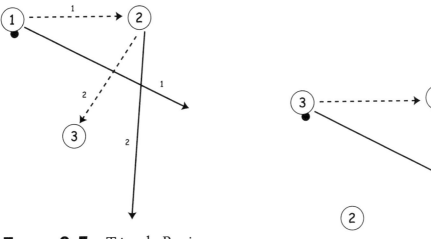

FIGURE 6–5. Triangle Passing Drill *(see 6-5 and 6-6)*

FIGURE 6–6

Triangle Passing

As shown in Figure 6-5, 1 passes to 2 and goes between 2 and 3 to create a new triangle. Then, 2 passes to 3 and runs between 1 and 3, after which 3 passes to 1 and goes between 1 and 2 (Figure 6-6), and so on, with the players moving constantly to new areas to create new triangles in this pass-and-move drill that introduces players to the concept of running to open space.

The Dutch (or Circle) Drill

This drill, which originated with the Dutch national team in the 1970s, is both a conditioning activity and a quality passing/receiving drill. Best performed in a large area measuring at least 40 yards × 40 yards, the drill features our old reliable inner/outer circles of players practicing such skills as dribbling, one- and two-touch passing, heading, and receiving.

Initially, all of the players except the goalkeepers (who are working elsewhere) are spread out along the perimeter of one large, outer circle—each player with a ball. After counting off 1-2-1-2, and so on, around the circle, the 1's put down their soccer balls and move toward the center to form an inner circle facing outward. In effect, then, each of the 2's has two soccer balls at her disposal, thus reducing the time lost when one of the balls is kicked away from the circle.

On a signal from the coach, each of the 1's calls a 2 by name, sprints toward that player at full speed but under control and one-touch returns her pass, then turns and jogs all the way back to the middle, looking for a new passer as she goes. When she spots a 2 who isn't already passing to someone else, she calls *that* player's name and sprints toward her to receive and return her pass. Play continues in this fashion—find a passer, call her name, sprint to her, return her pass, then jog back to the middle while searching for a new passer—for 60 seconds, at which time play stops while the 1's and 2's trade places and the 1's get to rest for one minute.

Besides its obvious value as a high-speed pass/return pass activity, the Dutch Drill also teaches players to keep their heads up and time their movements to avoid colliding with other players. Sometimes, we put our keepers in the middle to give them a workout, too.

It's important to emphasize that players jog all the way back to the middle every time; otherwise, they'll call the name of the next 2 in line and work their way around the circle at a jogging gait. While that's okay in some cases, we like to use the Dutch Drill as a high-speed, conditioning activity, featuring quality passing and receiving.

Overlapping Runs

It is also necessary for players to practice overlapping runs—which, in the present case, consist of movements around or behind a teammate to create space in which to receive the ball.

As 1 passes to 2 in Figure 6-7, 3 overlaps around 2 and receives 2's pass. Continuity consists of 3 passing to 1 and 2 overlapping around 1 to receive 1's pass (Figure 6-8), and then 2 passing to 3, with 1 overlapping around 3 to receive 3's pass (Figure 6-9). Since the triangles are constantly moving and changing shape, be sure to space your groups far enough apart so they won't interfere with each other.

Two-Player Passing Triangle

The drill shown in Figures 6-5 and 6-6 can be done with two players instead of three, with the third point of the triangle being the open space toward which the passer runs.

At the start of the action, 1 has the ball (Figure 6-10), and 2 can run to either side of 1. Depending on which way 2 goes, 1 will direct his pass, not at 2, but to the *open space* toward which 2 is running. After passing, 1 will run to either side of 2 who, as before, will pass, not directly to 1, but to the open space toward which he is running (Figure 6-11).

Although we normally think of pass-and-move sequences like those shown in Figures 6-10 and 6-11 as being directed toward the opponents' goal, players should understand that they can and should pass and move in the direction toward the open space.

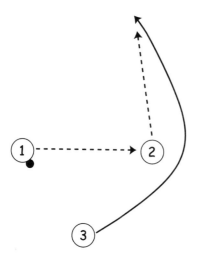

FIGURE 6–7. Overlapping Runs Drill (*see 6-7 and 6-9*)

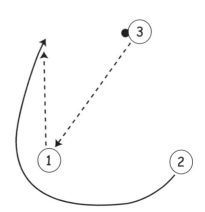

FIGURE 6–8

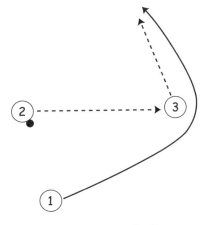

FIGURE 6–9

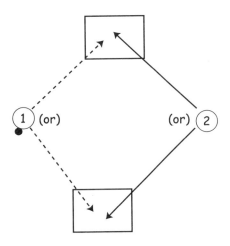

FIGURE 6–10. Two-Player Passing Triangles *(see 6-10 and 6-11)*

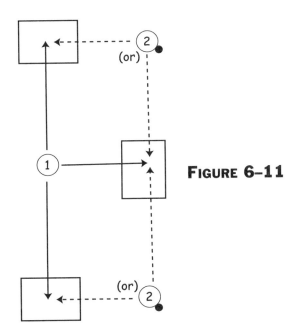

FIGURE 6–11

Coaching Tips: Passing/Receiving

1. Any passing drill is also a receiving drill. Don't overlook receiving when you're working on passing. You can either have an assistant coach monitor the receiving phase of your passing drills or do it yourself. As the late Frank Sinatra observed, "Ya can't have one without the other."

2. The *push pass* is the basic pass of soccer. Coach your players to keep their push passes on the floor and aim them at their receivers' feet.

3. Quality passing requires a combination of *mechanics* and *field awareness*. Mechanical efficiency results from prolonged and rigorously applied practice; field awareness is achieved by keeping one's head up and looking around to see what's going on elsewhere. Stress mechanics in your drills and field awareness in your mini-games and scrimmages.

4. Coach receivers to look the ball onto their feet, thighs, chests, or heads. Field awareness is always important, but collecting the ball cleanly can be an even higher priority.

SHOOTING DRILLS

Shooting is overrated, at least, as a practice activity. There. We've said it, and we're glad—WAIT A MINUTE! DON'T CLOSE THE BOOK! Hear us out!

Okay, we'll concede that *yes*, shooting is important. If you don't shoot, you won't score, and if you don't score, the best you can hope for is a scoreless tie. Also, unless you structure your practice sessions carefully (as you should), your shooting drills and scrimmaging may be the only real work your goalkeepers get.

When stripped down to its essentials, shooting is nothing more complicated than making an accurate, hard pass toward the net instead of a teammate. If your players can't dribble and pass well enough to set up shots on goal, they won't get enough shots to justify large expenditures of practice time devoted to improving shooting.

We spend 20 minutes a day practicing shooting. Players rotate every five minutes between four stations with goals equipped with rebound nets. The drills we use most often are shown in Figures 6-12 through 6-15; they can be simplified for beginners in early preseason practice by omitting the keeper, or made more difficult for more experienced players by extending the distance from which shots may be taken. We call these drills our *net work*.

Shooting Station Drill 1

Like our other net work drills, this drill features a passing line, rebound net and a receiving/shooting line (Figure 6-12). Although unassisted goals are not unheard of, we think it's important to initiate these drills with a moving ball in order to train players to shift their attention instantly from the ball's path to its new target—*the goal*.

Rotation is simple: 1 passes to 2 via a rebound net and goes to the back of the shooting line, while 2 collects the ball on the rebound and attacks down the middle on the dribble, attempting to drive the ball past the keeper from various distances. Then, 2 goes to the back of the passing line and the ball is relayed to 3, who passes into the rebound net for 4 to begin the next sequence.

Players should practice collecting the ball, dribbling and shooting with either foot, of course. You'll get more concentrated practice by alternating days between right- and left-foot shooting than by alternating feet with each shot.

Shooting Station Drill 2

This is the same drill as the previous one, but with the attack coming from a different angle. The positions of the passing and shooting lines shown in Figure 6-13 are used only to illustrate the angle of attack; the lines can be anywhere you want them to be (e.g., passing or attacking from the goal line), and should be changed frequently. Be imaginative in where and how you set up the shots.

Shooting Station Drill 3

In the previous drills, the shooter either took a two-touch shot (i.e., collecting the pass [one] and then shooting from that spot [two]), or else dribbling to set up the shot). In this drill that we call "Quick Shot," however, the receiver uses a one-touch shot directly off the pass (Figure 6-14). It's just "Wham!-Bam!-Thank-You-Ma'am!" or "Whirr!-Grr!-Thank-You-Sir!" and the keeper digs the ball out of the net.

As before, the location of the passing and shooting lines should be varied frequently, and players should practice one-touch shooting with either foot.

Shooting Station Drill 4

In this drill (Figure 6-15), 1 passes to attacker 2 via the rebound net and becomes the defender in a 1-v-1 matchup. (Actually, it's 1-v-2 because 2 must beat both 1 and the keeper.) Defense may need to be passive with inexperienced players and aggressive in other cases. As before, the location of the 1-v-1 confrontations should be changed often.

Other Drills

Let's back up for a moment. In the earliest phase of shooting practice with beginners, start with a dead ball and stationary shooting—with and without a keeper—using different angles and distances. The same technique should be applied in practicing long drive shots and corner kicks. Players can practice stationary volley and half-volley shots initially by dropping the ball and kicking it toward the goal.

A simple way to initiate your moving-shots practice is to place a pop-up goal beyond the last cone in your Slalom Dribbling drill.

Beyond the most basic level, players should be prepared to shoot from passes that come across their bodies, from behind them, directly at them, and from crossing passes from wingers. They should also practice shooting quickly after collecting shots directed at them when they are facing away from the goal. All of these situations can be set up in the station drills previously described.

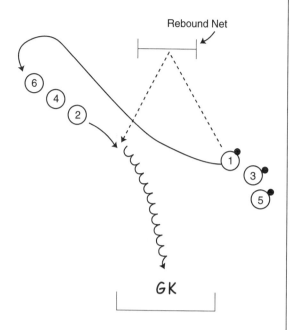

FIGURE 6-12. Shooting Station Drill 1

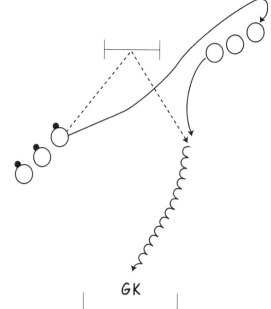

FIGURE 6-13. Shooting Station Drill 2

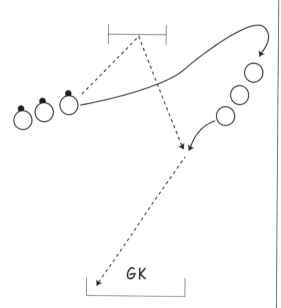

FIGURE 6-14. Shooting Station Drill 3

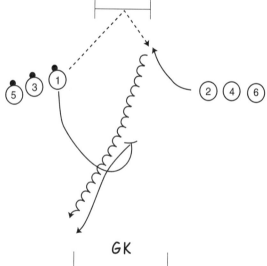

FIGURE 6-15. Shooting Station Drill 4

The THC (Throw, Header, and Catch) Game

Although this game does not conform to the strict rules of soccer, it's an activity that can be fun for beginners and that accomplishes the dual purposes of getting young players used to (a) executing headers without being afraid of the ball, and (b) moving around on the field rather than standing around watching the player with the ball.

THC is played on a 40 yard × 40 yard grid, with regulation goals at either end and two teams attempting to score by advancing the ball toward their opponents' goal via headers. Play starts with one player throwing the ball to a teammate, who attempts to head it to anyone on her team. If the ball is caught, that player will throw it to a teammate who heads it to another teammate, and so on, with the ball advancing goalward until it is sufficiently close for someone to shoot—using a header, of course.

If the ball is intercepted, the other team will initiate its own throw-header-catch sequence, hoping to set up a shot at their opponents' goal.

If a header is not caught, the other team gets the ball at the spot where the ball landed.

Coaching Tips—Shooting

1. Stress shooting quickly. To paraphrase Mayberry's illustrious deputy Barney Fife, *There are two kinds of shooters: the* quick *and the* dead. *Quick* is better.

2. With few exceptions, the hardest shots to defend against are low, hard drive lines. Teach your players to keep their shots (and push passes) low, especially in shots taken inside the Box.

3. We can't say this often enough: Vary the shots, their location, and the circumstances under which they are created and taken in your shooting station drills. It's trite, but true: *You don't win by luck; you win by preparation.* The more often your players practice a given shot from a given spot under simulated game conditions, the more comfortable they will be in executing that shot in actual game situations.

4. Although we haven't mentioned it—a clear case of overlooking the obvious— you'll want your players to practice taking penalty kicks. Have them devote equal time to kicking to either side of the keeper in order to avoid their developing a preference for one side of the goal. We once lost an important game because the opponents' keeper played on the same club team as our kicker and knew that he always kicked to the right side of the goal on penalty kicks.

TACKLING DRILLS

The ability to tackle the ball without fouling is one of the most important skills a defender can possess. Players should be drilled 1-v-1 in slide tackling from the front and side, block tackling from the front, shoulder-to-shoulder tackling from either side, and tackling from behind using the poke tackle. We neither practice nor encourage slide tackling from behind because of the risks involved, both injury and punitive risks (i.e., getting red-carded).

One way to practice slide, block, and poke tackling is, after pairing up players, to stipulate that the player with the ball must move *one speed slower than the defender,* at least until the defender is comfortable with that tackling style.

The "Dead Cockroach" Drill Series

In theory but not in practice, soccer is primarily a noncontact sport. To be considered legal, contact must be nonviolent and incidental (in the sense of not being intentional); still, Law XII of the FIFA rulebook, *Laws of the Game,* refers to "charging fairly, i.e., with the shoulder" when the ball is within playing distance and the players are attempting to play it. To practice *shoulder-to-shoulder tackling,* we use a series of drills we call the Dead Cockroach.

Players are paired up, given one ball per pair, and then separated into two lines as shown in Figure 6-16. In the drill's basic form, when the players come up for their turn, they give you the ball and then lie down on their backs, facing each other with their hands and feet up in the air like a cockroach who has enjoyed its last foray into the kitchen for a midnight snack.

When you roll the ball between them, the players leap to their feet and charge the ball, jockeying and jostling each other for possession. When one or the other of them finally takes possession, the drill may take any of several forms, depending upon what you're working on: (a) You can make it a breakaway fast break for a shot on goal, with or without keeper; (b) you can practice delaying the attacker via close marking; or (c) you can practice shoulder-to-shoulder, slide, block, or poke tackling in the manner described at the beginning of this section. However you use the drill, its attention-grabbing value and tendency to generate contact of the sort we're looking for should prove helpful in developing tackling skills that every defender should have.

You shouldn't have the players lie on their backs every time you use this drill, of course, since the novelty of imitating dead cockroaches tends to wear off rather quickly. You can also have them

a. Start out sitting, kneeling, or squatting;

b. Stand side by side, facing away from the direction you intend to throw the ball;

c. On the command "Go!" run to a given spot, where they turn around to find the ball already coming at them, whether in the air, on the floor, as a line drive, or bouncing; or you can otherwise vary the drill by

d. Moving to other areas to create different angles to the goal (Figure 6-17), or

e. Changing their routes to the ball, as shown in Figure 6-18.

In Figure 6-18, on command the first pair of players sprint to their respective corners of the penalty box, touch the line, and sprint to the penalty kick line, where the ball will be thrown or rolled by the coach. Normally, the ball is thrown when one of the players reaches his line; if one of the players is quicker than the other, however, you can either delay the throw or direct the ball closer to the slower of the two players.

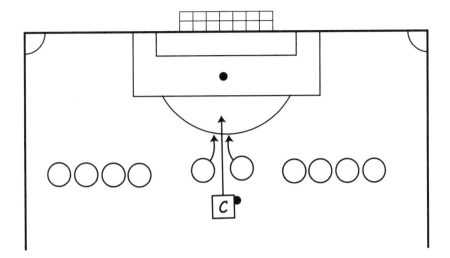

FIGURE 6–16. The Cockroach Drill

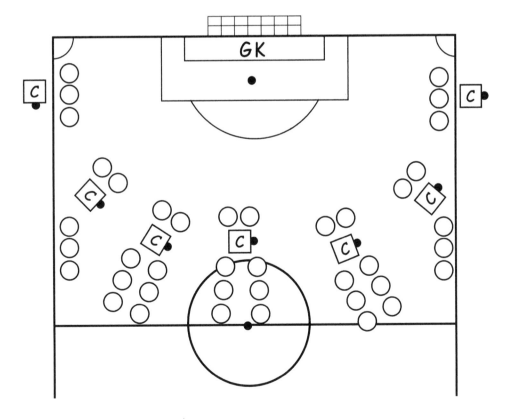

FIGURE 6–17. Varying the Location, Cockroach Drill Series

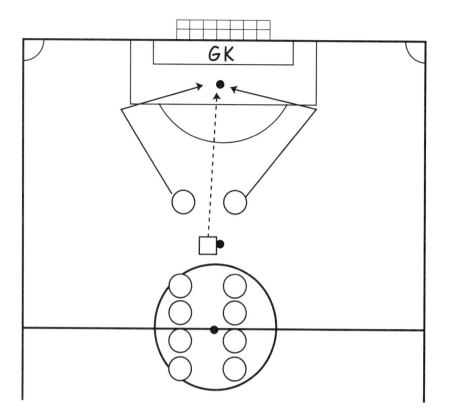

FIGURE 6–18. Varying the Players' Routes, Cockroach Drill Series

Coaching Tips—Tackling

1. Carefully explain the rules regarding legal and illegal contact before you start working on tackling.

2. Don't start off at full speed. Work up to game speed by practicing the various tackles at walking and jogging paces.

3. In working on slide tackling, stress positioning, technique, and regaining one's feet quickly. A perfectly executed slide tackle won't count for much if the tackler is out of position or fails to bounce up to pursue the free ball.

MINI-GAMES

Teaching players to handle pressure without committing physical or mental errors is one of the most difficult tasks and important priorities we face. As more than one coach has noted, "To err is human; to find someone to blame it on is even more human."

There are many ways of teaching players to handle pressure, all of which involve increasing the resistance the players face. It is important to understand, though, that simply providing greater challenges will not succeed unless the players are prepared to meet those challenges with a reasonable opportunity for success.

Mini-games provide an excellent format for training players to perform under increased pressure. Reducing the size of the field brings offensive and defensive players closer together and speeds up the action everywhere; this in turn forces the participants to pay attention to what they and their teammates are doing, and to make quick, accurate decisions.

Open-ended and less highly structured than drills, mini-games permit players to be creative within the context of team strategies. And because *you*, the coach, decide how large the playing area will be and how many players will be on it at any given time, the mini-game concept is highly flexible in terms of tailoring the games to your players' needs.

Be advised, though, that, like all forms of scrimmaging, mini-games are a supplement to your basic instruction in offensive and defensive skills, and not a substitute for teaching.

Micro Soccer

We play this fast-paced, challenging mini-game on a 20 yard × 20 yard grid with small, pop-up goals at opposite ends. There are no goalkeepers, just players going at it 2-v-2, 3-v-3 or 4-v-4, depending on what you hope to accomplish.

Micro Soccer is possibly the most versatile activity we use in our daily practices. In all versions, the absence of a goalkeeper intensifies the pressure on individual defenders to avoid getting beaten in 1-v-1 situations. Micro Soccer can also be used to teach players to respond quickly to changes from offense to defense, or vice versa.

The 2-v-2 version of the game gives players ample room to apply dribbling and ballhandling skills; it also provides an ideal format for inexperienced dribblers to practice extending their focus beyond themselves and their own situation to include a teammate. The basis of all team approaches to offense begins with 2-v-2 situations and dribblers' reacting, not just to their defenders, but to their teammates' and other defenders' movements as well.

In its 3-v-3 and 4-v-4 forms, Micro Soccer ups the ante in two ways: first, by further reducing the players' maneuvering space, and second, by bringing more defensive players into the mix. These factors, combined with the relatively small size of the playing area, dramatically increase the pressure on individual attackers to play heads-up, team-oriented soccer or suffer the consequences. The 4-v-4 format is especially well suited for players who, although they possess effective open-field dribbling skills, do not respond well to defensive pressure in tight spaces.

Big Dog

We got this up-tempo, mini-field form of scrimmaging from former Cornell University player John Landis. Played in 4-v-4, 5-v-5, or 6-v-6 fashion on a reduced field measuring, say, 60 yards × 50 yards or 50 yards × 40 yards—the dimensions can be whatever you want them to be—Big Dog features regulation goals, four teams, and two keepers who don't switch when the teams do. Each team wears jerseys contrasting in color with those of the other teams, so you'll need four sets of different-colored practice jerseys.

In Big Dog, two teams play, and the other two teams wait beyond the goal lines for their turn. Play continues until one team scores. The team that scores becomes the "Big Dog," and stays on the attack to meet its next opponent, while the other team exits, as shown in Figure 6-19.

The Green and Gold teams are playing; let's say the Green team scores. Three things happen simultaneously: (1) The Gold players exit and move to the other end beyond the goal line; (2) the Green team—the Big Dogs—gets the ball back and reverses field to go on the attack at the other end; and (3) the Blue team hustles out onto the field to play defense at their end.

If Green scores, Blue will exit and move to Red's end, as Green again reverses and attacks the Red team. If, however, Blue scores, Green will exit and go to the other end, while Blue reverses field to attack Gold.

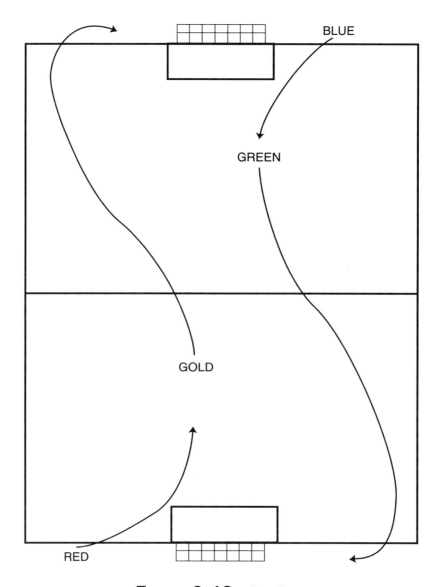

FIGURE 6–19. Big Dog

Normally, if the teams are relatively equal in ability, you won't have the same Big Dogs scoring five or six times in a row, and every team will get roughly the same amount of playing time. However, if two teams fail to score in a reasonable amount of time, you can declare that game a draw, switch both teams and install a 60- or 90-second time limit for scores, using a manager to keep the time. If one team remains Big Dog through several opponents, you can either (a) eliminate the keeper at their goal, (b) swap players around to equalize the talent, (c) declare that team the winner and start over with the two other teams, or (d) play "Little Dog" (see Figure 6-19). Installing time limits will help to ensure that teams are not overlooked in rotation.

In the "Little Dog" variation of the game, the team that scores leaves the field, and the team that was scored on goes on attack against its next opponent at the other end of the pitch.

Like Micro Soccer, Big Dog and Little Dog are extremely versatile. Ideally suited for practicing fast breaking, they also keep the teams alert that are waiting to play since, after scores, the next team has at most two to three seconds to find its marks and organize its defense to stop the attack. Eliminating the goalkeepers makes games even more challenging.

To make Big or Little Dog self-motivating, you can keep score and (a) reward the team with the most points with an extended or extra water break, (b) punish the team(s) with the least points with extra laps around the field or whatever else you may consider appropriate, or (c) combine the two.

Chapter 7

SYSTEMS OF PLAY AND THEIR ASSOCIATED STRATEGIES

Playing catch-up ball is a way of life for us. We like to get behind early, because it gives us more time to catch up.

—Fred Rossi
Pee Wee League Coach

The term *playing system* refers to any offensive or defensive alignment of the ten field players,[1] along with strategies and tactics arising out of that alignment.

Soccer fields are far too large for the field players to roam indiscriminately from goal line to goal line and touchline to touchline; as a result, it is customary to align players defensively in horizontal layers that define and delimit their roles and responsibilities. Alignments are expressed in numerical form (e.g., 3-4-3). The first number refers to the fullbacks, stoppers, and sweepers, whose basic positions are closest to the goal, and whose roles are primarily defensive. The last number refers to the forwards and wingers, whose basic positions are nearest to the halfway line, and whose roles are primarily offensive. The middle number refers to the midfielders, whose basic positions lie between those two layers; they may be attackers or defenders, depending on coaching strategy and who has the ball. A shorthand version of alignment description uses the last two numbers to identify the system (e.g., "42" to denote the 4-4-2 system).

All systems of play are extremely flexible and may be modified to provide additional attackers or defenders. Alignments simply define roles and organize a team's offense and defense, ensuring balance between them.

To avoid needless repetition in this chapter, we should note here that, *unless otherwise stated, all strategies associated with a given system also apply to all other systems, although modifications may be necessary in some cases.* For example, Figure 7-21 shows a stopper run from a 4-4-2 alignment; that same run can also be applied to any other formation that features a stopper.

---

[1] Since goalkeepers are generally but not necessarily confined to the goal box area, they are not regarded as field players.

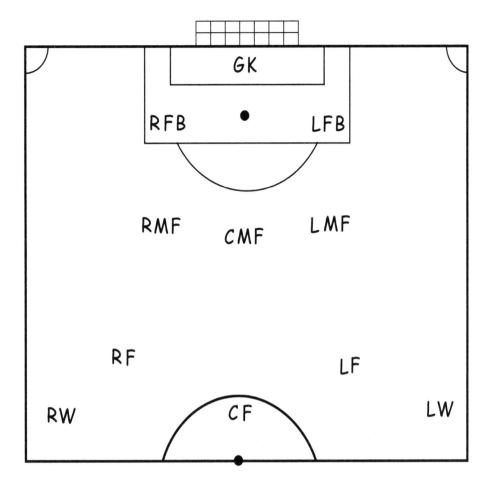

FIGURE 7–1. The 2-3-5 Alignment

THE 2-3-5 SYSTEM OF PLAY ("35")

Possibly the oldest organized playing system, the 2-3-5 alignment enjoyed great popularity during the early 1900s. As shown in Figure 7-1, it consisted of two full-backs, three midfielders, and five forwards. With as many as eight players involved in the attack, the 2-3-5 alignment was highly potent offensively but lacked defensive balance.

In 1925, the Federation International de Football Association (FIFA) amended its offside rule to require that two players rather than three must be between the attacking player and the goal he is attacking. This rule change, along with growing recognition that greater emphasis on defense was needed, led to the development of the 3-4-3 alignment that extended teams' defensive capabilities. Other systems have largely replaced the 2-3-5 and 3-4-3 in modern times.

THE 3-4-3 SYSTEM OF PLAY ("43")

Herbert Chapman, manager of Arsenal, one of England's leading soccer clubs, introduced the concept of the third fullback, or *stopper*, as featured in the 3-4-3 alignment.

As originally designed, the 3-4-3 stacked the "4" players in pairs, with a forward and a midfielder on either side of the pitch. This alignment, sometimes referred to as a "W-M" formation due to its shape (Figure 7-2), had the forwards forming a capital *W* and the midfielders, fullbacks, and stopper forming a capital *M*. In reality, however, those players had to realign themselves defensively with every ball movement into the defensive third in order to mark attackers along the sidelines between the wingers and fullbacks. Eventually, this led to modification of the basic 43 alignment as shown in Figure 7-3. The W-M alignment is still there, but in greatly elongated form.

Defensively, both versions of the 3-4-3 featured a stopper (ST), who functioned as the center fullback and marked anyone in his area (or else he covered the opponents' best attacker, depending on team strategy). The right fullback (RFB) and left fullback (LFB) marked the opponents' front runners (forwards). The left and right midfielders—LMF and RMF, respectively—were primarily defenders whose coverage responsibilities lay within the defensive half of the midfield third; they marked whoever entered their areas (e.g., wingers or outside forwards). The inside forwards—ILF and IRF in the diagrams—marked opposing midfielders. Such assigned responsibilities permitted the defense to match up regardless of whether the opponents sent two, three, or four players in the vanguard of their attack.

At first glance, 3-4-3 alignments appear highly versatile, suggesting as many as seven players in the defensive third (the "3-4") and seven attackers (the "4-3"). Even if such a scenario were realistic, however—and in most cases it isn't—having seven attackers would leave you with only three defenders other than the keeper; and seven interior defenders would require that your inside forwards and midfielders possess sprinters' speed and the endurance of marathon runners in order to fill the dual roles of covering on defense and supporting the offense.

The key to success in using the 43 system hinges, of course, on the capabilities of the inside forward-midfielder quartet. Marking attackers in the defensive third is a challenging task for any player; filling the offensive slots in the attacking third is equally demanding. Both tasks require a total effort and total concentration from everyone involved. Finding four players who possess the diverse offensive and defensive skills *and* the physical stamina to go both ways in covering a large portion of the field for more than a few minutes at a time is highly unlikely; that's why the 43, like the 2-3-5 system that preceded it, is not the system of choice for most coaches. It can be done, of course—but starting out your offensive runs and defensive stands with one less player than the opponents means that your inside forwards and midfielders are always going to be hustling to catch up with the action.

One possible way to make this system more user-friendly might be to alter the alignment slightly to favor either your offense or defense (i.e., by moving up an inside forward to run your 3-4-3 as a 3-3-4 with four attackers, or dropping back a midfielder to run it as a 4-3-3 with an additional fullback in the penalty area). However, such changes are largely cosmetic; they don't solve the problem nearly as efficiently as using another alignment would.

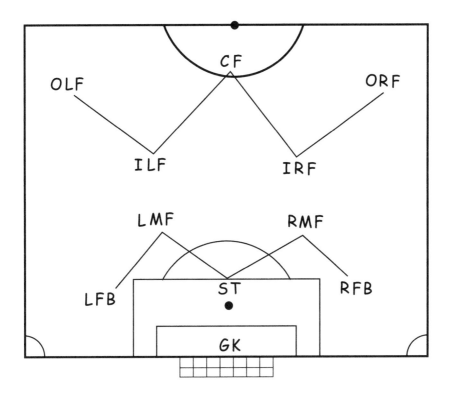

FIGURE 7–2. The 3-4-3 ("W-M") Alignment

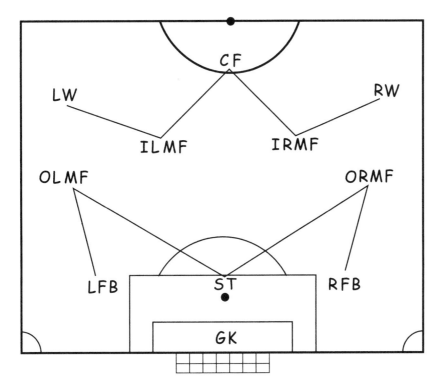

FIGURE 7–3. Variation in 3-4-3 Alignment

MODERN CONCEPTS OF SOCCER

The first and most important principle to bear in mind about systems of play is that *no playing system is a sure winner;* you won't win with a given system just because someone else is winning with it. Alignments and strategies don't win games; players do. If it were otherwise, every soccer team would be using the same system, every team would be undefeated, and no one would ever lose a game.

In modern soccer, at least four basic systems of play have evolved: the 4-2-4, 4-3-3, 4-4-2, and 5-3-2. Like the earlier 2-3-5 and 3-4-3 systems, all of them have strengths and weaknesses. Which one is best for your team depends on, among other factors, how well your players' strengths and weaknesses match those of the various systems.

Specifically, the successful incorporation of any playing system requires the following:

❐ You must understand all of the systems well enough to know which one might be best suited to your players; you must also understand the preferred system well enough to teach it to the players, and believe in it strongly enough to convince the players that it represents the best way for them to play the game.

In Mayberry, deputy Barney Fife's brief stint as a salesman, his "You-wouldn't-want-to-buy-a-set-of-encyclopedias, would-you?" approach to the art of selling was singularly unsuccessful, for obvious reasons. To sell your players on the merits of a given playing system, you must first convince yourself that it's what your players need.

❐ You must be aware of your players' strengths and weaknesses, both individually and as a team. Qualities such as team speed, physical conditioning, experience, leadership, individual skills, and attacking and defending capabilities must be considered in determining which system is preferable, and how players should be aligned within the system.

System Priorities

To take the previous statements a step further, the playing system you adopt should account for the following priorities:

1. It should maximize your chances of hiding whatever weaknesses your team possesses. If you can't hide your weaknesses, opponents can defeat you in either of two ways, by attacking your weaknesses directly or by ignoring them and concentrating their efforts on nullifying your strengths—say, by double-teaming your best attacker.

The more weaknesses you have, the more important it becomes to play conservatively. As you probably noticed in our brief look at the 2-3-5, with only two fullbacks and the keeper to protect the goal, the 35 offers only minimal chances for playing conservatively on defense. Oh, you can let it all hang out offensively in a 2-3-5, of course, but at the other end of the field, the opponents are likely to ring up goals like a K-Mart cashier ringing up sales when a "Blue Light Special in Aisle Five" is announced. And since all but the very best teams have defensive weaknesses of some kind or other, it's hardly surprising that 2-3-5 alignments are seen as rarely today as rumble seats and running boards on automobiles.

The last thing you need with an inexperienced team, or players who are weak defensively or slow in transition from offense to defense (or vice versa), is a high-powered, aggressive offense and pressure man-to-man defense. If your players are slow afoot, slow to react, or generally unsure of themselves offensively and defensively, you need a system that sacrifices a measure of your attacking potential in return for increased defensive concentration in the midfield area and your defensive third.

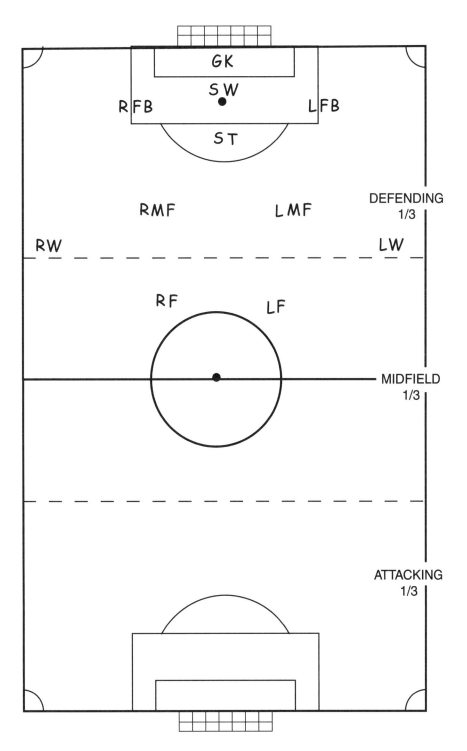

FIGURE 7–4. 4-4-2 Alignment with Sweeper/Stopper

We had five starters missing from our lineup in a 1995 high school playoff game. We knew we couldn't play our normally aggressive game under the circumstances, so we conceded most of our attacking potential, used a compact 4-4-2 sweeper-stopper system similar to the one shown in Figure 7-4, and played conservatively at both ends of the pitch, hoping to keep the game close enough to give us a chance of winning a low-scoring match. All we wanted offensively were a few shots on goal off fast breaks by our forwards, and maybe a couple of defensive fouls and penalty kicks along the way.

The strategy almost worked; we scored a fast-break goal early, missed a penalty kick, and led at halftime, 1-0. We eventually lost the game, 3-1, when the opponents tied the score midway through the second half and then pushed across two more goals in the last four minutes of play. In the final analysis, though, switching systems and strategies to accommodate our severely depleted lineup gave us a shot at winning a playoff game that we could not possibly have won otherwise.

Depending on the extent and severity of your team's weaknesses, you may or may not be able to hide them all. Skills aside, however, one area where you should *not* be weak is physical conditioning. As football's Vince Lombardi noted, "Fatigue makes cowards of us all." Fatigue is a preventable error.

We've always liked John Wooden's idea of preparing his players to play *three* halves of basketball, not two. Players may be tired at the end of matches, but they should not be exhausted; if they are fatigued to the point of exhaustion when the clock runs out, they'll be dead in the water if the game goes into overtime.

Regarding the notion of hiding your weaknesses, the best place to hide an especially weak player in your lineup is at a wing position. After all, you don't want to use that player as a keeper, sweeper, stopper, or fullback, where his mistakes will shred your defense. You don't want him as a midfielder, since that area is where attacks develop; if you play him as a midfielder, your attacks will break down before they ever reach your attacking third. And you don't want him at forward because he is incapable of leading the attack. His best role is simply staying out of the way until he acquires the skills necessary to become a more integral part of your team offense or defense—all of which leaves the wing position to him by the process of elimination.

It's not what you'd like to do, of course, but it may be what you must do for the team's sake. Such a strategy may weaken your offense somewhat; still, having a strong interior defense means that you won't need a high-powered offense to keep games close or to defeat opponents. Hiding weaknesses is a normal and accepted part of coaching strategy in all team sports. In most cases, you won't get any argument from the players in question; after all, if they are grossly unskilled they probably don't want to have the ball in the attacking third any more than you want them to have it there.

2. Your system should permit you to focus on your strengths. Assuming that whatever weaknesses exist are hidden away where they will do the least harm to your defense or offense, your next priority lies in finding ways to maximize your strengths. Defensively, your strengths might include team speed, experience, fundamental soundness, an aggressive attitude, ability to control dribblers and/or take the ball away from them, and quick transition from defense to offense.

The more skilled defenders you have, the less important it becomes to have extra defenders in or around the 18 (penalty box). Solid interior defense permits a team to extend its defense to aggressive marking in the midfield third and beyond; it also increases the chances of takeaways and fast breaking with more than just one or two attackers.

Playing to your offensive strengths refers, first of all, to using a system that permits your key attacker(s) to become involved in the offense early and often. The more players you have who are skilled at dribbling, passing, creating space with or without the ball, and shooting, the more effective your offense will be. Given sufficient numbers of highly skilled attackers, it doesn't really matter how you play your offense. With just one or two skilled attackers, however, it becomes critical to take advantage of every ball possession or scoring opportunity, whether by attacking relentlessly with those players or by working the ball around carefully and patiently and waiting for scoring opportunities to arise. In either case, your chances of success are greatest when your team is playing at its own best tempo and not the opponents'.

3. Your system should permit you to attack opponents' weaknesses and/or negate opponents' strengths—assuming, of course, that your players are capable of doing so. The last part of that sentence explains why this is only the third priority regarding ways to use playing systems.

It is axiomatic to all coaching that, before you can win a game by doing things right, you must ensure against losing it by doing things wrong. For weak teams—those that are likely to lose most of their games—this usually means adopting a conservative playing style that emphasizes defense and careful, low-risk ballhandling on offense. What the other team does is important, of course, but since you aren't likely to overpower superior opponents with your few strengths, the best you can do is try to hide your many weaknesses; stack your defenders deep in the defensive third and slow down the game tempo offensively to run time off the clock and keep the ball away from them. It's not an exciting or pretty way to play the game, but it is better than getting steamrolled by scores like 14-0 or 19-1. It's a fact of life that you won't beat superior opponents at what they do best. To think otherwise is to reduce your chances of ever defeating a superior opponent.

If we appear to be harping on a theme—well, we're sorry, but we've known too many coaches over the years who treat games as if the better team has a divine right to win by whatever score it chooses. We don't buy that argument. While every coach's goal is to win as many games as possible, with weak teams there's another, more fundamental goal involved, namely, keeping the score close and your players competitive.

Players who are used to losing will hustle and work hard only for as long as they think they have a chance to win. With such a team, your only realistic chance of remaining competitive against better teams for longer than it takes your players to work up a sweat is to protect the ball like Fort Knox when you have it and use eight or more defenders to protect your goal like Fort Knox the rest of the time.

The opponents probably won't like it if you slow down the game against them, especially if they're used to beating your team by nine or ten goals; still, whether they like it or not is *their* problem, not yours. Your problem is to ensure that the game is played in such a manner that your players are continually making progress toward becoming the sort of team you want them to be. You can't do that by coaching as if getting beaten 17-0 is no worse than losing by a score of 5-0. It matters. You can build pride even in defeat by keeping games close that were supposed to be runaway losses.

If all you want is to be liked by opposing coaches, send them get-well cards when they're sick, exchange Christmas presents, and let their teams score all the goals they want to every time you play them—but if you want those same coaches to *respect* you, forget what they want and do what's best for *your* team.

With a good team—one that is capable of winning at least half of its games—you can expand your goals accordingly. You won't entirely eliminate or negate the strengths of a superior opponent, but you *can* exploit and attack the weaknesses of weaker teams or those of equal ability. With a great team—one that is capable of winning most (or all) of its games—you can either exploit opponents' weaknesses or use your own strengths to create weaknesses.

Exploiting Opponents' Weaknesses

There are many ways to exploit opponents' weaknesses, depending on the nature of those weaknesses. If their ballhandling is shaky, you might extend your marking aggressively into the midfield third or beyond in order to force takeaways or turnovers that your attackers can translate into fast breaks and quick shots on goal. If an opponent has only one or two effective attackers, you can either play them closely or double-team one or both of them, whether to keep the ball away from them or to take it away from them when they get it.

If the opposing team is slow afoot, or if its players are either out of shape, slow to react to sudden changes in ball possession, or unskilled offensively or defensively, playing aggressive, pressure man-to-man defense and fast breaking will exploit any or all of those weaknesses and place great pressure on the opponents to play error-free ball. The weaker the team, the more likely they will be to fall apart under constant pressure. When they lose their composure, their mistakes will increase, as will the pressure to avoid further mistakes.

Tempo is a great equalizer in soccer. Whoever controls the tempo of the game or any section of it also dictates how the game will be played. The old coaching phrase "playing within yourself" refers to playing at your own best tempo; it can also refer to playing at whatever tempo the opponents prefer not to play at, as long as you're better at it than they are.

Speed isn't everything. What matters most is *effective speed*, or speed under control. It doesn't matter if a girl runs 11-flat in the 100 meters if she can't control the ball offensively (or control her mark defensively) at high speed. With effective overall team speed, however, we recommend taking chances offensively and defensively to keep the pressure on opponents throughout every second of the game. This strategy will automatically defeat any opponent who lacks the stamina to run with you for 40 minutes. Fatigued players will want to rest and find breathing room; applying constant offensive and defensive pressure all over the field will ensure that they don't get it. If *your* team is playing fresh and *ours* is bone-weary, it doesn't take an Einstein to figure out where the advantage lies, or who will profit from it. Fatigue cannot be overcome by telling players to work harder.

An up-tempo, high-speed strategy may also force opponents to concentrate longer and harder than they're used to doing, and to make accurate high-speed decisions that could be made easily without constant offensive and defensive pressure. If, through proper conditioning and training, your players are used to playing under those conditions, your system will function virtually as another player on the field for your team, giving you an enormous advantage against teams who aren't prepared to play that way. It takes highly conditioned, experienced players to use "run-and-gun" tactics; with such players at our disposal, however, we wouldn't play the game any other way.

Against a weak team, we'll attack with reckless abandon and pressure the opponents all over the field when they have the ball. And if they're really weak, we'll set as our goal not just shutting them out, but keeping the ball out of our defensive third for the entire game. It's our way of keeping our players motivated against weak teams.

The converse of this theory applies to weak teams: *Avoid at all costs the temptation to run with a superior running team.* If they're better at it than you are, they'll eventually destroy you, because they are more familiar with that tempo than your players are. As the late cartoonist Walt Kelly *(Pogo)* once noted, "When you eat with a tiger, the tiger eats last."

Negating Opponents' Strengths

All other things being equal, the team with the most strengths wins the game. Among teams of equal ability or nearly so, effective coaching consists of finding ways to negate opponents' strengths without depleting your own strengths to the point where they are no longer strengths.

If your team is weak defensively, you can bolster it by retreating deeper into your defensive third and adding players as necessary in and around the 18—*but you can do the same thing to negate opponents' strengths, if they are potent offensively.* You can also play "loose" (i.e., positional) defense on the ball and elsewhere by staying between the dribbler and the goal in on-the-ball marking, and either overplaying toward the ball elsewhere to cut off the passing lanes or applying zone defensive principles away from the ball to reduce the number of openings to which opposing attackers can make a run.

Perhaps the best way to reduce opponents' defensive strengths is to use the entire midfield/attacking two thirds of the field offensively rather than limiting your attack to one area of the field. If the opponents are superior defensively, they probably are also aggressive in their marking. Spreading your attack vertically brings them farther out from their goal and penalty area; spreading it horizontally via crossing passes from one touchline to the other will further extend the defense, stretching it to (or possibly beyond) the limits of effective coverage.

THE 4-2-4 SYSTEM OF PLAY ("24")

The 4-2-4 alignment offers the sort of versatility that the 3-4-3 only hinted at. With four players in position to attack immediately, the 24 can improve a team's fast-break potential even with players of average speed. It's also a good system to use in playing catch-up ball when you need to score in a hurry, with the four players up front pressuring the opposing players to get a quick turnover and shot on goal. In either case, having four defenders in or around the penalty area reduces the chances of your being burned by your own team's offensive mistakes.

Like the 3-4-3, the 24 can be played either of two ways, with four fullbacks (Figure 7-5) or with two fullbacks and a sweeper/stopper tandem aligned in I formation with the keeper (Figure 7-6). Either system is fine; with a high school team we happen to prefer the sweeper system—which, incidentally, is known as a *Catenaccio* formation in reference to its Italian origin; it features tight man-to-man marking—because it reduces confusion regarding coverage in and around the penalty box. With younger players (i.e., below junior high or middle school age), we might prefer the four-FB alignment, placing our two best fullbacks on the left side of the field since most young players are predominantly right-footed and are more likely to attack to their right (our left).

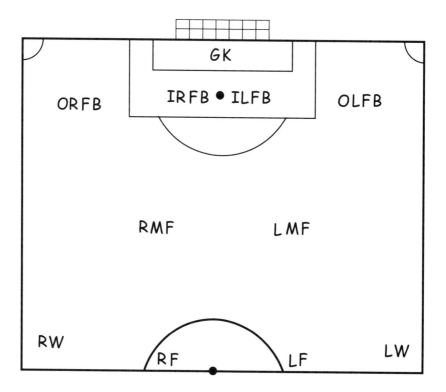

FIGURE 7–5. 4-2-4 Alignment with Four Fullbacks

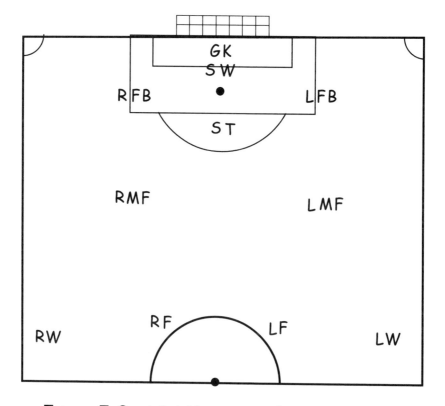

FIGURE 7–6. 4-2-4 Alignment with Sweeper/Stopper

In a four-fullback defensive alignment, wingers mark wingers, forwards pressure fullbacks, midfielders mark midfielders, and the four FBs mark forwards.

In a Catenaccio defensive alignment, the two FBs mark forwards and the stopper either marks the opponents' best offensive player, or else he marks the extra player if the opponents send three players on attack. If the opponents send only two forwards in their attack and your stopper is marking one of them, one of your fullbacks will be free to help out defensively and make runs in your offensive attacks (Figure 7-7).

The sweeper, or *libero*, is—as the Italian term suggests—literally a "free player" on defense, with no specific defensive responsibilities. The sweeper is the last line of defense short of the keeper. Playing zone defense and marking any unmarked attacker who penetrates the coverage and threatens the goal, the sweeper is the field general of the defense. He or she directs and organizes the other players and supports them throughout the defensive third.

Even a cursory glance at Figures 7-5 and 7-6 reveals the greatest area of potential weakness of the 4-2-4: the midfield area. It's a large area—too large, in fact, to be covered by only two players unless they are Clark Kent and Bruce Wayne when they aren't playing Superman and Batman on the soccer pitch; that's why, in using this system under normal circumstances, you'd probably want your outside forwards (wingers) dropping back to support the defense in the midfield third. When you regain possession of the ball, the wingers will move up and out to create space in the ensuing attack (Figure 7-8).

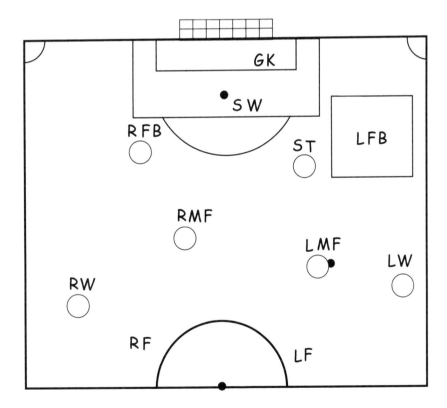

FIGURE 7-7. A Free Fullback, 4-2-4 Defense

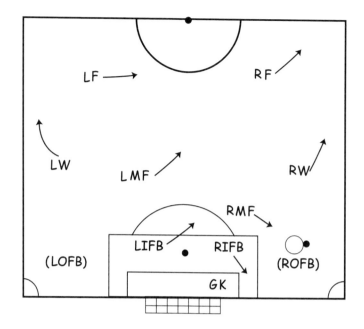

FIGURE 7–8. Offensive Flow in Transition, 4-2-4 System

Even with support from the forwards, your midfielders must be nonstop go-getters and workhorses in order to maximize the potential of the 4-2-4 alignment. If your midfielders possess the qualities necessary to play tough defense *and* to support the offense, the 4-2-4 gives you the equivalent of 13 players on the field rather than 11: the keeper, six players on defense, and six players on the attack. (And if you're really pressed for time and nothing else but a goal will do, you can send two fullbacks on offense to give you eight attackers, as shown in Figure 7-9.)

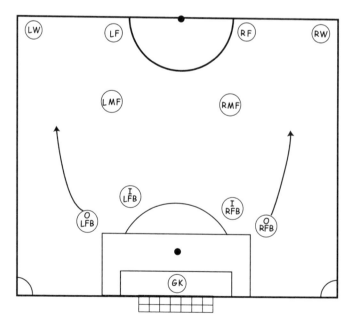

FIGURE 7–9. Attacking with Fullbacks, 4-2-4 System

Using eight attackers is not the sort of strategy you normally want to employ, or else you'd be using a 2-3-5 system; still, it's something to consider on a situational basis. We said earlier that the margin of defeat matters—and it's true, in broad terms. It's better to lose to a superior opponent by a score of 5-1 than to get blown away, 22-1; but if you absolutely, positively must score *right now* to have a chance of catching up in a close game, you may have to let it all hang out offensively to get that score. In such cases, losing 3-0 with eight to ten players on attack is no worse than losing 1-0 with fewer attackers. It won't affect how your players feel about themselves.

Organizing a 4-2-4 Attack

The number of players involved in your offensive attack depends on two factors, namely, how many effective attackers you have and how many players are in position to become involved in the early stages of the attack. The 24 alignment suggests four lead attackers—the forwards and the wingers—with the midfielders next in line and either the stopper or a fullback trailing the play, possibly to enter the action as the ball advances. In Figure 7-10, MF_2 is racing ahead to join the first wave of attackers.

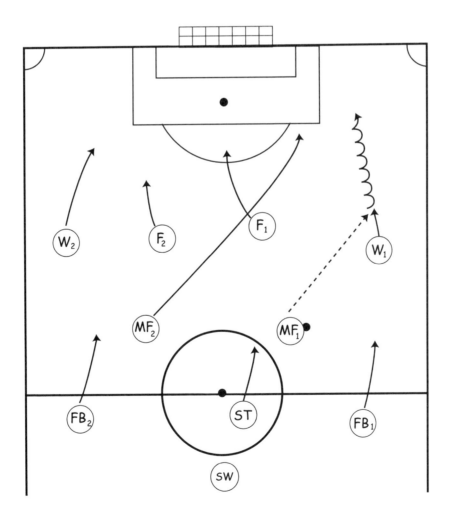

FIGURE 7-10. Sideline Attack with Forward Overlap, 4-2-4

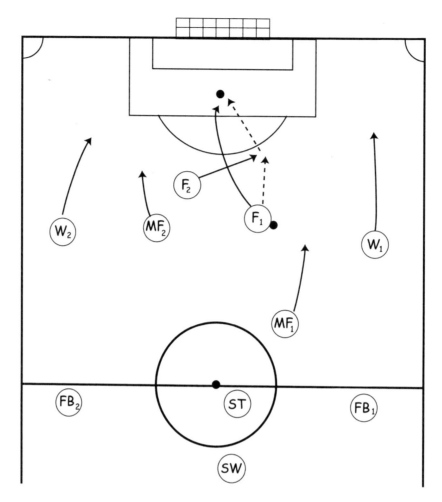

FIGURE 7–11. Forwards Give-and-Go, 4-2-4

W_1 has five options after receiving MF_1's pass and dribbling along the sideline. He can (1) use his speed or dribbling skills to get past his defender; or he can (2) pass to MF_2, who is joining the attack, (3) pass to F_1 in the middle,[2] (4) pass to F_2 on the far side of the penalty box, or (5) switch-pass to W_2 near the opposite touchline. All of those players are direct threats to the defense; that is, upon receiving W_1's pass they will be in position to shoot on goal if the defense falters.

An understanding of what is and is not shown in Figure 7-10 is critical to understanding team offensive strategy in soccer. Nine players are moving in the diagram; what is *not* shown is that they will keep on moving, either toward or away from the goal or open areas of the field, depending on what W_1 does. They will not stand still in the area indicated by the arrowheads, because no offense functions effectively with

---

[2] F_1's movement is called an *overlap away from the ball*. It serves three purposes: creating space for the dribbler, threatening the middle of the defense, and opening an area for a trailing attacker (e.g., MF_2 in Figure 7-11).

attackers standing still. The diagram simply shows that W_2, F_2, F_1, and MF_2 are not sprinting toward the opponents' goal ahead of the ball, in which case they would be offside when W_1 passes the ball. W_1 will not pass to them where they are, but rather *to where they are going.* Which player W_1 passes to will depend on which player is open, and on W_1's ability to find and connect with that player as well.

The spectrum of offensive skills ranges from rank beginners who can see only the ball and the grass below them, to players whose field awareness encompasses the locations of all their teammates and their defenders as well. Such skills are not easily come by, but they can be developed over a period of time through the combination of hard work and patient coaching. It takes time for players to develop an instinctual feel for what their teammates are going to do, but when that point is reached, your offensive horizons are virtually unlimited.

Your tasks here are to teach your players where and how to move to create and use space wisely, and to let them know where they can expect to find their teammates in given situations.

Figure 7-11 shows a simple give-and-go sequence involving two attacking forwards. Since F_2 could not possibly receive the ball while stationary, she runs across F_1's line of sight to collect the pass as shown; then, when F_2 has passed, F_1 makes a run toward the goal to collect F_2's pass—hopefully, for a shot on goal. Failing that, F_1 will look first for W_2, W_1, or F_1 in an attempt to press the attack; if those passing lanes are closed to attack, she will probably look to one of the midfielders who are moving up to support the attack, or to the fullbacks or stopper along the perimeter if she finds it necessary to kick the ball out or reorganize the attack.

It's important that players avoid crowding the ball. Movement away from the ball is far more likely to be productive than either a lack of movement or movement toward the ball. The ball changes directions so frequently in a given offensive sequence that constant, purposeful (as opposed to random) movement is necessary to keep attacks alive. Playing offensive soccer via random player movements is no more likely to be effective than balancing your checkbook by putting down random numbers. It might be possible, but your creditors and the bank probably wouldn't be satisfied with the results.

With a veteran team that is strong offensively and defensively, the 4-2-4 alignment offers great possibilities for controlling opponents all over the field—provided, of course, that the midfielders are superior athletes and versatile performers. Within the 24 alignment, you can move players forward to enhance your attacking potential, back them up to strengthen your defense in midfield, or go all out in pressuring opponents throughout the field, offensively and defensively—*and you can do any or all of those things simply by changing your strategy but not your alignment!*

That's what we mean by calling the 4-2-4 system *versatile!* (But your players must be versatile to handle it.)

THE 4-3-3 SYSTEM OF PLAY ("33")

As shown in Figures 7-12 and 7-13, the 4-3-3 is a simple variation of the 4-2-4 in which a forward has been dropped back to strengthen the midfield area defensively.

In 4-3-3 defense, fullbacks mark forwards, midfielders mark midfielders, wingers mark wingers, forwards pressure the opponents' fullbacks—and in sweeper/ stopper (Catenaccio) coverage the stopper (ST) marks the opponents' third forward or playmaker out of midfield. The sweeper (SW) should always be kept free to help out, and should avoid the temptation to cover an unmarked forward. If the opponents have a numerical advantage in their attack, a midfielder should drop back to mark the extra attacker. The sweeper is too valuable to the defense to be wasted by marking any player who is not a direct threat to the goal. With the sweeper occupied elsewhere, the only defender left to protect the goal is the keeper—and *that* is a situation to be avoided at all costs.

The key player in determining how versatile—and thus ultimately how useful—the 4-3-3 will be is the center midfielder (CMF). If he or she can fill the role of a center forward (CF) on attack as shown in Figures 7-14 and 7-15, the 33 will function offensively in the same manner as a power-oriented 4-2-4 system; still, the primary responsibility of the CMF in the 33 system is always defense.

When the CMF joins the attack to form a four-player front, the stopper moves up to cover the space vacated by the CMF, and the fullbacks move into support positions.

The player movement in Figure 7-15 is similar to that shown in Figure 7-10, only with four lead attackers rather than five. W_2's options are the same, as are the overlap away from the ball by F_1 and the filling move by CMF_1. The stopper fills CMF_1's position and MF_2 supports W_2.

© 1999 by Parker Publishing Company, Inc.

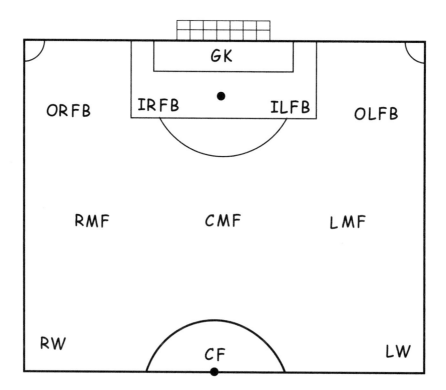

FIGURE 7–12. 4-3-3 Alignment with Four Fullbacks

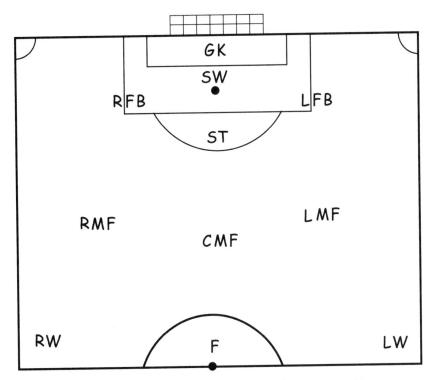

FIGURE 7–13. 4-3-3 Alignment with Sweeper/Stopper

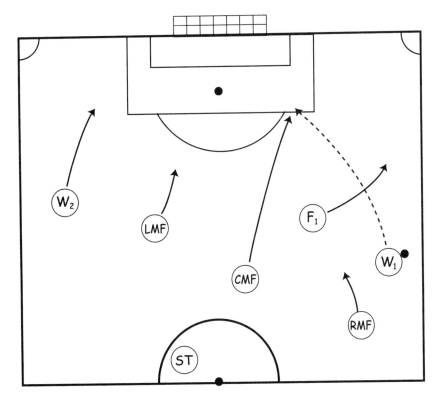

FIGURE 7–14. Center Midfielder Attacking, 4-3-3

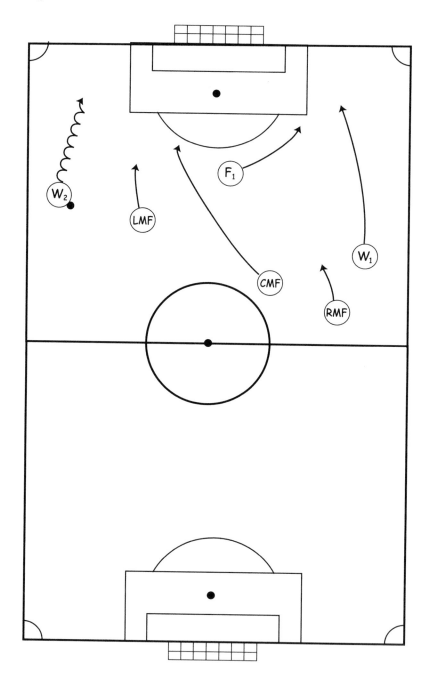

FIGURE 7–15. Wing Option, Forward Overlap. 4-3-3

The Rubber Band Principle

Timing is a crucial factor in all offensive runs. If F_1, CMF_1, or W_2 mistime their runs or reach the box too soon and stand around waiting for W_2 to make his move, they become easy marks and eliminate themselves as receivers. We use the easily understood principle of the rubber band to teach our players how to keep moving: you *check in* (make your run), and if you mistime it or otherwise fail to gain an advantage, you *check out* (reverse field to clear the area), and then *check back in*, somewhat in the manner of a rubber band stretching out and contracting.

There are a number of ways that this principle might be applied. In Figure 7-15, the CMF could check out and then make his own overlap run to set up F_1's run to ball side—or F_1 could check out and advance toward the sideline to set up W_1's run to the middle. The important things for the players to understand are that *continuous offensive movement generates defensive uncertainty,* and that *lack of movement stalls the attack like a flat tire.*

The 4-3-3 system is slightly more defense-oriented than the 4-2-4; that's why a coach might prefer it to the 24 with a team that has trouble controlling the midfield third defensively.

THE 4-4-2 SYSTEM OF PLAY ("42")

Sir Alf Ramsey, coach of England's 1966 World Cup champions, is regarded as the "Father of the 42 System." His system, shown in Figure 7-16, was primarily defense-oriented, featuring four fullbacks (two of whom served as stopper and sweeper), four midfielders—actually, two MFs and two wingers—and two forwards.

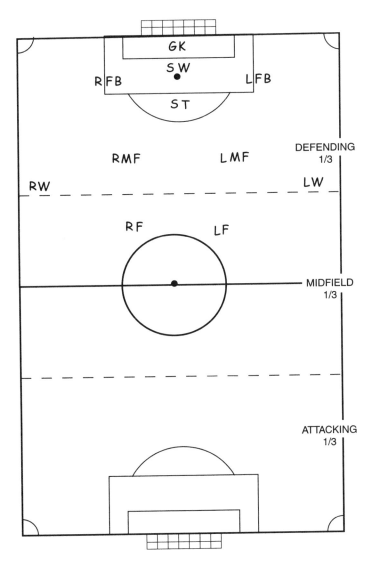

FIGURE 7–16. 4-4-2 Alignment with Sweeper/Stopper

Figure 7-17 shows the four-fullback variation of the 42. Like the Catenaccio (sweeper) formation, it packs eight defenders in and around the penalty area, and thus offers strong defensive possibilities. However, the four-fullback alignment contains two problem areas: the large open space in midfield between the MFs and forwards, and the fact that having four fullbacks can be confusing in terms of matchups and coverage. Those factors serve to explain why the Catenaccio formation is more widely used than the four-FB alignment.

In both variations of the 42, wingers mark wingers and midfielders mark midfielders. The forwards roam and are always ready for a quick counterattack; they also put immediate pressure on the ball when they lose possession, and one of the forwards can drop back to support the defense in midfield if necessary, leaving one forward up front.

Because of its primarily defensive nature, the 4-4-2 is likely to be the system of choice for coaches who are basically defense-minded, or whose teams are weak defensively. However, many coaches who use other systems turn to the 42 in the latter stages of games in which they are protecting a lead and don't need a score to win. The 4-4-2 gives them additional bodies in midfield, and thus reduces the chances of their giving up fast-break goals or being outnumbered in the defensive third. Offensively, they may use long, clearing kicks to get the ball out of their area, or they may elect to spread the field and maintain ball possession to run out the clock.

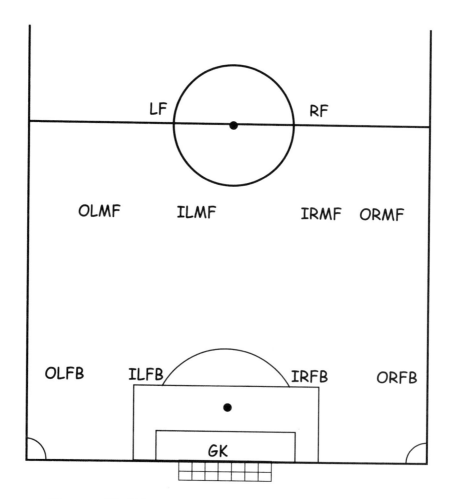

FIGURE 7–17. 4-4-2 Alignment with Four Fullbacks

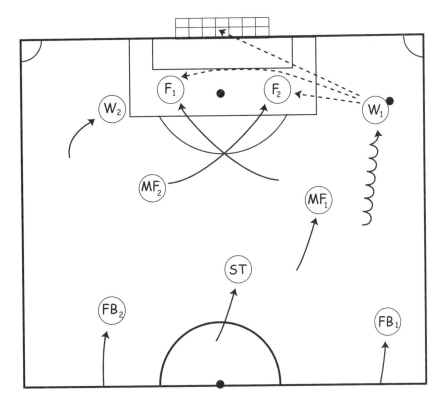

FIGURE 7-18. Options at the End of the Overlap, 4-4-2

In the original Ramsey system, the wingers did not attack; instead, the midfielders and fullbacks raided areas in front of the wingers. Today, however, the wingers are expected to participate in the attack, along with the forwards, midfielders, and possibly even the stopper or a fullback, depending upon the situation and the opponent. The wingers must be speedy, the forwards capable of scoring, and the midfielders adept at passing and playmaking if the offense is to avoid being overwhelmed by the defenders' numerical superiority. The stopper and fullbacks generally play supporting roles on offense by being available to help out when the attack bogs down, whether by relaying the ball from one side of the field to the other or simply by supporting attackers in trouble. Sometimes, they may even surprise opponents by making runs through the heart of the defense (see Figures 7-21 and 7-22).

Building a Team Offense, 4-4-2

Figure 7-18 offers a different perspective of the forward overlap/winger option play shown in Figures 7-10 and 7-15. This time, we're showing where the players are at the end of their movements. MF_1 has passed to W_1 and filled his position when W_1 dribbled deep. F_1 has overlapped away from the ball, and F_2 delayed his run into space until the area was cleared.

As the diagram shows, the attack is nicely balanced. W_1 has the same options as before, that is, taking a shot on goal or passing to F_1 or F_2. The other players, not directly involved in the attack, assume support positions: W_2 moving up but staying outside the 18 to pick up any short clearing kick by the opponents; MF_2 advancing to support the forwards; MF_1 supporting W_1; the stopper filling the middle, supporting the midfielders and looking for an opportunity to make a run (Figure 7-22). The fullbacks watch their marks but remain in position to support or make a run (Figure 7-22). The sweeper supports the stopper and fullbacks.

Essentially, then, attacking movements consist of certain players leading the advance and other players advancing behind them in layers, with each player prepared to assist the player(s) ahead of him if necessary. If it hasn't been made abundantly clear by now, that is what is meant by "supporting" the attack or any given player within it.

While it is customary to refer to two attackers in the 4-4-2, or four attackers in the 4-2-4, and so on—or to six attackers in the 42 or 24 if you include the midfielders—a coordinated attack involves all ten field players thinking offensively, mindful of their responsibilities (some of which are defensive) but looking for ways to press the attack or help out their teammates.

Overloading

In basketball, teams overload one side of the court to create a numbers advantage on that side. Soccer teams do the same thing but for a very different reason—to create space for another player to run into. In Figure 7-19, the forwards are overloading the left side to create space for W_1.

If MF_1 had the ball, the procedure could be reversed by overloading F_1 and F_2 to their right to set up a run for W_2.

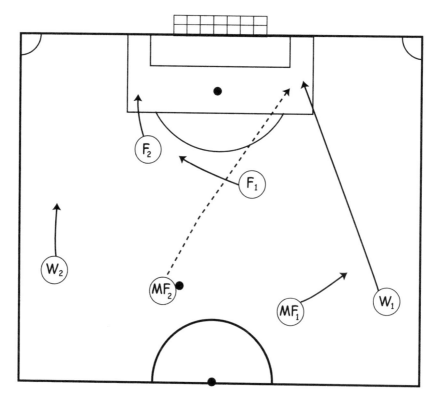

FIGURE 7-19. Forwards Overlapping, 4-4-2

Theoretically, the same thing could be done to set up a pass from MF_2 to W_2 in Figure 7-19, but in practical terms it wouldn't work as well because of W_2's location on the ball side of the field. Off-the-ball defenders normally play toward the ball side of their marks in order to prevent runs inside them; creating space away from the ball stretches defenses and helps to ensure that defenders don't "cheat" toward the intended receiver.

Midfielder Runs

In Figure 7-20, MF_2 and MF_1 have joined the attack, making runs from their midfield positions to become primary receivers in the penalty area. When FB_2 passes to F_2, W_2 and both midfielders initiate their runs to open space as F_1 drops back to support F_2. W_1 stays outside to maintain space for F_2's crossing pass to MF_1.

Midfielder runs are most likely to be productive when the defensive coverage is focused on the forwards and wings.

Stopper/Fullback Runs

If, as many coaches do, you prefer man-to-man defense, one of the first decisions you'll make in every game is who marks whom on defense. If you use a Catenaccio (sweeper-stopper) defensive formation, you might want your stopper to mark the opponents' best attacker. You'll also want reliable defenders marking the forwards and wingers, since those players are most likely to represent the vanguard of their team's attacks. If you're using a 4-2-4 system, you'll thus have your fifth- and sixth-best defenders marking their midfielders, which explains why midfielder runs are likely to be productive.

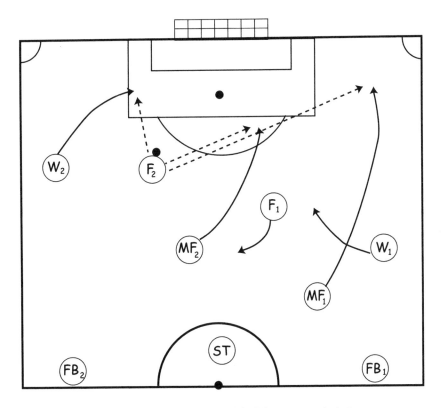

FIGURE 7–20. Midfielder Run, 4-4-2

The problem becomes even more acute if the opposing coach decides to sneak his stopper or a fullback into the offense via a run, in which case you're covering the runs with, at best, your seventh- and eighth-best defenders. In such cases, if those defenders can't mark a tree without tripping over their own feet, you're in a heap o' trouble whenever a stopper or fullback decides to make a run on the goal.

In Figure 7-21, the stopper makes her run down the middle *after* the ball is relayed from the sweeper to MF_1 to W_1. Timing is important because, if the stopper makes her move too soon, she will reach the 18 before the pass is made, and she will eliminate both the element of surprise and herself as a potential receiver.

The same holds true for the other receivers, F_2 and W_2: W_1's pass should be to open space ahead of them, and if they arrive too early there will be no open space to pass to.

Reading the play, MF_2 will drop back to cover the stopper position and the other players will support their teammates accordingly, with the sweeper directing the support.

In Figure 7-22, FB_1 makes a run past W_1 as F_1 and F_2 run away to create space. MF_2 can pass directly to FB_1, or pass to F_2 or F_1, who can make their own move on the goal or relay the ball to the fullback. In either case, FB_1 should be unmarked, because no one really expects the fullback to make such a bold move.

MF_1 will drop back to cover the fullback slot on that side.

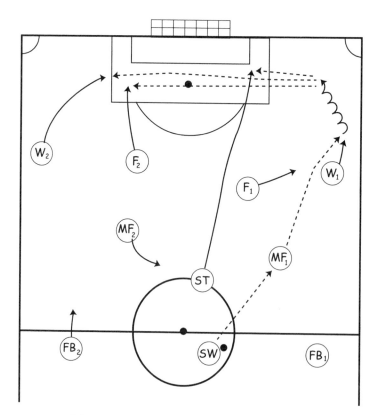

FIGURE 7–21. Stopper Run, 4-4-2

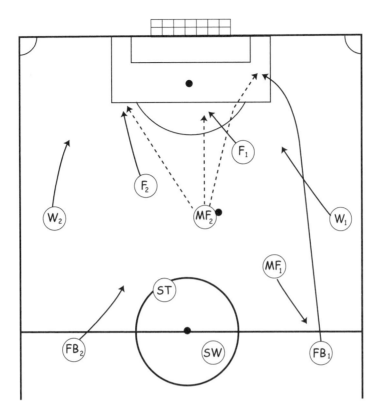

FIGURE 7–22. Fullback Run, 4-4-2

Switching the Ball

Attacking doesn't consist entirely of fast breaking with numbers up on the opponents, nor is it necessarily a matter of ramming the ball forcefully down opponents' throats. In many (if not most) cases, it also involves finesse: picking and choosing when, where, and how to attack, and setting up the opponents for 1-v-1 confrontations that they aren't prepared to handle. Runs by the stopper and fullback are essentially finesse tactics, as are overloads, to cite two examples.

Players must know when to call off attacks and reorganize the offense; failure to do so when the attack has bogged down usually results in takeaways or turnovers. Probably the best way to reorganize the offense is to vary the point of attack. One way to do this is to use switch passes across the pitch (e.g., from wing to wing); another, slower and more methodical, technique involves a series of switching passes to work the ball around the perimeter, as shown in Figure 7-23. The passing sequence is rather cut-and-dried, with FB_1, the SW, FB_2, and W_2 moving to meet the ball in turn. Meanwhile, the forwards and midfielders are moving to space and setting up runs when the ball is established on the other side of the field.

FIGURE 7–23. Working the Ball Around the Perimeter, 4-4-2

MIXING SYSTEMS

There's no rule that says you have to maintain the same alignment on attack that you use on defense; in fact, few teams do so, at least, not as a planned strategy. You attack with whoever is in position to attack when your team recovers the ball. The actual number of attackers in the initial offensive movement toward the opponents' goal is likely to change with every ball possession. Actual team attacking alignments (as opposed to the positioning and spacing of players leading the attack) come into play only when the initial thrust has been blunted. Defensive alignments are far more likely to remain constant from one possession to the next.

For example, we generally prefer a 4-4-2 alignment defensively because we're basically defense-oriented and we like the idea of having eight defenders to cover attacks in our defensive third. It increases our chances of controlling opponents defensively.

With a weak defensive team, we'd attack with our forwards and keep everyone else back (i.e., maintaining the 4-4-2 alignment); with a good defensive team we'd try to add at least two attackers—probably the wingers—to the attack, in effect changing the 4-4-2 to a 4-2-4 on attack. With a superior defense, we might add one or both midfielders (and maybe even a fullback as well) to the mix, trying to overwhelm opponents offensively as well as defensively. But it all starts with protecting the integrity of your defense.

Such changes in alignment are not uncommon, and arise spontaneously. They are planned only in the sense of your telling certain players (e.g., the wingers or midfielders) that you want them to become involved in your fast breaks. Of course, you wouldn't tell them that unless they were capable of doing so and still fulfilling their defensive responsibilities at the other end of the pitch.

THE 5-3-2 SYSTEM OF PLAY ("32")

When selecting a defensive alignment for your team, it is important to recognize that changes you make in that alignment from defense to offense require versatility on the part of certain players if an acceptable balance between defense and offense is to be maintained. The more versatile players you have, the more players you can involve in your attacks without weakening your defense. Even then, though, you must match your players with the positions requiring versatility if your strategy is to succeed. An excellent example of how versatility can enhance a team's attack can be seen in the 5-3-2 system of play (Figures 7-24 and 7-25).

As might be expected, the 32 is extremely potent defensively, with five interior defenders—three central defenders (CDs) and two wingbacks (also called *fullbacks*) in one version (Figure 7-24), and two CDs, two WBs and a sweeper in the other (Figure 7-25)—covering the goal area like a tarpaulin. If left unchanged, this alignment is simply an even more defense-oriented version of the 4-4-2 alignment in which the sweeper and the central defenders play zone defense and the wingbacks play man-to-man.

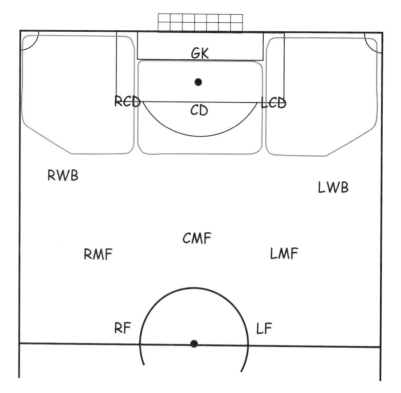

FIGURE 7–24. 5-3-2 Alignment with Three Central Defenders

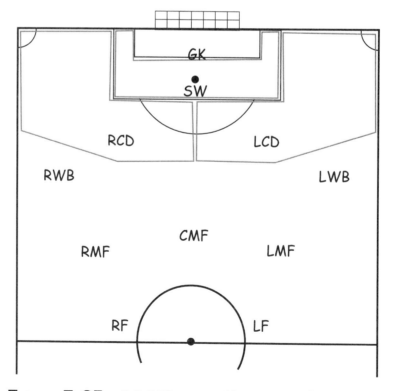

FIGURE 7–25. 5-3-2 Variation (Sweeper and Two CDs)

In both versions of the 32, the three interior defenders play zone defense and the wingbacks, or halfbacks, play man-to-man. The difference between the two approaches lies in the location and shape of the three individual zones of responsibility: With three central defenders, the interior alignment is side by side along the outer edges of the penalty box (Figure 7-24); with a sweeper present (Figure 7-25), the two CDs are aligned outside the penalty area and have broader (but not deeper) zones to cover.

Versatility arises when you have wingbacks who are capable of joining the attack.

Since the alignments shown in Figures 7-24 and 7-25 are interchangeable, we'll use the three-CD version here (Figure 7-26). If the wingbacks are capable of supporting the midfielders on attack, the alignment changes to 3-5-2; and if the wingbacks are bona fide racehorses who can go on attack with the forwards, your original 32 alignment becomes a 3-3-4 on attack—a massive switch from conservative defense to aggressive offense! Played in such a specialized, demanding fashion, the 32 is a highly potent playing system that adds security to your defense and numbers to your attacks.

There is, however, that very large **IF** to be accounted for. In order to join the frontrunners in the attack and still get back and play effective defense near the goal, those wingbacks must be capable of making 60- to 70-yard sprints up and down the field with the offensive and defensive flow. Even if they merely support the midfielders, they're going to be covering real estate in 40- to 50-yard chunks at a time.

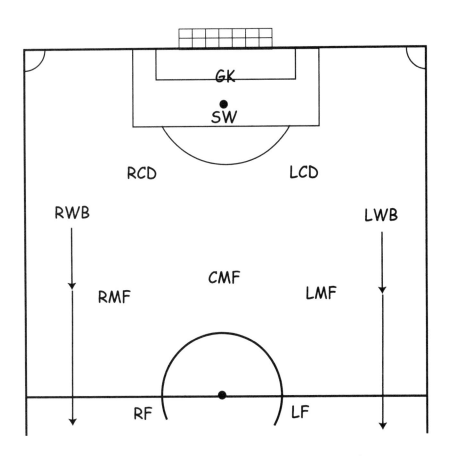

FIGURE 7–26. Changing the Alignment in Attacking, 5-3-2

We say this, not to discourage or deter anyone from using this system—or any other given system, for that matter—but to point out how personnel requirements within the various playing systems affect the probable success of those systems. If your wingbacks have the speed, endurance, and playing skills necessary to join your forwards in the attacking third and still get back to play tough "D" in your defensive third without tripping over their tongues after a few minutes of such extended wind sprints, then 5-3-2 is precisely the system you should be using.[3] It is, after all, extremely defense-oriented, if your wingbacks can get back to cover their marks after attacking.

Just don't forget about that **IF.**

---

[3] If your wingbacks don't have the kind of superior speed, endurance, and athleticism necessary to make the 5-3-2 go, you're probably better off using a *flat back 4* alignment (e.g., Figure 7-17) and zone defense.

Chapter 8

BASIC SOCCER STRATEGY

Playing offensively is the best defense. When you have the ball,
only you can score.

—Pele

RISKS AND THE THIRDS OF THE FIELD

Team strategy in soccer depends, first of all, on who has the ball, and where. For strategic purposes, coaches divide the soccer pitch into three equal sections separated by imaginary lines: *the defensive third* (i.e., the third of the pitch nearest your own goal); *the midfield area*—the middle third of the pitch; and *the attacking third*, or the third of the pitch nearest your opponents' goal (Figure 8-1).

Team quality and the coach's philosophy of how the game should be played ultimately determine a team's strategies. Generally speaking, however, the amount of risk a team is willing to take depends on where the ball is (and, of course, how much time is left in the game).

Most coaches consider their own defensive third of the pitch a *no-risk area;* if the opponents have the ball near your goal, you don't want your players taking unnecessary chances on defense that might lead to an easy shot on goal for the opponents.[1]

The midfield third is an area of *acceptable risk*, especially at the wings; if your players make a mistake here, the opponents still have roughly half the length of the pitch to go, give or take a few yards, in setting up a shot on goal. With effective marking to slow the ball's progress or delay the attack, you should be able to get enough defenders back to provide adequate deep coverage.

"Take calculated risks," Gen. George S. Patton advised. "That is quite different from being rash." The farther from your own goal those risks are taken, the less likely they are, when unsuccessful, to lead directly to opponents' scores—and, conversely, the more the pendulum swings in your team's favor if they succeed.

---

[1] "In *our* box, don't take chances; in *their* box, don't waste chances." —Coach Paul Gibbons.

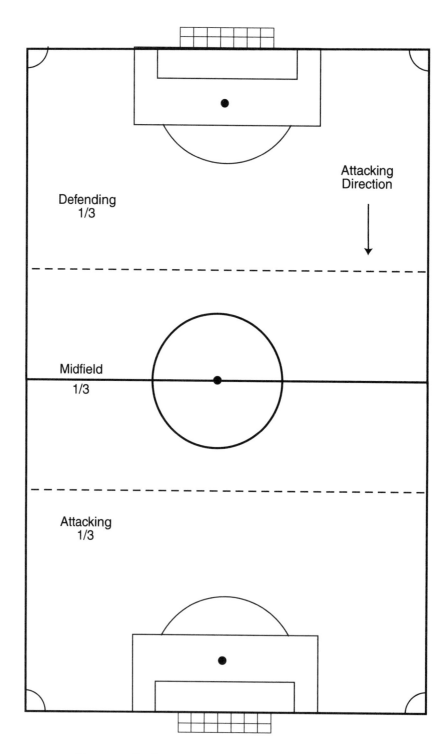

FIGURE 8–1. Dividing the Pitch into Thirds

The attacking third is generally regarded as an area of *all-out risk* since, as the Greek historian Herodotus noted, "Great deeds are usually wrought at great risk." (Or, as a coach we know put it, referring to reaching the state high school playoffs, "If you don't take the chance, you won't make the dance.")

Of course, not every team can or should always go all-out in the attacking third, since other priorities may take precedence (e.g., killing time on the clock or protecting a lead). Field balance is important, too; you don't normally want so many players involved in your attack that your defense will be weakened if the opponents take the ball away. And it's often necessary to call off the attack to reset the offense or search elsewhere for penetration points (the "rubber band" strategy: penetrate, and if nothing develops, check out, reset the attack, and start over). However, the principle still applies: *Generally speaking, you can take chances in the attacking third that you wouldn't attempt elsewhere.* Even if your aggressive tactics fail, the opponents still have to take the ball at least two thirds of the length of the pitch to score.

The Defensive Third

Because of the offside rule, the defense always starts out with a numbers advantage over the attacking team. In theory, at least, that advantage continues when the ball is established in *our* attacking third, since *you* can have eleven defenders in your defensive third and we're limited to a maximum of ten attackers, unless we're silly enough to bring our keeper up to your end of the field, and—believe us—we're not!

Defense begins, not in the defensive third of the field, but wherever and whenever a team loses possession of the ball. When that happens, every player must react immediately and switch to a defensive mode. In such cases, your team's first defensive priority is to deny and restrict our time and space—that is, pressuring the ball to deny us time to set up our attack free of defensive pressure, and jockeying the ball toward the touchline or other areas where our maneuvering space is limited and your support is strongest. While it isn't absolutely necessary for your on-the-ball defender to take the ball away from us, it is imperative that he delay ball penetration into your defensive third until his teammates have had time to fall back into support coverage.

In the same way that retreating armies give ground grudgingly via delaying tactics rather than retreating in wild, panicked disarray, you want your players to retreat in an organized manner, with your on-the-ball defender jockeying for position to control our dribblers' progress and your supporting players denying passes to other attackers or to openings where attackers could penetrate the defense.

The Second Pass. When the defenders capture the ball in their defensive third, they have the advantage of already facing the opponents' goal. To maintain this advantage, some of them will move laterally to open spaces to support their teammate's pass while others, anticipating the second pass that gets the attack moving into high gear, will probably delay their runs to create openings downfield (Figure 8-2).

In Figure 8-2, the sweeper has stepped up to intercept F_1's through pass to F_2. The defensive fullbacks, FB_2 and FB_8, immediately sprint wide to support SW_4. With forward momentum and the element of surprise in his favor, SW_4 could, of course, move ahead on the dribble, looking for a forward, wing, or midfielder to pass to. If, however, the sweeper opts for the safe, lateral pass to the fullback along the touchline because the retreating defenders are clogging the middle of the pitch, the attack will build via the second pass from FB_8 to W_9 as shown, or to another player—

probably a midfielder—making a run to open space. In either case, it is the *vertical* pass ahead to a teammate making a run that challenges the defense, especially if the first pass was made simply to move the ball out of harm's way.

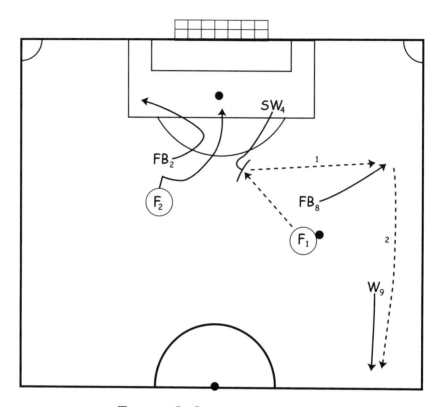

FIGURE 8–2. The Second Pass

The Midfield Third

Ideally, your defensive objective in the midfield area is to keep the ball out of the defensive third altogether; realistically, your objective may be similar to the old defensive football credo, *Bend, but don't break.*[2] The longer it takes the opponents to move the ball into your defensive third, the better your team's chances become of stopping them if or when they get there. Control is achieved by getting numbers up on the attackers early, maintaining defensive balance across the field, and funneling the ball into areas such as the midfield corner or the touchline where the defender can get help from her teammates. Off-the-ball defenders must always be prepared to offer support, whether by double-teaming the dribbler or moving quickly to contain a dribbler who has broken free of her mark.

Offensively, while speed is important in creating an attacking advantage, it is not the only consideration. Building the offense in the midfield area in an organized, controlled manner can prevent attackers from playing out of control and losing the ball prematurely. Once the attackers have the ball in the midfield area, their primary goal

---

[2] See the section "Delaying Tactics," p. 171.

is to advance to the attacking third in a rapid but controlled manner, whether by dribbling into open spaces or by using through passes or overlaps to connect with wings or forwards who have lost their marks and are looking for the ball.

The midfield area is, in a very real sense, the base of support upon which attacks rest. Every player—even those whose responsibilities are primarily defensive—is instrumental in maintaining possession. Remember the rubber band strategy, with players extending the attack goalward via change-of-pace dribbling, feints, or passing sequences, working the ball from player to player via combination passes and from one side of the field to the other, looking for openings in the attacking third but prepared to bring the ball back to the midfield third if necessary.

Total team support is necessary if the attack is to be sustained. Players in the midfield area cannot stand around idly watching the game just because the ball has advanced beyond them into the attacking third; rather, they must keep moving and maintaining adequate spacing in the midfield area to keep the field spread and to prevent one defender from covering two attackers. They must also be prepared to collect teammates' passes and move the ball out of danger whenever offensive thrusts bog down in the attacking third.

The Attacking Third

If, having reached your attacking third, your players have numbers up on the opponents, they should be moving at the highest speed they can maintain and still control the ball via dribbling or passing. Since it's generally easier to score when the defenders have only two or three players back than when the entire defense is packed in around the penalty area, coaches generally want their players to position themselves for a quick (and preferably high-percentage) shot on goal before the defense is fully organized to stop it. This may be done in any of four ways: (a) by having enough players involved in the early stages of the attack to overwhelm the defense by sheer weight of numbers; (b) by maintaining balance across the pitch to keep the defense spread out, and by crossing the ball to weak side if the defenders overplay toward the ball; (c) by using combination passes, through passes, or creative dribbling to set up 1-v-1 situations; and (d) by finishing attacks aggressively and confidently. The latter sometimes may be easier said than done, but is nevertheless vital to your team's chances of scoring. With numbers up on the defense, you *don't* want your players to call off the attack until they've gotten at least one good shot on goal.

Figure 8-3 shows a balanced attack against a well-organized man-to-man defense that has retreated quickly enough to stem the initial attack. The offensive team has a number of options here, all of which fall into one of two categories: The striker can call off the attack and check out to reset or reposition the attack, or else the players can continue the attack by using techniques like those described in Chapter 7. (See pp. 141–151 on the 4-2-4, 4-3-3, and 4-4-2 systems.)

As noted earlier, the attacking third is generally considered an area of all-out risk. Good defense can and will keep games close, but the only way to win consistently with your offense is for your midfielders, wings, and forwards to develop the attitude that the attacking third of the pitch is *their* turf and not the opponents', and to treat every chance they get to score as a *must-do* situation. That doesn't mean they should relentlessly press their attacks when no attacking advantage exists or can be created—but it *does* mean that they should treat every ball possession with the utmost respect.

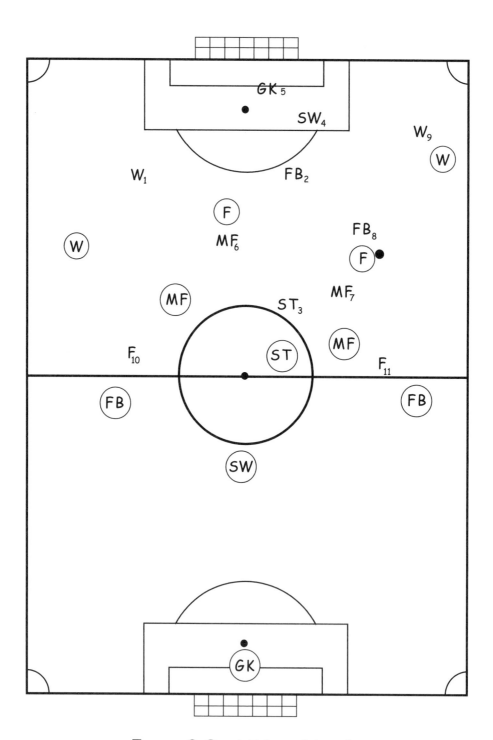

FIGURE 8–3. A Balanced Attack

MAN-TO-MAN DEFENSE

Although the situation is changing, most amateur soccer teams at the high school level and below in the United States still use man-to-man defense—and there's a very practical reason why they do. Elsewhere in the world—especially in Europe and Central and South America where soccer traditionally has been the No. 1 team sport—children play soccer from earliest childhood. In the United States, however, the traditional "Big Three" team sports of baseball, basketball, and football have commanded most of the attention and money over the years. Only recently have American club soccer leagues become a widespread alternative for youngsters who are starting out in sports.

Faced with relatively inexperienced players who scarcely know or understand the rules of soccer, let alone the skills and strategies of the game, American coaches at the club and high school levels have generally opted for man-to-man rather than zone defense. Otherwise, with eleven players in their defensive half of the field they might spend entire seasons teaching their players where the zones are located and how the defensive responsibilities within those zones overlap. It's quicker and easier just to tell them to mark the same player wherever she goes. (It's not quite that simple, of course, but it's a lot easier for inexperienced players to understand than concepts of zone defense as applied to soccer.[3]) Man-to-man defense incorporates many zone principles, as in the sweeper's play or the relatively loose marking given weak side attackers (e.g., W_1 in Figure 8-3).

Man-to-man defensive responsibilities are usually assigned as follows: Wings mark wings; fullbacks mark forwards; midfielders mark midfielders; forwards help out defensively in the midfield area, usually by pressuring the opponents' fullbacks; and the sweep, free of any specific marking responsibility, plays zone defense in the defensive third. The stopper either marks the opponents' best attacker or is not assigned a specific mark—but is free to assist any of her teammates on defense. If the opponents send only two forwards on attack, the fullbacks will cover them as mentioned previously; however, if three forwards attack, the stopper will mark the third forward.

In Figure 8-4, the fullbacks (FB_2, FB_8) are marking the attacking forwards; the stopper (ST_3) is marking the dribbler (in this case, a midfielder); the wings (W_1, W_9) are marking wings; one midfielder (MF_7) is marking an opposing midfielder, leaving the other defensive midfielder (MF_6) free to help out in coverage, whether by double-teaming the dribbler with ST_3 or marking the opposing sweeper if he makes a run; and the forwards (F_{10}, F_{11}) are back playing support defense, prepared to cover any runs made by the fullbacks or to go on attack if there's a turnover. The sweeper (SW_4) will step up to mark any attacker who breaks through the defense and becomes a threat for a shot on goal.

Sorting out the individual coverages is of paramount importance to the defensive unit.

---

[3] The major exception to this rule involves *corner kicks*. Many teams defense corner kicks by stacking the majority of their defenders inside the goal box in zone fashion (see Figure 8-27, p. 199), reverting to man-to-man coverage if or when the attack on goal fails and the attackers take the ball outside to reset their offense.

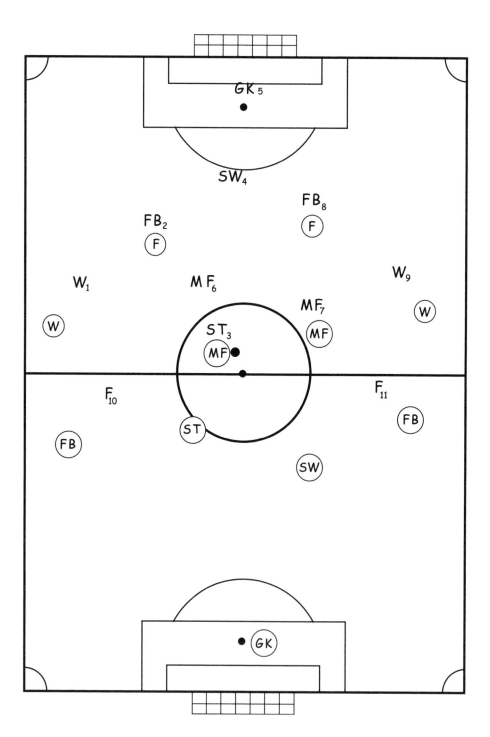

FIGURE 8–4. Man-to-Man Defensive Responsibilities

Delaying Tactics

It is often necessary to slow down the ball's progress in order to give one's teammates time to retreat to the defensive third and organize the team defense after turnovers. There are two ways to delay the ball's progress downfield—by *high-* or *low-pressure* delaying tactics.

High-pressure delaying involves tight marking on the ball that forces the dribbler to watch the ball rather than looking downfield for passing opportunities. In order for high-pressure marking to be effective, the defender must be close to the attacker *before he receives the ball*. It is extremely difficult for a defender to control or contain a skilled attacker who already has the ball under control with his head up, surveying the field ahead of him.

In Figure 8-5, F_{11} is pressuring the ball and trying to force the dribbler away from the middle; F_{10} and MF_7 are covering the fullbacks, and the other defenders are closely marking the other attackers to prevent the downfield pass that allows the attackers to gain momentum vertically.

High-pressure marking can become low-pressure marking without changing any of the defenders' responsibilities or any of the basic principles involved; in fact, the high-pressure coverage shown in Figure 8-5 becomes low-pressure marking (on the ball, at least) when the sweeper passes to the goalkeeper, since neither F_{10}, F_{11}, nor MF_7 is in position to immediately apply pressure defense to the keeper.

Low-pressure delaying involves loose marking on the ball that allows the attacker to dribble but not to make uncontested passes ahead. Dribbling advances the ball more slowly than passing does, and thus gives off-the-ball defenders additional time to get back on defense—and the more dribbling the attacker does, the more vulnerable he becomes to being double-teamed or losing the ball.

Before we lose sight of our objective here, however, we should remind you that this is, after all, a *delaying* tactic. In Figure 8-6, F_{11}, marking loosely, will continue to retreat if the stopper dribbles, but will gradually close the distance between them. F_{10} will drop back and the rest of the team, waiting beyond the halfway line, will pick up their marks as they cross the line. The closer the opponents get to their attacking third (i.e., *our* defensive third), the greater the defensive pressure on all of the attackers will become.

The dribblers will not simply be encouraged or permitted to dribble wherever they want to go and at whatever speed they desire, especially in the defensive third; rather, their defenders will, through careful positioning and hard work, attempt to influence them toward the touchline or toward known areas of team support. The latter underscores the absolute necessity of communication between defenders. Ball and player movement in soccer is so rapid, constant, and impromptu that it is virtually impossible for defenders to keep up with everything that's happening around them unless they help each other out by shouting instructions, warnings, and the like.

In order to keep a loosely marked dribbler from passing the ball in the defensive third, secondary defenders (i.e., those marking receivers who are nearest to the ball) must be close enough to their marks to deny those passes. Defenders whose marks are two or more push passes away from the ball (e.g., weak side attackers) may play somewhat looser—but alert—team defense. Their coverage cannot be *too* loose, though: if they play too far off their marks, the dribbler may cross the ball and attack the defense from behind. Players away from the ball must be in position to see the ball and their marks at all times. Failure to do so, whether by turning their backs on the ball or by watching the ball but not their marks, is a defensive cardinal sin, since it offers the opponents an unnecessary attacking advantage.

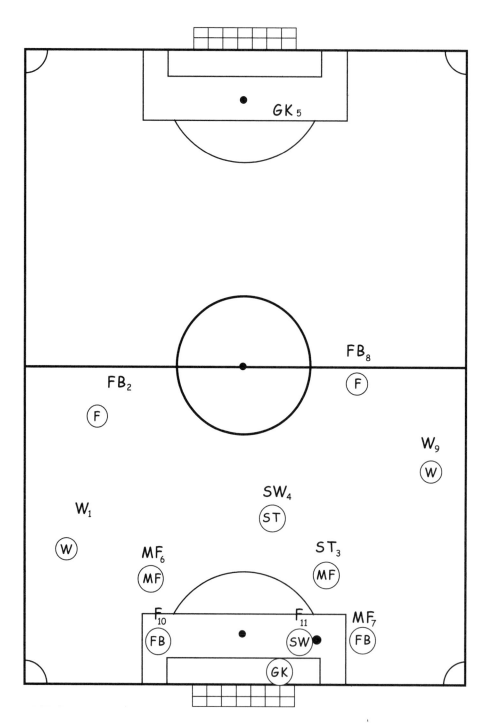

FIGURE 8–5. High-Pressure Man-to-Man Defense, Full Field

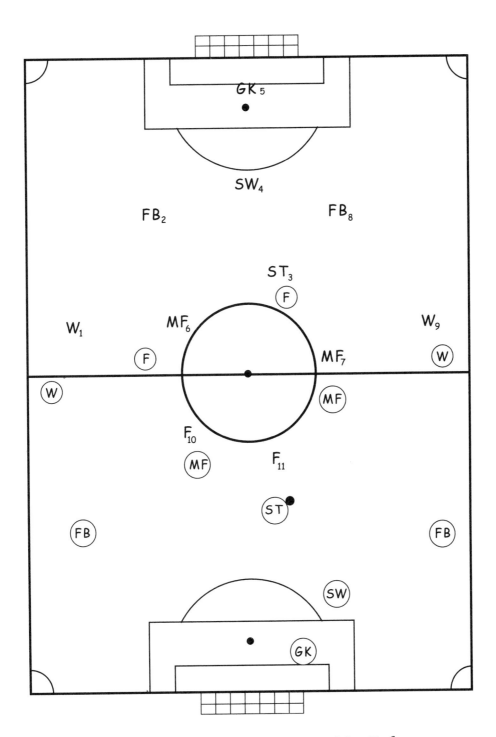

FIGURE 8–6. Low-Pressure Man-to-Man Defense

Desperation Delaying

In high-pressure defense anywhere on the pitch, or in low-pressure defense in the midfield third or defensive third, there are times when a teammate must step up to delay an attacker who has beaten his mark. When such occasions arise, communication between defenders is an absolute *must*. The defender who was beaten must sprint back behind the ball to take up the space that was vacated by whichever teammate stepped up to cover the ball (Figure 8-7).

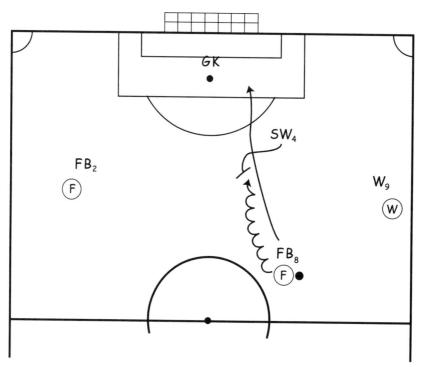

FIGURE 8–7. Picking Up a Dribbler Who Has Broken Free of His Mark

In Figure 8-7, the sweeper (SW$_4$) steps up to cover the forward who has beaten FB$_8$, whereupon the fullback races back to take the sweeper's place in coverage. The fullback will probably be late in arriving unless SW$_4$ announces the change loudly and forcefully. Communication and teamwork enhance the effectiveness of any defense.

Double-Teaming

Double-teaming is an aggressive defensive strategy in which two defenders work together to contain a single attacker, especially the dribbler, and preferably in areas such as the corners or along the touchline where support for a square pass—one that travels parallel to the touchline or goal line—or through pass is limited. When the double-team is executed in the corner or by the touchline, the boundary lines themselves serve as a third defender, hemming in the dribbler (Figure 8-8).

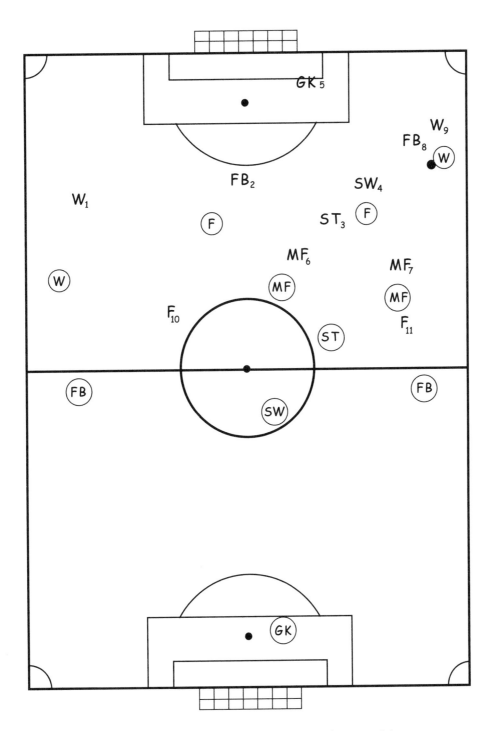

FIGURE 8–8. Double-Teaming at the Touchline

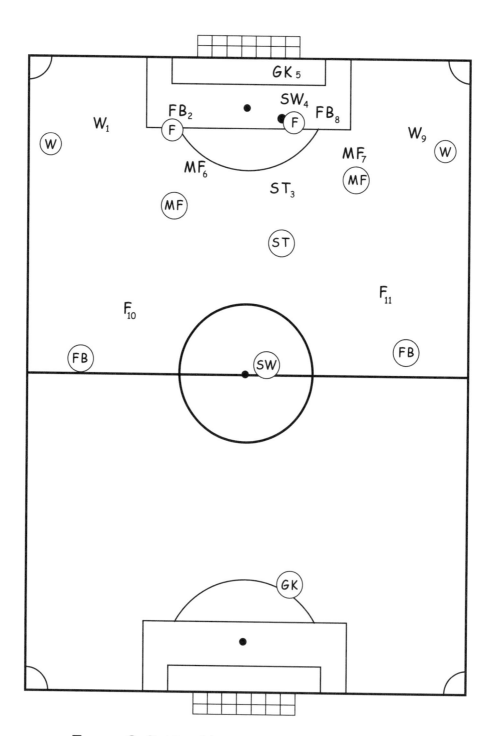

FIGURE 8–9. Double-Teaming in the Penalty Area

Double-teaming also frequently occurs when an attacker is outnumbered in front of the goal (Figure 8-9). Such double-teams must be executed quickly, while the dribbler is looking down at the ball or having difficulty in controlling the ball. Without the elements of surprise and proper spacing between the defenders, the double-team is unlikely to produce a turnover or contain the ball. If the dribbler sees the double-team coming, he may be able to maneuver the ball out of danger; if the defenders are too close together, he may go around them and continue his attack; and if they are too far apart, he may dribble or pass through them.

When the opposing team has only one outstanding attacker and little in the way of a supporting cast, a coach may elect to double-team that player wherever he goes, hoping to keep the ball away from him and force the responsibility for attacking on the rest of the team. Such double-teaming won't work against a team that is loaded with skilled, aggressive attackers, but when deployed against a team with only one skilled attacker it can disrupt their offensive game plan, frustrate the player being double-teamed, and make him work harder than he is used to working.

Those old standbys *communication* and *teamwork* are the primary ingredients in any double-teaming situation.

ZONE DEFENSE

In a best-of-all-possible-worlds, your team would be stocked with an endless supply of tireless, highly skilled defenders capable of controlling their marks on a man-to-man basis, and zone defense would be unnecessary. After all, why would you want your players standing around marking thin air and watching their cuticles grow when no one is in their zones for them to mark?

In that sense, at least, the use of zone defense is basically negative, since if your team has no defensive weaknesses, you need merely to attack opponents with your defensive strengths to defeat them. However, that statement also defines the chief limitation of man-to-man defense, namely, that it takes *eleven*—and not four, eight, or even ten—players working together as a team to render man-to-man defense effective.

What sort of weakness might lead to the use of zone defense? Well, it might be a lack of depth or team speed, chronically poor transition from offense to defense, inexperienced players who are easily beaten by their marks, weak interior defense, or the like. Many coaches—for example, in Europe where zone defenses flourish—simply prefer the conservative nature of zone coverage.

We don't mean to imply that zone defense is in any way inferior to man-to-man defense; it isn't. Zone defense is simply a different approach to defense that, like man-to-man, will enhance the play of some teams and adversely impact the play of other teams. Part of the art of coaching consists of knowing which type of defense is best for *your* team. It's not quite that simple, however, because zone defense incorporates elements of man-to-man defense and vice versa. (We offer a brief comparison of the two defensive styles on p. 185.)

In zone coverage, players' defensive responsibilities are defined by specific areas (zones), as shown in Figure 8-10. Rather than marking a specific attacker wherever she goes, the defender stays in her zone and marks any attacker who enters her zone. When a mark leaves a defender's area of responsibility, that defender stays put and looks for someone else to mark in her zone.

The midpoint between two zone defenders is known as the *seam* of the zone, and it is here that opponents are most likely to attack. When an opponent passes through her zone, the defender will mark her man-to-man until she reaches the seam, at which time marking responsibility passes to the next defender. Communication between teammates is imperative in effective zone defense.

If two attackers are in one zone, they tend to cancel each other out in many instances by permitting one defender to cover both of them; if not, the defender will mark the one who is nearest to the ball.

Except for ball coverage, which may be tight or loose, marking is generally looser in zone defense than in man-to-man coverage—and necessarily so, since the off-the-ball defenders must constantly evaluate and respond to threats posed by attackers moving into or through their zones. However, any attacker who penetrates the zone will be closely marked.

Like man-to-man, zone defense can be used with any playing system or alignment; it can also be played in a variety of ways, many of which are beyond the scope of this book. Appendix A suggests books that will tell you everything you could possibly need to know about the nuts-and-bolts operation of zone defenses. For our purposes, however, it should suffice to select one alignment and show a few of the ways that it can be used or adapted for zone defense.

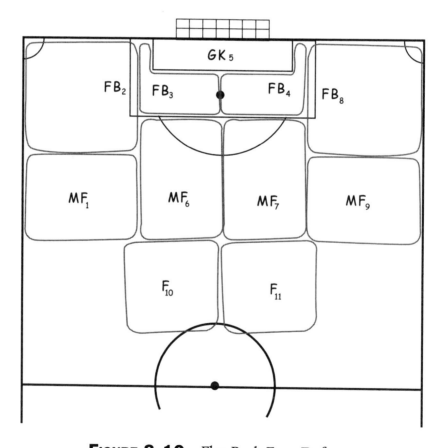

FIGURE 8–10. Flat-Back Four Defense

Zone Defense From a 4-4-2 Alignment

With four interior defenders inside the penalty area and four more defenders stationed just outside its boundaries, the 4-4-2 alignment is ideally suited for zone coverage with a team that needs interior defenders in abundance: No matter where the ball is located, at least three of the four fullbacks—and at least two midfielders as well—will be in position to defend the goal area.

The interior defense shown in Figure 8-10 is known as a *flat-back four*—"flat" because, in their basic positions, the fullbacks are arrayed in a line across the pitch.

The basic philosophy underlying zone defense can be seen in the defensive movements and coverage shown in Figures 8-11 to 8-13: defenders on the ball side of the pitch shifting toward the ball and defenders on weak side dropping back toward the goal to support the team defense. These simultaneous movements are intended to produce layers of defensive support between the ball and the goal while providing continuing coverage in areas that might otherwise be vulnerable to attack. With the players positioned as shown in the early stages of an attack in Fig. 8-11, the midfielder with the ball has five defenders aligned between him and the goal; if he beats F_{11}, he still has four more defenders to beat—MF_7, FB_4, FB_3 and the goalkeeper.

Several other points regarding Figure 8-11 merit our attention. First, the defensive shifts by FB_3 and FB_4 create a Catenaccio (sweeper/stopper) alignment, which is itself a form of zone coverage. Second, one of the defenders—FB_8—hasn't needed to move at all in covering his zone, and none of the other defenders have moved very far from their basic positions; this economy of player movement in response to ball movement is typical of zone defense and suggests one of its chief advantages. Third, *six* of the defenders—MF_1, FB_2, FB_3, FB_4, FB_8, and MF_7—have no one to mark. This situation will change as the attack advances or more offensive players join the attack, of course—but as long as the ball remains in its present location, all of the defenders will remain in place, looking for attackers to mark within their individual zones and releasing them when they leave.

Figure 8-12 is a simple continuation of the action involved in Figure 8-11, with the defense covering a forward who is making a deep run toward the touchline. And while this simple, isolated run by a single attacker is hardly representative of the complexity of team offense in soccer, it shows how zone defenses contract goalward—and shift ballward—as the ball moves closer to the goal, leaving certain attackers and vast areas of real estate uncovered (e.g., the weak side winger in Figure 8-13) to intensify coverage elsewhere when those players present less of a threat to the defense than other attackers do.

Figure 8-12 also shows how defenders cover attacking runs through their zones. MF_6 covers the forward to the halfway point between him and FB_8; then, his responsibility completed, he drops back to a position slightly more goal-oriented than previously. FB_4, immediately picking up the forward, does likewise, eventually releasing the forward to FB_8 and dropping back to support the team coverage. Dropping back is necessary because their movements in covering the run created gaps in the defense behind them.

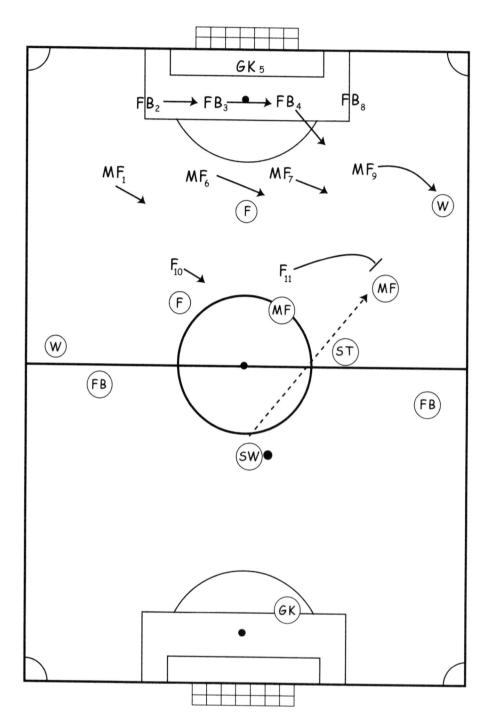

FIGURE 8–11. Defensive Movement with Pass that Establishes Ball Side

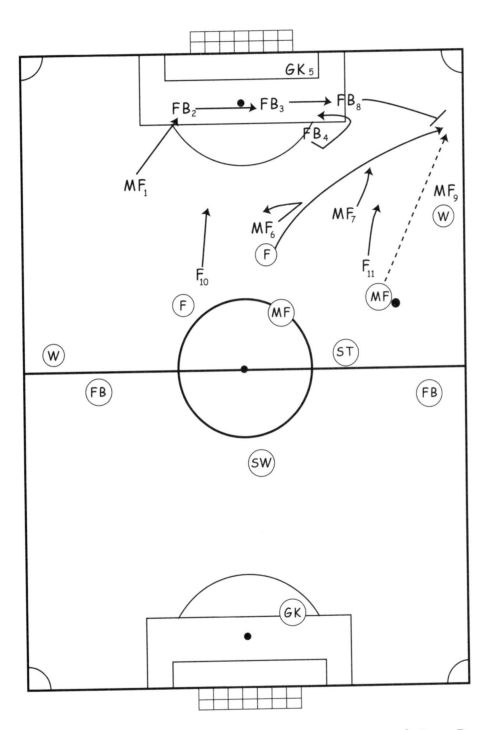

FIGURE 8–12. Continuation of Defensive Movement with Deep Pass Along the Touchline

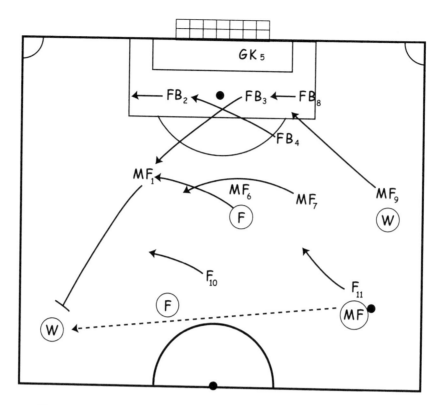

FIGURE 8–13. Defensive Rotation with Crossing Pass

Figure 8-13 shows one type of zone defensive adjustment to a crossing pass in the midfield area, the defenders simply biding their time and waiting for the attack to come to them.[4] Of the five attackers in Figure 8-13, only the winger and the forwards are receiving any kind of pressure—the winger because she has the ball, and the forwards because they are in position to extend the attack goalward. The winger could try to cross the ball back to the other, deeper winger at the opposite touchline—but to do so she has to loft the ball over F_{11} without MF_9 intercepting the pass. And *that* is precisely what zone defense is all about: playing the percentages, giving up what won't hurt you in order to keep from getting burned elsewhere, and keeping players in position to offer solid defensive resistance and numbers up on the attackers in areas where you're most vulnerable to attack.

In all phases of zone defense, the main concern is *marking players* versus *marking space*. The nearer defenders are to the ball, the more important it becomes for them to mark players rather than space—assuming, of course, that someone is available to mark in their zones. MF_1 could mark the winger closely in Figure 8-11—but how would that help his team? The defense is better served by playing off his mark to cover the open space behind him, than for him to closely mark a player away from the ball, who cannot possibly initiate an attack on goal from that spot.

---

[4] A variation of this coverage consists of FB_3 sliding over and filling FB_2's slot, and FB_4 moving across to cover the area FB_3 is shown moving to in Figure 8-13. We prefer the coverage shown in the diagram because FB_3 has a better angle of approach to the zone that was vacated by MF_1.

In any case, since most attacking sequences are based on creating spaces or attacking openings in the defense, it is imperative that zone defenders know, not just where their zones are located but also where the seams between their zone and adjacent zones are located. (The seams are located halfway between any two adjacent defenders.) They must also know where to shift with various ball locations. Failure to recognize those points can result in defenders' failing to cover players along the edges of their zones, failing to shift with ball movement, or shifting too far and thus creating openings in the defense that aren't supposed to exist at all.

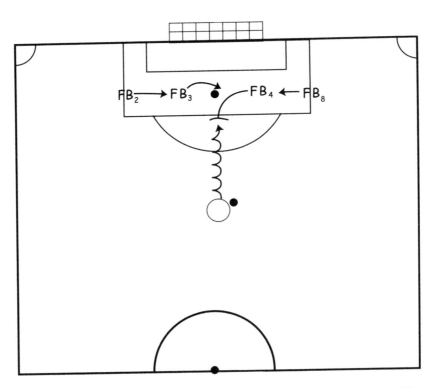

FIGURE 8–14. Interior Zone Defense: Covering the Middle

Focusing on the Fullbacks

With the ball and attackers located along the defensive perimeter, the fullbacks will maintain their positions roughly as shown in Figures 8-10 to 8-13. But if one or more attackers penetrate, with or without the ball, the fullbacks will alter their defense to meet the threat(s) in a manner similar to that shown in Figures 8-14 to 8-16.

If the attack comes through the middle (Figure 8-14), FB_3 and FB_4 will go to Catenaccio coverage—one of them moving up to mark the ball and the other moving over to support the area behind him. The other two fullbacks will take their places, compressing the interior defense to protect the goal area.

If the attack shifts to a diagonal rather than a direct frontal assault on the goal (Figure 8-15), FB_2 will mark the receiver, FB_4 will stay on his mark, and FB_3 and FB_8 will shift one zone toward the ball, covering the goal area. (A midfielder will drop back to cover the weak side post area.) FB_4 is still in Catenaccio alignment, but that doesn't matter; what matters is covering an attacker who is a direct threat on goal.

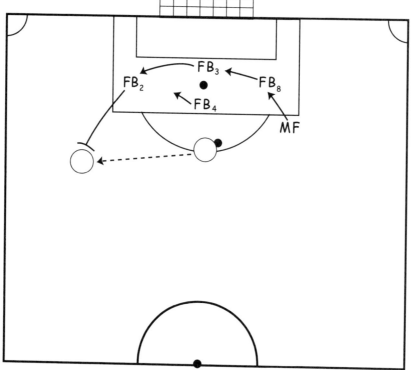

FIGURE 8–15. Interior Zone Defense: Covering the Diagonal Attacking Angle

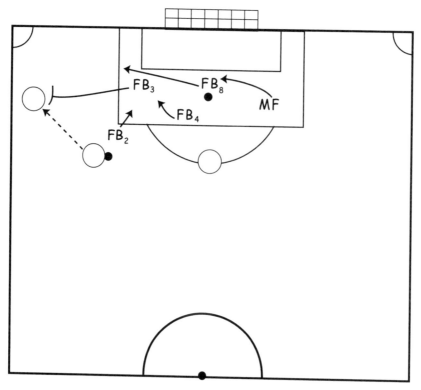

FIGURE 8–16. Covering the Deep Side of the Pitch

If the attack shifts to the side of the pitch (Figure 8-16), FB_3 will cover the ball, FB_8 will cover the zone vacated by FB_3, and FB_2 and FB_4 will stay with their marks. The midfielder will support FB_8.

If all of this sounds complicated—well, it can be if you're not used to playing this way, but not if you understand the zone concept and what it's designed to do for your defense. If you've ever played or coached zone defense in basketball, it's the same in soccer, only with more players involved.

Fullbacks don't leave their marks in or around the penalty area to cover a zone vacated by another fullback—but if they have no one to mark they will quickly abandon their own zones and shift over to cover a zone left open by a teammate who is closer to the ball.

Combination Defense

There are two ways to play combination defense. One way is to play zone defense part of the time and man-to-man defense the rest of the time. This style of combination defense is somewhat rare, and is seen most frequently as a 9-man zone defense against corner kicks (see p. 199), after which the defenders revert to their usual man-to-man or zone defense. Another usage involves playing zone defense in your own attacking third and midfield third, and switching to man-to-man defense in your defensive third; or the converse of that strategy; that is, using man-to-man coverage in the attacking and midfield thirds and playing zone defense in your defensive third.

The other way of playing combination defense is more commonly encountered; it consists of some of the defenders' using zone coverage while the rest play man-to-man. The flat-back four is ideal for such usage, with the fullbacks playing zone defense as shown in Figures 8-14 to 8-16, and everyone else marking up man-to-man. Such coverage, while ensuring that the deep defenders remain in position to defend the goal at all times, can be somewhat risky with inexperienced fullbacks who are slow to recognize necessary changes in coverage responsibilities.

Comparing Man-to-Man and Zone Defense

Which, then, is better—zone defense or man-to-man? The answer depends on what you hope to accomplish defensively.

- ❐ *All defenses incorporate both man-to-man and zone defensive principles.* In zone defense, players mark man-to-man within their zones. Even in high-pressure man-to-man defense, the goalkeeper (and sweeper, if used) plays zone defense; weak side defenders along the wing may sag away from their marks when the ball is at the opposite touchline; and teams may use strictly zone coverage in defending corner kicks regardless of whether they normally play man-to-man or zone defense.

- ❐ *Man-to-man coverage simplifies defensive assignments and ensures that every defender—except the keeper (and the sweeper in Catenaccio coverage)—is marking someone.* In zone defense, players are assigned (and confined to) specific areas, or zones, marking any attacker who enters their zone and automatically switching defensive responsibilities whenever that player leaves their zone. This is radically different from man-to-man coverage in which defenders mark specific attackers and follow them wherever they go. Man-to-man defense is best suited to teams that have relatively minor defensive weaknesses or want to play an up-tempo game.

❐ *Zone defenses are, by their very nature, more compact and goal-oriented than man-to-man defenses.* This can be either a blessing or a hindrance—a blessing because zone defenses tend to be difficult to penetrate, and a hindrance because the compactness tends to reduce defensive pressure along the perimeter of the defense. Without defensive pressure along the perimeter, opponents may be able to keep the ball longer and dominate time of possession. Applying pressure away from the ball along the perimeter is generally considered unwise because it spreads and enlarges the interior zones.

In any case, zone defense is ideally suited to teams that require increased defensive manpower near the goal on a continuing basis, or slow teams, or teams with little depth.

❐ *In man-to-man defense, any player who has no one to mark is free to help out elsewhere.* In zone defense, that same player is confined to his zone (although his position within that zone changes with various ball and player locations).

❐ *The very concept of zone defense, however, implies that help is never far away.* When an attacker passes through one level of the defense she faces, not open space, but the next defender in line. Zone defense would be useless if it were not layered to provide continuing resistance to penetrating runs by attackers. The only openings in zone defenses are likely to be found along the seams—the spaces between individual zones where defensive responsibilities sometimes overlap.

Man-to-man coverage has no seams; except for the sweeper's zone coverage it offers no guarantees that defensive help will be immediately available if a defender is beaten by his mark.

❐ *Man-to-man defensive concepts are easier to learn (e.g., stay with your mark wherever he goes), but its techniques require greater individual skills.*

❐ *Zone defensive concepts are generally more complex[5] but allow for a greater margin of error because there is always someone behind you to take up the slack if you're beaten by your mark.*

❐ *Because players sometimes have no one in their zones to mark, zone defense can foster lazy defensive habits.* On the other hand, so can low-pressure man-to-man defense.

❐ *Aggressive, high-pressure man-to-man defense offers the easiest way to dominate opponents—but it is likely to be effective only when your players are (a) fundamentally sound defensively, and (b) at least as fast and well conditioned physically as the opponents.* We've already referred to the futility of racing plowhorses against racehorses; well, zone defense offers one way to combat speed and quickness advantages when they're stacked against your team.

---

[5] They are complex in the sense that the boundaries of individual zones consist of imaginary lines that are not marked on the pitch, but must be memorized or at least recognized.

SITUATIONAL STRATEGIES

Kickoffs

Once upon a time, you couldn't score a goal directly from a kickoff. Well, you can now, but it doesn't happen often. More often, quick scores result from set plays involving a series of passes that penetrate the heart of the defense and produce a shot on goal in a matter of seconds. We call such quick scores "first blood"; our high school varsity boys' team record for drawing first blood is ten seconds.

Of course, good teams aren't going to stand by idly watching your attackers waltz through them for an easy shot on goal; normally, in order to mount an instant attack, you must first draw the defense toward the ball. In most cases, the best way to do this is to initiate the action with a short kickoff, with ball location or diversionary runs by some of your players disguising the true nature, intent, and thrust of your attack. But let's not get ahead of ourselves.

Prior to the kickoff, your offensive players should survey the opponents' defensive positioning, searching for areas of vulnerability or weakness. If such an area can be identified, *that* is precisely where your attack should be directed.

If, as is often the case, the defenders' alignment and spacing reveal no vulnerable areas in terms of depth, width, or field balance, you'll have to draw them out of position—in effect, creating a weakness where there was none. Figures 8-17 through 8-21 show a variety of attacking strategies from kickoffs. Each of them is based on a penetrating pass to an open space vacated by one or more defenders. Which strategy to use in creating that opening is determined by the defensive alignment and coverage.

We line up three attackers near the ball on our kickoffs, spread our other attackers, and (usually) initiate the action with a very short, safe forward kick.

The two-pass sequence in Figure 8-17 is designed to get the ball to our best striker (F_1) in the area just behind the outermost defenders. If it succeeds, F_1 will advance the ball for either a shot on goal or a pass to one of the wingers attacking wide.

In Figure 8-18, we're attacking through the wing position, hoping to get a quick shot on goal from W_1 or from F_2 or W_2 on weak side. We don't expect MF_1's run through the heart of the defense to get him the ball, but we'll take it if the defense fails to cover his run. F_1's delayed run probably won't produce a quick shot on goal, but it allows us to get into our regular offense quickly if nothing productive develops in our initial pass-dribble sequence.

Ball and player movement sequences such as those shown in Figures 8-19 and 8-20 can pull defenders out of position and spread the defense to create areas of vulnerability. Both plays feature the same deceptive strategy—a *drop pass* (also called a *back pass*) from F_2 to MF_2—that may lull the opponents into thinking that your attack will develop and advance in a methodical, leisurely fashion; after all, you can't very well attack by moving the ball backward toward your own goal, can you?

Well, yes, you can if the defenders are overly aggressive in your midfield area. If that happens, the pass to F_1 in Figure 8-19, or to W_2 in Figure 8-20, may catch the opponents out of position to cover the resulting offensive surge.

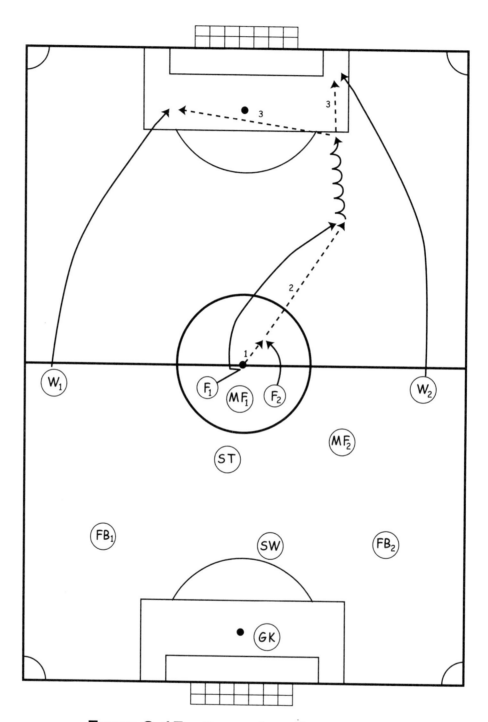

FIGURE 8–17. Getting the Ball to F$_1$, Kickoff

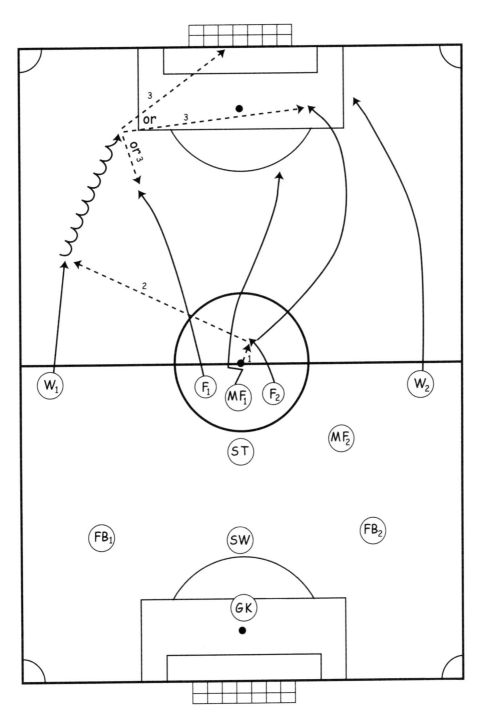

FIGURE 8-18. Attacking at the Wing, Kickoff

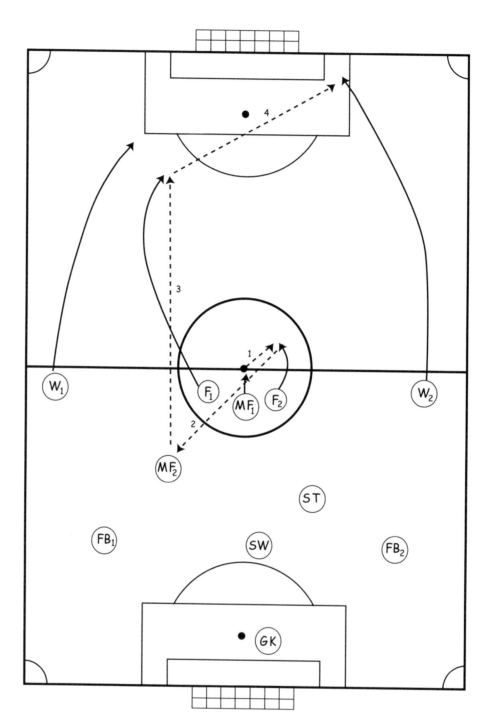

FIGURE 8–19. Drop Pass Attacking Sequence, Kickoff

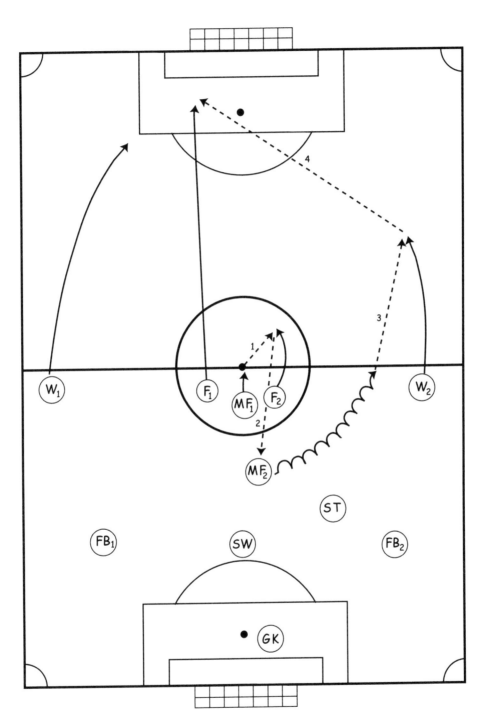

FIGURE 8–20. Drop Pass Attacking Variation, Kickoff

This strategy, known as *slingshotting* because the attack appears to be retreating until it suddenly "slingshots" past the unsuspecting defenders, fits in perfectly with much of what we do in our regular offense: advancing the ball in a given area, looking for openings or ways to attack, bringing the ball back out when the attack fails to produce a shot on goal, and checking back in or setting up our attack elsewhere—always prepared to check out again and reset the offense if the defense threatens to overwhelm the ball. Given the high caliber of our varsity teams in recent years, we'll *always* attack by slingshotting against a team that comes out to challenge us when we call off an attack and bring the ball out to midfield.

Figure 8-21 features decoy runs toward the ball side of the pitch by three attackers to disguise the attacking team's true intent, that is, to get the ball deep to W_1, the winger on weak side. Using a midfielder to relay the ball to W_2 is a nice touch, because that player is often overlooked as a factor in attacking on kickoffs and may not be marked by one of the opponents' best defenders.

Although we did not invent these strategies,[6] we have used and adapted them with our teams for many years as organized approaches to attacking opponents aggressively right from kickoffs. All of them have proven effective for us.

A point that bears repeating: *Plays and patterns don't win games; players do.* When plays work as designed, it's because players make them work. No matter how good a play or pattern looks on paper, you'll probably have to adapt it to your players' skills in order to make it work. Most teams have three to five kickoff plays.

Defensing Kickoffs. Since the shortest distance between two points—the center spot and the goal in this case—is a straight line, your first priority is to protect the middle. Our 10-second goal occurred when an opponent failed to stop our two forwards from going straight up the middle of the pitch in a series of give-and-go passes.

Assuming that you have enough defenders in the middle to deter such frontal attacks, your next task is to see that they don't get suckered out of position and set up a slingshot-type play for their opponents in the area they vacated (see Figures 8-19 and 8-20). Further assuming that your players know better than to do that, you—and they—should be aware that *teams often attack wide of the middle to draw the defenders outside and spread the coverage,* after which they will look for a crossing pass to a player making a deep run behind the defense on the other side of the pitch (e.g., W_1 in Figure 8-21). The odds in favor of your team's successfully defensing this ploy will increase dramatically if you teach your players to position themselves in their individual markings in such a manner as to be able to see the ball and their marks at the same time. Defensive players should never turn their backs on the ball.

With a very weak team, we offer the following advice, not just for kickoffs but in any defensive situation in which your players are likely to be overwhelmed by the opponents: *When in doubt, retreat toward your own goal.* It may not solve the problem, but it will at least increase the number of defenders near your goal.

---

[6] We originally borrowed most of these concepts from James P. McGettigan's excellent *Complete Book of Drills for Winning Soccer* (West Nyack, NY: Parker Publishing Co., 1980); where he borrowed them from is anybody's guess. Probably, like Topsy in *Uncle Tom's Cabin*, they "just growed"—part of the ever-expanding body of knowledge in our sport that every soccer coach contributes to and draws from.

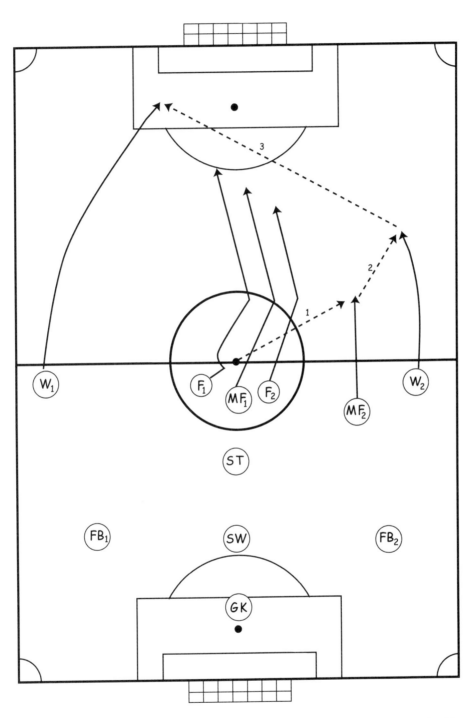

FIGURE 8–21. Decoy Moves to Set Up Weak Side Pass, Kickoff

Throw-Ins

As in virtually every phase of soccer, quickness, anticipation, timing, and spacing are key ingredients in successful throw-ins. The person making the throw-in must scan the field quickly, noting the location of teammates and opponents alike, and then deliver the ball quickly to an unmarked teammate or to an open space toward which a teammate is heading. The best throw-in usually is the *safest* one, because the attacking team's primary consideration is always to maintain ball possession. Simply throwing the ball into a crowd does nothing to ensure continued possession of the ball.

Offensive players must be able to create space to receive the throw-in; young, inexperienced players should be taught to look for open areas to make runs to, and to time their runs to coincide with the thrower's being given the ball. We tell our young players: *If you make your run too soon, there won't be an opening to run to.*

We recommend using no more than two to three players on throw-ins. Overloading a given area of the field with five to six players is unwise, not just because it reduces spacing and brings defenders closer together, but also because your team needs field balance in case the opponents intercept the ball.

Throw-ins should be directed toward receivers' feet (for easy possession), toward the head (for passing), or to open space where a teammate can collect the ball. A simple signal from the target player can suggest which pass the thrower should use.

Whenever possible, throw-ins should be made forward (i.e., toward the opponents' goal line). Throwing the ball *back* to a teammate—toward your own goal line—is acceptable only if that player is open and can gain possession easily without pressure. The most effective throw-in, in terms of gaining an offensive advantage, is likely to be the ball that is played ahead of the wing and down the line into space (Figure 8-22).[7]

In Figure 8-22, MF_1's movement is a decoy run toward the touchline. The *real* action involves W_1 faking toward the ball and then checking out rapidly away from the ball along the touchline to collect the fullback's throw to open space ahead of her.

When your team is making a throw-in in the attacking third, they can have an enormous edge if you have a player who can throw the ball into the Box. If you have such a player, use your tallest offensive player(s) as target(s).

Goal Kicks

As shown in Figure 8-23, there are two strategies for playing goal kicks. One way is to kick the ball as far downfield as possible, hoping to gain possession and go on the attack immediately, or at least to move the ball far enough away from your goal to be able to mount an effective defense—to take the ball away or slow down the opponents' attack. The other way is to kick short to a fullback and build your attack.

Long goal kicks should be directed toward a teammate—probably a winger—located far downfield along either touchline. Kicking down the middle is usually inadvisable because defensive coverages tend to be heavily concentrated in that part of the pitch.

---

[7] Players should bear in mind that, unlike basketball, in soccer, the referee doesn't have to handle the ball prior to the throw-in, and that they don't have to wait for the defense to get set before making the throw-in.

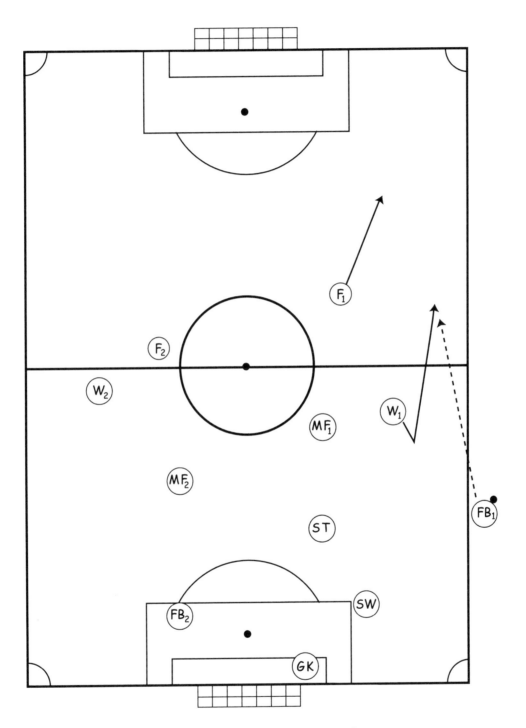

FIGURE 8–22. Throwing in Down the Line

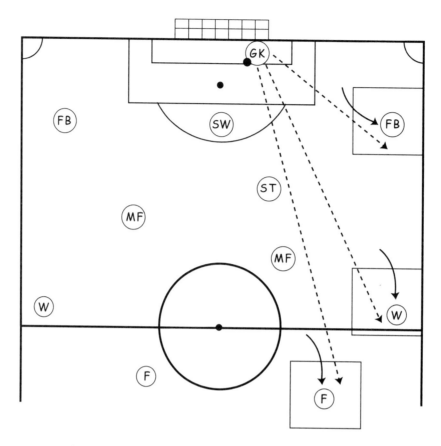

FIGURE 8–23. Receivers' Routes, Goal Kick

If your team loses possession, the opponents will probably try to attack quickly or build up their attack before your defense is organized. Your player nearest to the ball can help to counter that strategy by aggressive on-the-ball marking to give her teammates time to find their marks and move to goal side on defense.

Short goal kicks aren't always as easy or safe as they might appear to be. They are most effective when the opponents are playing "soft," low-pressure defense, or when your players are skilled enough to handle pressure and still maintain ball possession. Since losing the ball in its defensive third places a team in severe jeopardy of surrendering an open shot on goal, we spend part of every daily practice working on maintaining possession and building up our attack after short goal kicks.

Always use your goalkeeper to execute goal kicks.

Corner Kicks

Like direct free kicks and penalty kicks, corner kicks are always scary affairs because, no matter which team you're pulling for, they always seem to be governed by Murphy's Law.[8] You just hold your breath and hope for the best.

---

[8] Anything that can go wrong, *will*.

Offensively, you want to try to get a shot on goal; in defensing corner kicks, gaining possession of the ball is at best a minor consideration compared with getting the ball away from your goal and clearing it far downfield.

The offensive team has several options in trying to set up a shot on goal. Figures 8-24 and 8-25 show two of our favorites, the former featuring five attackers and the latter sending six attackers into or through the Box.

We call the play shown in Figure 8-24 the "Two-Man Drag"; we identify the field players by numbers rather than by position because the positions don't affect the play. We want our tallest attackers or best leapers at 3, 4, and 5.

On a signal from the kicker, 1 and 2 run across the Box, and then turn around and face the goal; when they reach the middle on their runs across the Box, 3, 4, and 5 begin their runs from the back of the penalty area. The kicker chips or drives the ball toward the area shown in the diagram, and each of our attackers attempts to be the first player to the ball and head or kick it into the net. We don't normally kick toward the goal itself because the goalkeeper will catch the ball.

We call the play in Figure 8-25 the "Wave." Instead of making runs across the Box, 1 and 2 initiate the action by making decoy runs as shown to make the defense think we're going ball side. (We *will* go to 1 or 2 if the defense fails to cover their runs.)[9]

On a signal from the kicker, 3, 4, and 5 make staggered runs into the Box from beyond the penalty area, hoping to confuse the marking assignments. (The order of runs is determined by the players themselves prior to the play.)

The critical attacking areas are the *back post* and the *middle of the goal*; those areas are especially difficult to cover because the defenders cannot follow the ball and their marks at the same time, and thus may have trouble timing their moves to the ball.

The short corner kick (Figure 8-26) is simply a short pass from the kicker to an open teammate nearby when attacking the goal area directly is impractical for any reason. Short corner kicks usually travel no more than 10 yards. Normally, the receiver will chip or drive the ball toward the goal and into the mix of players from both teams.

Figure 8-26 also shows a variation of the inside movements by 1 and 2 in Figure 8-24; instead of going all the way across the Box and pivoting, they stop and pivot halfway across, an action that may or may not screen the goalkeeper away from the ball if the kick is directed toward 3 or 4. Technically, it's a violation of the obstruction rule for 1 or 2 to screen off the keeper when not playing the ball; still, in our 17 years of club and high school soccer coaching, obstruction has never been called against our team or any of our opponents on a corner kick. And that brings to mind the comment of a born-and-bred Georgian who has coached soccer for many years and knows whereof he speaks: "It ain't obstruction if they don't call it."

If you're wondering whether to use this sort of ploy, the penalty for intentional obstruction is an indirect free kick for the opponents from the spot of the infraction.

---

[9] The runs of 7 in Figures 8-24 and 8-25 are decoy; they will become short cornerkick runs (Figure 8-26) if, for whatever reason, 6 cannot drive the ball toward the Box.

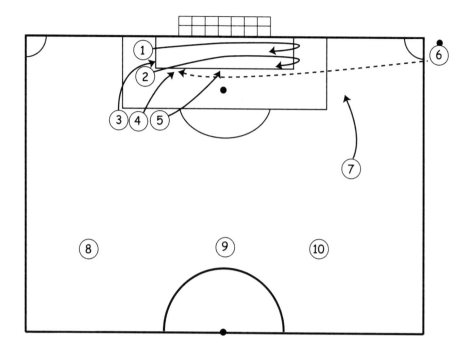

FIGURE 8–24. "Two-Man Drag" Set Play, Corner Kick

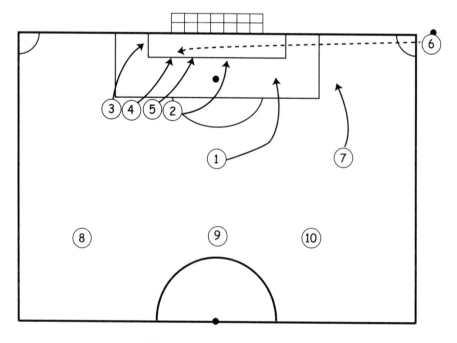

FIGURE 8–25. "Wave" Set Play, Corner Kick

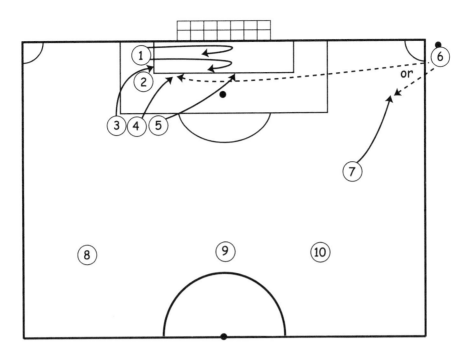

FIGURE 8–26. Short Corner Kick

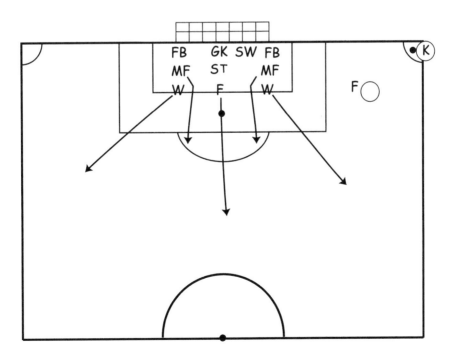

FIGURE 8–27. 9-Man Zone Defensive Alignment, Corner Kick

Defensing Corner Kicks. In defensing corner kicks, teams usually either use a compact, 9-man zone defensive alignment like that shown in Figure 8-27, or else they play man-to-man; either way, their primary objectives are to be the first to the ball and clear it out. We align our players as shown in the diagram to facilitate our laning assignments in organizing our attack when we intercept the ball.

Direct and Indirect Free Kicks

The difference between an indirect and a direct free kick is, of course, that the former (IFK) must be touched by two players before a goal can be scored, whereas the latter (DFK) requires only one kick to score. In either case, the ball is in play after the first kick, and may be played by either team thereafter. Direct free kicks may result in scores directly off the kick—but they are equally likely to involve two or more kicks, especially since the opponents will set up a defensive wall of players 10 yards away between the ball and the goal.

Beyond those basics, the first thing to remember about DFKs and IFKs is that *neither the referee nor the kicker is required to wait for the defense to get ready.* The tempting conclusion to be drawn from this fact is that taking the kick quickly before the defense is properly organized can result in a score, and it's true—but not always. Our rule of thumb regarding DFKs and IFKs is this: *If you see an opportunity to shoot quickly or set up a goal, take it; if not, set up and relax; don't force it.* Do it right.

The second thing to remember regarding direct and indirect free kicks is that, if you decide not to quick kick—say, if the defense is organized or you're farther out than about 30 yards from the opponents' goal—you're entitled to ask the referee to move the defenders 10 yards away from the ball. The referee is obliged to honor that request.

Most teams have at least one set play for free kicks. Assuming that whatever play(s) you use requires at least two kicks (or else you wouldn't need a play at all), you can use the same play(s) for direct as well as indirect free kicks. (For IFKs, at least, start out with two players on the ball.) While the temptation always exists to devise complex plays involving a number of players and runs, we've found that simplicity is better.

Timing is critical in setting up shots from free kicks. In Figure 8-28, 1's decoy run is intended to draw defensive attention away from 3 and 4, at least momentarily. When the ball is kicked—it will be a chip pass over the defensive wall—3 and 4, originally facing the ball, pivot toward the goal and attempt to head the ball past the keeper. If they move before the ball is kicked, they'll be offside. We use a verbal command by the kicker—GO!, loudly announced as the ball is kicked—not just to signal to 3 and 4 to start their moves but also *to alert the linesman that we aren't offside when the ball is kicked.*

In Figure 8-29, 3's decoy move clears the area for 2's quick one-touch pass to 4's feet; 5's move is also decoy, since it occurs in plain view of the defense, and 2 will be facing 5 until the last second when 2 passes to 4.

As before, 4's run cannot begin until 2 kicks the ball.

Defensing Free Kicks. The defenders must organize themselves quickly, setting up a wall of players 10 yards away from the ball and on a direct line between the ball and the goal. In the case of DFKs, no matter how hard the ball is kicked, the defenders must be willing to block the shot with their bodies.

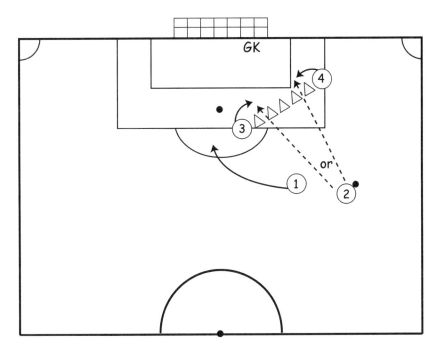

FIGURE 8–28. Set Play, Direct Free Kick

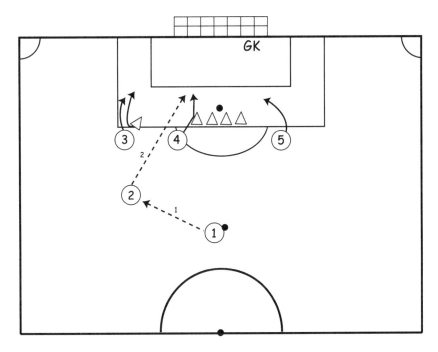

FIGURE 8–29. Set Play, Indirect Free Kick

The number of defenders in the wall depends on the ball's location; the closer to your goal the kick will be taken, the more players you need in the wall. We use the following guidelines:

Yards from Goal	*Players in Wall*
40 or more	1
35	2
30	4-5
20	5
In penalty area	5-6
6-yard line	8-10

Penalty Kicks

With only one defender—the goalkeeper—between the ball and the goal, penalty kicks should be as automatic in soccer as extra-point kicks are in American football. Your team can, after all, choose its penalty kicker. You want your best penalty kicker taking the shot—and that player is the one who can block out the emotional stress of the situation and execute the kick accurately and forcefully under pressure. Skills aside, not every attacker is equally adept at handling the pressure of penalty kicks.

The kicker should have decided where she is going to aim her kick before she begins her approach to the ball. The best place to aim is low to one side of the goal—preferably, toward a corner if your kicker is skilled enough to kick the ball where she's aiming it (see Figure 8-30). Keepers usually guess which way the ball is going and commit themselves entirely to that side; even if they guess correctly, though, they still should have trouble deflecting a low, hard kick toward the corner of the goal. Your kicker's objective should be to drive the ball hard enough and accurately enough to score regardless of whether the keeper guesses correctly or dives toward the wrong side of the goal.

Drop Balls

Relatively rare among the special situations, drop balls are superficially akin to face-offs in hockey. Drop balls result from stoppages in play in which the referee is unsure which team was in possession of the ball when play stopped. When a drop ball is announced, any number of players from either team may position themselves around the referee in an orderly fashion to prepare for the drop; the ball must hit the ground before it can be played by any player.

Strategies for playing the drop are few, but important. In our experience, neither team normally has an advantage over the other in drops, except when the ball is being dropped relatively near one of the goals.

If the drop occurs in your defensive third, play the goal side, mark up, and organize your defensive coverage quickly.

If the drop occurs in the penalty area, be extra careful and think about a quick shot or pass to a flanking player. Depending on how desperate you are defensively, you might even consider that your keeper can use his hands in the penalty area; would you risk his participating in the drop?

The first offensive priority in drops near the goal is to get possession of the ball; your chief defensive priority is to clear the ball out of danger.

With drops that occur in or around the midfield area, you just hope that one of your players gets a foot on the ball. After the drop, play progresses as in any other phase of the game.

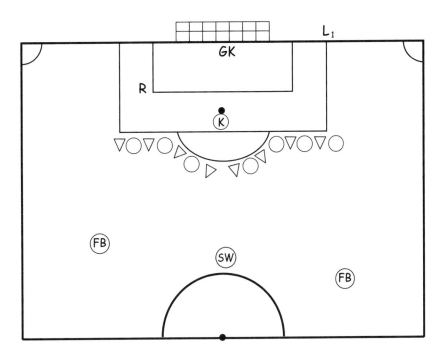

FIGURE 8–30. Penalty Kick

Part 3

COACHING YOUR TEAM

Coaches are like politicians:
They have to be smart enough to understand the game,
and dumb enough to think it's important.

—Eugene S. McCarthy,
former U.S. Senator

Chapter 9

TEAM TRYOUTS AND SQUAD SELECTION

*I realized early that I may never become adept at controlling
the ball with my feet. Therefore, I would have to make up for it
in other ways such as speed, willingness to make contact,
the ability to leap into the air, and hustle.*

—Kyle Rote, Jr.

RECRUITING

In an established soccer program, your varsity team will consist almost exclusively of players who have come up through the local club program, with perhaps a year of jayvee experience behind them. This gives you a terrific advantage if, as we do, you work very closely with the club-level teams because (a) the players will know you and understand your coaching methods and playing system long before they ever reach the varsity level, (b) you'll have a pretty good idea what your team will be like before tryouts begin, and (c) you won't have to beat the bushes looking for recruits from the general school population, who have never played soccer, to fill out your varsity squad. The more extensive your club soccer is, the more selective you can be in filling available varsity slots.

In 1984, our first year of soccer coaching, 26 boys (only a couple of whom had any real prior exposure to the game) tried out for the varsity soccer team; in 1998, we had 100+ candidates trying out for 15 positions on the varsity and jayvee teams, and many of them had extensive playing experience. The difference between those two numbers reflects the difference in what you can expect or hope to accomplish with either group.

In organizing a team for the first time at your school, you literally may have to take any warm bodies that show up for tryouts exhibiting a pulse; even so, you can lay a groundwork for team tryouts in advance of the starting date by advertising your tryouts via public service announcements over local radio and television stations, signs prominently displayed in the school halls, articles in the school and local newspapers, announcements over the intercom or in-school television, talking with students in P.E. classes, and the like.

Figure 9-1 contains a notice that we post in the halls and gymnasium and send out to the players we expect to attend tryouts.

FIGURE 9–1
TRYOUT NOTICE—GRIFFIN HIGH SCHOOL SOCCER

If you want to play soccer for the Griffin Bears, you should start by running and training on your own during the months of November, December, and January and be ready to go full speed from the first day of tryouts. Formal conditioning work will begin on January 19, _____.

The physical and mental qualities we're looking for include:

1. Quickness, agility, and familiarity with soccer's basic skills.

2. Playing experience and an understanding of how the game is played.

3. Fitness and a positive attitude toward working and playing hard.

4. Loyalty, mental toughness, and coachability.

5. Ability to meet at least minimal requirements sufficient to maintain academic eligibility.

We'll hold training sessions with Paul and Ken two nights per week (conditioning and scrimmaging) and weight training sessions with Coach Graves in the GHS weight room on Tuesdays and Thursdays at 4:00 P.M.

CONDUCTING TEAM TRYOUTS

The more organized your practices are, the more you'll accomplish. Drills and activities should be organized within specific, predetermined time frames, at the end of each of which you move on quickly to something else. Two kinds of evaluative drills are necessary, those that involve specific soccer skills and those that reveal players' basic athleticism (e.g., quick feet, agility, leg strength, vertical jumping ability, speed, and endurance). Quickness and agility can be measured using the President's Council shuttle run, leg strength on a leg press machine, vertical jumping ability via a jump-and-reach test, speed via timed 40s, and endurance via timed mile runs.

If you want to find out in a hurry where you stand in terms of players' overall soccer skills and athleticism, spend part of every tryout session scrimmaging. (This is especially important if you have a large turnout and cannot devote individual attention to every player.) Make the scrimmages long enough to give all candidates a fair chance to use whatever skills they possess, and carefully evaluate their individual performances. (Bear in mind, though, that some of the players who weren't involved in club soccer may not be in shape to play for long stretches without suffering from fatigue that will adversely affect their performances.) Keep those evaluations; by comparing them with your evaluations of other scrimmages, you may get an idea of how quickly the players learn and adapt to your coaching style.

Many (if not most) of your drills should be competitive in nature (1-v-1, 2-v-2, etc.) since soccer is, after all, a competitive sport; however, you should also devote part of every session to teaching basic skills and evaluating the players' ability to listen and to learn. Players who are unreceptive, unmotivated, or unwilling to learn from their mistakes at this stage of the game are unlikely to be magically transformed into eager learners after squad selections are announced. *This* is the time to identify those individuals who are likely to make life miserable for you later with their uncoachability, and evaluating their responses to teaching-learning situations is an excellent way to do it.

What to Look For in Young Players

Soccer skills—ballhandling, dribbling, receiving, passing, heading, shooting, defense, and tackling—are of primary importance, of course, and athleticism is always a plus for any player (except goalkeepers, for whom it is a necessity).

In the absence of soccer skills, look for youngsters who display general athletic ability. Of the traits listed, endurance is the least important, because it can be developed through conditioning. The others are all associated in one way or another with one general trait—*quickness*. Quickness is important because, while it can be improved to a certain extent through training, it cannot be taught. (If you doubt that, ask any track coach.) Among players of equal skills, the quicker player will win most of the time.

You should also be looking for mental and emotional qualities such as mental toughness, aggressiveness, competitiveness, alertness, willingness to work hard and follow instructions quickly and unquestioningly, eagerness to learn, and receptiveness to criticism. Collectively, these attributes denote a positive attitude toward competition and self-improvement. The ability to handle pressure is a form of mental toughness and an important attribute for any player—but not necessarily at this point, since players who are deficient in basic skills are unlikely to handle pressure situations well and players who are fundamentally sound can be taught to handle pressure.

Selecting Your Team: Five Guidelines

The tryouts process is essentially a matter of weeding out those candidates who lack either the necessary skills to compete at the varsity level or the kind of positive attitude toward their coaches, teammates, hard work, self-improvement, and the pursuit of team goals that will render their selection worthwhile for everyone connected with the team. While we can't tell you whom to select, we can offer five guidelines to player selection for your consideration:

1. *Among players of equal skills or ability, go with the one(s) who respond best to your coaching.* As we've noted, until effective leadership arises from among your players *you* are the team. You owe it to yourself and the team to make your job as easy as possible by surrounding yourself with players who respect you, believe in you, and will remain loyal to you through good times and bad.

2. *Among players of equal skills, go with the younger players, who will benefit more from the experience than upperclassmen who cannot possibly learn all that needs to be learned about soccer in only one or two years.*

    The only viable reasons for keeping unskilled upperclassmen might be (a) to fill out the team roster when the turnout for tryouts is low,[1] or (b) to model desired attitudes when such attitudes are otherwise lacking—players who are loyal, hard-working, and committed to you and your goals despite their lacking superior skills.

3. *Among players of equal skills, go with the players who possess greater athletic ability.* With a long way to go, a short time to get there, and a lack of talented players, your best available shortcut to success lies in selecting players whose athleticism can make up in part for the skills they lack. For skilled, experienced players, superior athletic ability is a bonus that enhances their effectiveness; for unskilled players, it is a necessity.

4. *Consider the positions you need to fill and look for players who possess the qualities necessary for those positions* (Figure 9-2).

5. *If possible, avoid selecting players who are disruptive, lazy, or likely to exert a negative influence on their teammates.* Such players are fairly easy to spot; they're the ones who are chronically late arriving at practice; forget their gear; grumble or complain about how hard you're making them work; blame others for their mistakes; give a half-hearted effort in drills and run at an easy, relaxed pace in scrimmages; argue with the coaches or other players; constantly ask you how much longer practice will last; or expect special treatment or consideration based on the quality of their skills or supposed importance to the team.

    Real soccer players love to play the game, and to practice the skills that will make them more effective players. *They're* the ones you want to keep, and not those who consider daily practice a chore rather than a challenge.

---

[1] Even then, you should be careful to avoid selecting players who are likely to turn on you later if the team doesn't win as often as they might like.

FIGURE 9-2
SKILLS ASSOCIATED WITH SOCCER POSITIONS

Position	Skills Necessary
Goalkeepers	Quickness; agility and lateral mobility; jumping ability; good hands; ability to punt the ball far downfield with accuracy; defensive anticipation and focus; and ability to coordinate and direct the team defense.
Fullbacks	Quick feet; ability to play tight 1-v-1 defense without diving in after the ball; heading skills; and dribbling skills sufficient to maintain possession of the ball and get it out to a teammate or clear it.
Sweepers	Speed; 1-v-1 marking skills and ability to organize and direct the defense; good judgment in supporting teammates defensively; dribbling skills and a strong leg for clearing the ball; ability to receive the ball and head or pass it quickly and accurately; and ability to support attacks.
Stoppers	Playing air balls; dribbling and passing skills, and ability to support attacks; and effective 1-v-1 marking and tackling skills.
Midfielders	Tireless, hard workers on either side of the halfway line; dribbling and shooting skills; good first touch on the ball; and ability to make accurate penetrating passes ahead to teammates in the attacking third.
Wingers	Speed; dribbling skills; and a strong leg for making crossing passes or shooting from beyond the 18.
Forwards	Controlled speed and quickness; dribbling and passing skills; ability to play air balls; good first touch on the ball; an aggressive attitude on attack; ability to control the ball in pressure situations and create scoring opportunities for self and teammates; shooting with accuracy; and ability to make quick transitions from attacking to defense and challenge the ball before the opponents can organize their attacks.

211

How Long Should the Tryouts Last?

Your tryouts should probably last between three and five days. Less than that may not give the candidates time to shed their initial nervousness and exhibit the full range of their potential; it also overlooks the possibility that a given player may be having a bad start or a bad day; more than that cuts into your preseason practice and unnecessarily prolongs the candidates' suspense regarding their status.

To return to an earlier point, your tryouts should include the teaching of skills to help you determine how well the candidates react to instruction and criticism; however, you should also include plenty of rigorous, demanding drills and activities that will challenge the players physically and set the tone for the kinds of practices the team will face when tryouts are concluded. Setting a demanding pace in tryouts will help your selection process by driving off the pretenders who underestimated the challenges of playing varsity-level soccer.

With a good team, it is *very* important in tryouts to expose the candidates to competitive situations that will reveal how well they respond to pressure, since if they are already highly skilled, all they'll need is fine-tuning and the ability to use those skills effectively in the pressure-cooker environment of game situations. The more skilled players you have, the more the ability to handle pressure should factor into the selection process.

Even if you have a good idea starting out as to which candidates are going to make the team and which are not, you should still take at least three days for tryouts, if for no other reason than to be able to say that you gave everyone who tried out a fair chance to display her or his skills.

Because an unusually large number of students showed up for our 1998 team tryouts, we decided to focus entirely on conditioning activities over a five-day period, to weed out the less dedicated candidates and get the remaining players in shape to play the best soccer of their lives. It worked; we didn't have to cut anyone, and of those who stuck it out enough were ninth-graders to enable us to form a junior high team to complement our jayvee/varsity program. In earlier years, those players would have been involved in club rather than school soccer.

ANNOUNCING PLAYER SELECTIONS

Of all the responsibilities associated with coaching, none is more difficult or dreaded by coaches than telling youngsters that their services are not needed on this year's team.

Some coaches post a list at the end of the final day of tryouts, telling who has made the team and who has not; others prefer to announce their selections verbally in one way or another. The former is easier, but we prefer the latter because we think it's important to talk to the rejected—and dejected—candidates, preferably individually, but at least collectively if there are too many to make individual conferences feasible.

The way we see it, every youngster who attends our tryouts deserves our thanks and our respect for having cared enough to try out for the team, and we owe it to them to ease them gently through the dismissal process. Besides thanking them for their hard work, telling them that the selection process was extremely difficult—it always is—and offering our sympathy for their disappointment, we'll tell them honestly but tactfully why they didn't make the team (e.g., *You need more playing time than you could get with us because we have so many talented players this year*). If they're underclassmen and good kids who lack soccer skills, we'll either ask them if they might consider being a team manager if there's a position available or encourage them to play rec soccer, work hard on improving their skills, and try out for the team again next year. Such treatment probably won't win us many friends among the ones we're cutting, but we hope it won't gain us any enemies, either.

Before announcing your cuts, don't forget to check the players' eligibility (i.e., age, residency, and academic status) as defined in your state high school association handbook and contained in school records and transcripts. It makes little sense to reserve a spot on the team roster for a player who is ineligible unless the player's eligibility can and will be restored during the season.

Chapter 10

PRESEASON PRACTICE

Everything is practice. I made lots of goals with the head.
I knew it was very hard to score with the head in Europe,
but I made many goals because I practiced that shot.

—Pele

THE FIRST TEAM MEETING AND OTHER PRELIMINARIES

After congratulating those who have made the team, you'll want to take time to outline your expectations and team goals for the season, including the rules you'll expect the players, coaches, and managers to live by. If you use a player handbook, now's the time to give each player a copy. The handbook should contain, among other things, a copy of the current year's schedule, a checklist of what the players and managers should do and bring with them in preparation for daily practices and games (see Appendixes E, K, and L), the coaches' home and school telephone numbers, a description of your system of play, and any other pertinent information you want your players to have.

It's important to get the preliminaries behind you as quickly as possible in order to avoid wasting valuable practice time. Those preliminaries include eligibility reports, medical examinations, and other paperwork. As you probably already know, *no one on your team is eligible to play jayvee or varsity soccer until both the state office and a licensed physician certify that he or she has been cleared to play.*[1] You can fill out in advance the returning players' eligibility forms and those of last year's jayvee squad whom you expect to make the varsity team, get the physical examinations out of the way, and then fill out the remaining forms at your first team meeting.

---

[1] In our state, players cannot even try out for teams unless they have been medically approved to do so.

214

We mail the completed eligibility reports ourselves as soon as the principal signs them, having known one coach whose school secretary failed to mail them in on time. If there is one thing we've learned over our years in coaching, it is this: You don't tug on Superman's cape or spit into the wind, and *you don't mess around with your high school association!*

The rest of our paperwork consists of (a) materials contained in our GHS athletic packet (including forms relative to the school's $15 athletic assessment fee, insurance, parents'/guardians' permission to participate, and release for medical treatment; (b) an individual soccer information sheet; and (c) a medical history form to be signed by the student and a parent or guardian (see Appendixes F through H).

PRESEASON PRACTICE

Preseason begins when tryouts conclude and a physician has examined your athletes and signed their medical forms (Appendix I); it ends when the team plays its first game. How much you accomplish in that brief span depends on several factors, the most important of which are (a) the level of your players' technical and tactical skills, their experience, and their familiarity with you and your playing system; and (b) your ability to organize your practice sessions in such a manner as to get in everything that must be covered.

Desirable Individual Skills-Team Preparation Ratios

Basically, three aspects of player and team preparation must be taken into account in preseason: conditioning, individual skills development, and installing the team offense and defense. In an established system with a good club-level program in place, the former should be your least difficult obstacle to overcome, since the players are likely to be in good shape from their recent participation in off-season club soccer. One aspect of your team development, *scrimmaging*, will help to get and keep them in shape.

The ratio of practice time you'll need to devote to each of the three phases of team and player development will depend on how much work your players need in each area. With skilled, experienced players in abundance, you probably should devote a greater percentage of your practice time to team concepts, game strategies, and scrimmaging than if your players are inexperienced and lack basic skills.

As a broad rule of thumb, try an initial 20-60-20 percentage of preseason practice time devoted to conditioning, basic skills development, and work on team aspects of the game, respectively, with a weak team in early preseason. Those percentages are likely to change after the first week or so, however, if you are going to get in all that must be covered before the first game is played. (See the section on preseason practice schedules at the end of this chapter.)

With a team that can reasonably be expected to win half of its games, we might start out with and retain, say, a 10-40-50 ratio throughout preseason, focusing on team strategies because the players already possess skills sufficient to win games on a regular basis. With an excellent team, we might start out with a 10-40-50 time allotment and end up at 10-20-70 to ensure that the players thoroughly understand our system and how to apply their skills within it. The "50" and "70" percentages will probably consist primarily of 3-v-3 and 4-v-4 drills and scrimmaging—or even 3-v-4 or 4-v-5 if the starters are superior players who need such challenges to elevate the level of their game or improve their ability to handle intense pressure.

Desirable Offense-Defense Ratios

In installing your playing system, how much time you spend working on offense or defense will depend on two factors: (a) whether your coaching philosophy is basically conservative (i.e., defense-oriented) or offense-oriented, and (b) how much work your team needs in each phase. Whereas a defense-minded coach may spend as much as 80 percent of his or her time allotment for team preparation in building a solid defense that will keep the team competitive when the wheels fall off the offense, another coach may prefer a more equitable distribution between the two phases— and both of them may be right or wrong, depending on what their teams need and how they prefer to coach.

Don't just walk out on the practice field, flip a coin, and say to yourself, *It's tails, that means we work our tails off on defense today.* Effective coaching requires far more attention to detail than that. You should know what you hope to accomplish, and how you intend to accomplish it, before you ever set foot on the practice field. Your practice schedule may be as brief as a simple list of sequentially arranged drills or as complex as to include specific time allotments for each activity—but in either case it should serve as a roadmap to where you're going and how you plan to get there.

Practice Schedules

A good practice schedule will take at least 30 minutes to prepare. When you do it is immaterial—immediately after practice, at home in the evening, or after school and before practice—but *do it.* Consider that 30 to 45 minutes a small investment in your team's future, in the sense of focusing your thoughts on your team, its needs, and how those needs might be met.

We've known coaches who don't use practice schedules; their excuses for such laziness run from *I just don't have time for that sort of thing* to *I guess I'm just not very organized.* We've occasionally known such coaches to have very good teams, too— usually because they inherited someone else's talented players. We've never known any consistently successful coach who didn't attribute his or her team's success to preparation rather than to luck or chance. If you don't prepare to succeed, you'd better be prepared to fail.

Organizational ability is not, as some coaches seem to think, a talent; it is, rather, a habit. The more time you're willing to spend thinking about your team, the more organized you'll be. As the eminent scientist Louis Pasteur noted, "Chance favors the prepared mind."

A checklist of aspects of team offense and team defense to be installed during preseason appears in Appendix J. You don't have to—and shouldn't—try to work on all of them every day, but you must spend enough time with each of them during pre-season to ensure that your players understand how you want them to perform in each area.

Contrasting Emphases in Preseason Practice Schedules: A Case Study

When we fielded our school's first varsity boys' soccer team in 1984, our players possessed only rudimentary, kickball-like skills and little or no tactical sense. We had only four weeks to get them in shape and ready to compete at the varsity level. It quickly became evident that, even if we had eight or twelve weeks to prepare, we would not be ready to offer more than token opposition for the better teams in our region.

We started out using trial-and-error techniques to find out what was best for our team. We initially devoted 20 percent of our 2-1/2-hour daily practice time to conditioning activities, 60 percent—1-1/2 hours—to basic skills, and 20 percent to developing a playing system we could live with (Figure 10-1).

We badly needed a jump-start in skills development, but since there was none we found it necessary to sacrifice an increasingly large portion—up to 30 percent—of our conditioning and basic skills time in favor of team offense and defense during the last three weeks of preseason practice so we could look and play like a team when the season began. The players needed scrimmaging to get used to what game conditions were like, and to learn to recognize their responsibilities within the context of game situations.

We ended up with a 10-30-60 split between conditioning, individual skills, and team offense/defense (Figure 10-2). It was a difficult decision for us to make, especially since almost all of us, players and coaches alike, were relatively new to soccer and much of our system-oriented instruction involved walk-throughs. We told the players that, in order for us to have any hope of being competitive in our league, they would have to supplement our formal daily practices by working on the basic skills on their own time.

We hated to give up 45 valuable minutes of fundamentals practice and conditioning, but we had no choice. Since the players weren't going to master the necessary playing skills in a month, no matter how much supervised instruction they received, we felt that the team would be better served by concentrating on our style of play—especially our defense—and counting on scrimmaging to compensate for the lost conditioning time. Defensive skills are far more easily acquired than attacking skills. While that's not to say that playing defense is easy or that offense, whether team or individual, should be neglected, time spent practicing defense *is* likely to be more productive on a short-term basis than practicing individual offensive skills. It was simply a major decision that we faced; we still think it was the best choice we could have made under the difficult circumstances of trying to squeeze a year's worth of training into 50 hours of preseason practice.

A coach once told us, "My preseason practice time is critical to me; I can't afford to waste it working on things that aren't going to improve enough to help us win the next game. So unless our weaknesses are minor and can be adjusted in daily practice, I'd rather work on our strengths to keep us strong in those areas and use our playing system to hide our weaknesses, than to waste our time beating dead horses. The time to turn major weaknesses into strengths is during the off-season, not preseason." You may or may not agree with her, but it's something to think about.

Note that, although the activities didn't change between the schedules shown in Figures 10-1 and 10-2, the time allotments (and thus the depth of instruction we could reach in any given area) changed dramatically in our amended preseason practice schedule. Remember: Preparing practice schedules is important; it brings precision to your coaching and organizes your thinking about your team. Even so minor a decision as dropping 5 minutes from one time segment and adding it to another poses questions: *What part of the activity to be reduced should be eliminated? Do you drop one or more drills altogether? Or do you retain the drills but reduce the amount of time spent practicing each drill?* Considering such questions will make you more efficient in your coaching.

FIGURE 10-1
1984: INITIAL PRESEASON PRACTICE SCHEDULE[2]

4:00-4:10   Warmups, stretching

4:10-5:40   Basic skills development

        A. Passing and receiving

        B. Dribbling skills

        C. Heading, chest, and thigh work

        D. 1-v-1, basic offensive moves

        E. 1-v-1, basic defense

        F. Shooting on goal (with keeper)

5:40-6:10   11-v-11 scrimmaging

        A. System of play

        B. Corners (offense and defense)

        C. Dead ball sets (offense and defense)

        D. Controlled scrimmaging

        E. Throw-ins

6:10-6:30   Conditioning activities

FIGURE 10-2
1984: AMENDED PRESEASON PRACTICE SCHEDULE[3]

4:00-4:10   Warmups, stretching

4:10-4:55   Basic skills development

        A. Passing and receiving

        B. Dribbling skills

        C. Heading, chest, and thigh work

        D. 1-v-1, basic offensive moves

        E. 1-v-1, basic defense

        F. Shooting on goal (with keeper)

4:55-6:25   11-v-11 scrimmaging

        A. System of play

        B. Corners (offense and defense)

        C. Dead ball sets (offense and defense)

        D. Controlled scrimmaging

        E. Throw-ins

6:25-6:30   Conditioning activities

---

[2] Based on a 20-60-20 ratio between conditioning, individual skills, and team patterns and strategies.

---

[3] Based on a 10-30-60 ratio between conditioning, individual skills, and team patterns and strategies.

PRESEASON PRACTICE SCHEDULES

We'll conclude this chapter with our first week's preseason practice schedules (Figure 10-3). You'll note that we don't spend as much time on fundamentals work as we did back in 1984, when everyone on the team was new to soccer. We don't have to; we've worked with these kids for practically all of their lives through club, jayvee, and varsity soccer, so by now they know what we want them to know about soccer's basic skills. All we have to do is apply a bit of fine-tuning about three times a week to keep the parts running smoothly. (You'll note, though, that we *always* reserve 10 minutes for our fast footwork drills.) It's the sort of luxury you can allow yourself after coaching in the same school and community for two decades. After all, if you can't build a strong program in that time span, odds are that you aren't ever going to do it.

FIGURE 10–3
PRESEASON PRACTICE SCHEDULE

Monday (4:00 p.m. – 6:00 p.m.)

4:00-4:20	Watching film of fast footwork drills (10)
4:20-4:25	Light jog (3 laps around soccer field)
4:25-4:40	Stretching exercises
4:40-4:50	Complex run—three groups (Indian run, boxes, steps)

4:50-5:00	Dutch drill
	    1-touch and pass back
	    2-touch and pass back
	    Thigh-instep trap and pass back
	    Chest-instep trap and pass back
	    Heading

5:00-5:20	Ball work (fast footwork, keeper work separate)
5:20-5:50	3-v-3 micro soccer with small goals/4-v-4 Big Dog soccer with regulation goals and keeper: same time, different areas
5:55-6:00	Sprints
6:00	Cool down

Tuesday (4:00 p.m. – 6:30 p.m.)

4:00-4:05	Light jog (3 laps around soccer field)
4:05-4:15	Stretching exercises
4:15-4:25	Fast footwork drills (keeper work separate)

4:25-4:35	2-man drills
	
	    1-touch instep
	    1-touch inside foot
	    1-touch outside foot
	    Thigh-instep pass
	    Chest-instep pass
	    Headers

4:35-5:05	3-v-3 micro soccer with small goals
5:05-6:05	4-v-4 Big Dog soccer with regulation goals and keeper
6:05-6:15	Sprints
6:15-6:25	Cool down
6:25-6:30	Team meeting

FIGURE 10-3 *(cont'd)*

Wednesday (4:00 p.m. – 6:00 p.m.)

4:00-4:05	Light jog (3 times around soccer field)
4:05-4:15	Stretching exercises
4:15-4:25	Fast footwork drills (keeper work separate)

4:25-4:35	2-man drills
	    1-touch instep
	    1-touch inside foot
	    1-touch outside foot
	    Thigh-instep pass
	    Chest-instep pass
	    Headers

4:35-5:05	Net work (4 keepers, 4 nets): 1-v-1 situations
5:05-5:45	4-v-4 micro soccer with small goals/4-v-4 Big Dog soccer with regulation goals and keeper: same time, different areas
5:45-5:55	Sprints
6:00	Cool down

Thursday (4:00 p.m. – 6:00 p.m.)

4:00-4:05	Light jog (3 times around soccer field)
4:05-4:15	Stretching exercises
4:15-4:25	Complex run—three groups (Indian run, boxes, steps)
4:25-4:35	Fast footwork drills—field players (keeper work separate)

4:35-4:45	2-man drills
	    1-touch instep
	    1-touch inside foot
	    1-touch outside foot
	    Thigh-instep pass
	    Chest-instep pass
	    Header

4:45-5:15	Net work
	    1-v-1
	    1-touch shooting
	    2-v-1

5:15-5:45	3-v-3 micro soccer with small goals/4-v-4 Big Dog Soccer with regulation goals and keeper
5:45-5:55	Sprints
5:55-6:00	Cool down

FIGURE 10–3 *(cont'd)*

Friday (4:00 p.m. – 6:00 p.m.)

4:00-4:05	Light jog (3 laps around soccer field)
4:05-4:15	Stretching exercises
4:15-4:25	Fast footwork drills—field players (keeper work separate)
4:25-4:35	2-man drills

                    1-touch instep
                    1-touch inside foot
                    1-touch outside foot
                    Thigh-instep trap and pass back
                    Chest-instep trap and pass back
                    Headers

4:35-4:45   Dutch drill
                    1-touch and pass back
                    2-touch and pass back
                    Thigh-instep trap and pass back
                    Chest-instep trap and pass back
                    Heading

4:45-5:45   2-v-2 micro soccer with small goals/1-v-1/4-v-4
                    Big Dog soccer: same time, different areas

5:45-5:55   Sprints

5:55-6:00   Cool down/team meeting

Chapter 11

ORGANIZING YOUR DAILY PRACTICES

Nobody ever mastered any skill except through intensive, persistent, and intelligent practice. Practice it the right way.

—Norman Vincent Peale,
American clergyman and author

CONDUCTING DAILY PRACTICES THAT *SIZZLE:* FIVE GUIDELINES

1. Coach with Intensity

Let your players know by your every word and deed that the quality of their daily performances matters to you. You should expect and demand that your players give 100 percent of themselves, physically and mentally, throughout every second of every practice session and every game. You don't have to be in their faces every second, shrieking like a banshee or shouting at them—but you *must* let them know when they're not giving the kind of effort, physical or mental, that you expect of them. When you're teaching them, they should be listening and watching intently and absorbing what you're saying; when they're performing, they should be concentrating intently, not just on what they're doing but on what the players around them are doing as well. Even their water breaks should be conducted intensely (i.e., timed within narrow limits), because intensity is a *habit*, and one that is more easily turned off than turned on. Your goal should be for your players to automatically turn on the intensity whenever the whistle starts the action.

At first thought, coaching with intensity may appear to take the fun out of the game for the players; in reality quite the opposite is true if you take the time to teach your kids that soccer is a series of competitive challenges to be met, and that only by giving their best effort, physically and mentally, can they hope to withstand those challenges.

2. Vary Your Practice Routine

You know you're in trouble when the players know what's coming next before you announce it. Adding new drills is one way of varying your routine; if they don't work as designed, you can always either alter or discard them. Another way is to rearrange the order of your drills and activities. Traditionally, coaches start out with individual drills and work their way up to team drills or scrimmaging—but there's no law that says it has to be that way every day. As a coach we know likes to say, *"I'm the law in these parts, podnuh!"*

Probably the biggest problem associated with daily practices is the tendency to do the same things over and over until they become tedious, boring, or frustrating to the players. The problem is partly unavoidable, since learning occurs through repetition of specific movements until they become automatic; still, part of the art of coaching consists of knowing when enough is enough.

Example: Frustrated that his players were consistently fouling up a 2-on-1 fast-break drill, a rec league coach told them they were going to work with that drill all day if necessary until they beat the defender and scored five goals in a row. They stayed on that same drill for 45 minutes—and when he finally dismissed his players in disgust, you could have scraped up what was left of their morale with a putty knife. Watching the players drag themselves off the field, you just knew they were dreading tomorrow's practice like a trip to the dentist for root canal work.

3. Look for Ways to Make Drills Self-Motivating

A drill is said to be self-motivating if it contains built-in incentives, whether rewards or punishments, that motivate players to work hard and concentrate without being urged to.

You probably already use self-motivating techniques at least occasionally (e.g., "Everyone who beats the keeper in three out of five penalty kicks doesn't have to run wind sprints today"); with a little thought, you can apply the principle to other drills.[1] However, such drills are useful only in teaching players to hustle and to focus on what they're doing; because they may involve immediate rewards and punishments that are distracting and possibly time-consuming, they do not necessarily adapt well to teaching situations, especially when the skills or concepts are new to the players.

4. If You're New to Soccer, Buy Some Drills Books (Appendix A)

One of the keys to having successful practices is to change your drills often. Of course, that doesn't mean abandoning your best drills, the "old reliables" that your players like and you find yourself going back to time and again because they *work;* rather, it means constantly looking for new approaches to teaching, learning, and drill-and-practice that accomplish your goals and give your daily practices a lively, fresh feeling. We recommend two relatively old, but tried-and-true, drills books, both by James P. McGettigan: *Complete Book of Drills for Winning Soccer* (Prentice Hall, 1980) and *Soccer Drills for Individual and Team Play* (Prentice Hall, 1987), as excellent sources for more than 500 individual and team drills in every phase of the game. Most of the drills can be adapted as necessary to meet your team's needs.

---

1 The controlled-scrimmaging drill in Figure 11-1 is a self-motivating drill.

If you've played organized basketball, you can also adapt many basketball drills to soccer. Just think of it as basketball drills with a lot more players on the field. That advice from coach John Rennie (Duke University) helped us to get through our first year of soccer coaching when we were as new to the game as our players were. It is as helpful now as it was then, and we don't hesitate to pass it on to you.

Unless you're far more creative than the rest of us, the bulk of your drills probably will come from other creative and successful coaches who have studied the sport and devised effective drills for teaching and practicing its skills and strategies. You could do it all yourself, of course, but why bother when, with a little research, you can borrow tried-and-true techniques from other successful coaches? Sir Isaac Newton acknowledged, "If I have seen further than [others], it is by standing upon the shoulders of Giants [who preceded me]." That's good advice for all of us.

5. Don't Just Scrimmage; Use Controlled-Scrimmaging Sequences

Scrimmaging simulates 11-v-11 full-field game conditions, and thus is a necessary part of every player's soccer training. If, however, your goal is to teach your players how to react to pressure situations that arise in games, controlled scrimmaging is superior because it focuses on specific pressure situations and permits instruction within the framework of those situations to the exclusion of all others. You just can't get that kind of repetitive activity in scrimmaging.

To set up a controlled-scrimmaging situation, identify any two situations in sequence and restrict your scrimmaging to them alone. For example, you may want to work on team defense and building the attack or fast breaking after transition; fast breaking and settling into the team offense when the initial attack stalls or breaks down; running the team offense and (delaying the ball/getting back on defense) when transitions occur; attacking (or playing defense) in dead-ball situations and continuing play until someone scores or transitions occur; or any of an infinite number of situations of your choosing.

Two ways to spice up these sequences are to time them and to devise a point system of scoring to make them more competitive. For example, if you're practicing your team offense, you might put 1:30 on your clock and station your managers out of bounds on either side of the pitch. Then, give the ball to the attacking team at the center spot and tell the players that they have a minute and a half to pass out of bounds to a manager on one side, collect the throw-in, move the ball to the other side of the pitch and pass to the other manager, collect *that* throw-in, and set up a shot on goal (Figure 11-1). Failure to do so in the allotted time gives the other team three points. The attacking team gets one point for every shot taken, and five points for a goal. The opponents get three points for a takeaway, two more points for clearing the ball to a teammate beyond the halfway line (or one point for building their own attack). When the ball goes out of bounds, a point is awarded to the other team, the attacking team maintains possession, and the clock stops until the ball is put in play. The sequence stops when attackers score or the other team crosses the halfway line in control of the ball. Then, reset the clock (but not the score) and do it again.

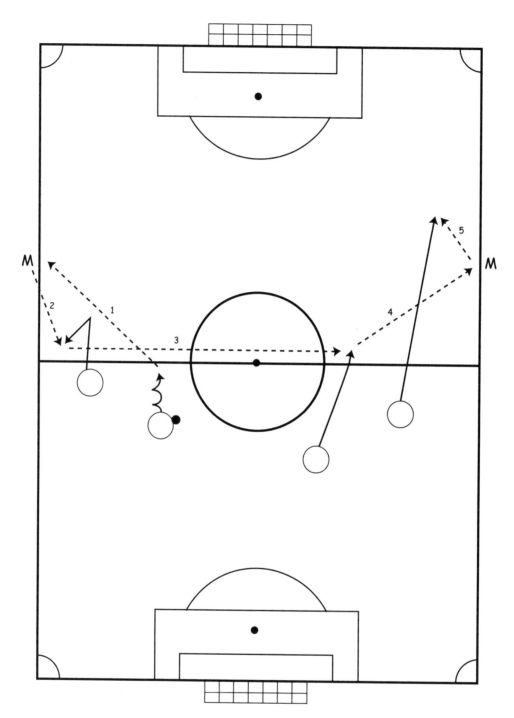

FIGURE 11–1. Typical Controlled-Scrimmaging Sequence, Offense

Admittedly, this approach does not conform precisely with the way games are actually played—but if that bothers you, leave out the time and scoring, and use the sequences as a teaching tool. The time and scoring add competitive pressure and a greater sense of urgency to the individual sequences than is present under normal circumstances.

Of course, all of this presupposes that your offense and transitional defense are already in place, or else you'd be going over them in walk-through fashion. The sequences and their scoring may appear complex at first, but only for awhile. The players will get used to them in short order, just as they'll get used to playing under the intense pressure that these kinds of controlled-scrimmage sequences provide.

We've described one such sequence in some detail; with a little imagination you can extend it to any phases of the game you want to work with in a team context. What we like best about controlled scrimmaging is that *it improves players' ability to concentrate for extended lengths of time without overloading them to the point of losing their ability to focus on essential tasks*, as is often the case in regular scrimmaging.

FINDING A DESIRABLE RATIO BETWEEN DRILLS AND SCRIMMAGING

Drills are activity sequences of relatively brief duration that involve repetitions of isolated, specific skills or movement patterns; as such, they are ideal teaching tools. Drills can and should be used in teaching new skills or patterned movements, or in correcting mistakes in execution.[2] Drills can simulate given aspects of game situations, but because of their repetitiveness, they cannot simulate the free flow of situations that arise constantly under actual game conditions. For that, you'll have to use scrimmaging. (Controlled scrimmaging is an intermediate step between drills and scrimmaging that incorporates elements of both activities.)

Scrimmaging provides an excellent way to get players in shape and keep them that way. Because it replicates game conditions, scrimmaging teaches players to see the game as a whole rather than as a series of isolated parts; however, its effective use requires that the players be familiar with all the components of team offense and defense that they will encounter in scrimmaging. For best results, then, scrimmaging should occur *after* your players are familiar with your playing system.

If your team is young and inexperienced, you'll probably want to devote considerable time to individual and team drills incorporating soccer's basic skills; if, however, your players already have a solid foundation in the fundamentals, you can afford to scrimmage or controlled-scrimmage as much as necessary to refine your players' tactical development. You should understand, though, that, because it is open-ended, nonspecific, and continuous-action oriented, scrimmaging does not lend itself well to specific teaching-learning situations. It is best reserved for practicing techniques and strategies that have already been learned.

We would be remiss if we did not offer a final warning about scrimmaging: It is not a desirable substitute for coaching or teaching. We've known coaches who use scrimmaging as the primary focus of their daily practices, not because their team

---

[2] After losing by a lopsided margin, a college coach was asked by a reporter, "What do you think of your team's execution today?" He thought about it briefly and replied, "I like the idea, but don't you think it's a bit harsh? What if we just run a few extra wind sprints after practice instead?"

needs it but because it's easy and requires little preparation. All you have to do is put 22 players out on the field, 11-v-11, and referee the proceedings. *Don't demand 100 percent from your players while you're taking the easy way out, substituting what is essentially free play for a more organized, instruction-oriented training session.* Whether drilling or scrimmaging, every phase of your training sessions should have specific objectives related to improving your team.

Scrimmaging isn't necessarily a lazy coach's way of avoiding the hard work of preparing a detailed daily practice plan—but it *can* be. Scrimmage all you wish, but not to the extent of overlooking the instructional aspects of your coaching. In a very real sense, coaching *is* teaching; aside from its conditioning value, the only real reason for scrimmaging—or anything else you do in daily practice, for that matter—is to promote your players' learning and make them more effective team players.

INSTALLING YOUR OFFENSE AND DEFENSE

Before attempting to install your offensive/defensive system, you must be absolutely certain in your own mind that it is the best system for your team and players. To achieve such certainty, you must know where your players stand individually and collectively in terms of their skills and understanding of the game; you also must understand whatever system you decide to use well enough to adapt it to your players, answer their questions, and formulate strategies that they can master through practice. Chapters 7 and 8 deal with playing systems and strategies; our concern here is how to install them with your team.

The Whole-Part-Whole Method of Instruction

This tried-and-true teaching method consists of (a) showing the players the complete package in walk-through fashion so they can see how it works, (b) breaking the package down into bite-sized chunks for drill and practice in each separate phase, and (c) putting it back together in scrimmage or controlled-scrimmage situations.

The Walk-Through

We like Bret Simon's[3] phrase, "painting a picture," to describe the coach's efforts to show how a playing system is designed to work. It can start with a brief chalk-talk, offering the players a diagrammed representation of what will be going on. Then, it's onto the field for a slow walk-through, in which the players should be encouraged to ask questions to clarify their understanding of the system. (It is precisely *here* that your system will begin to break down if you don't have total confidence in it, or if you don't really understand it well enough to teach it to your players.)

Breakdown Drills

Breakdown drills are nothing more than the entire system broken down into smaller segments for drill and practice. These, too, should begin as walk-throughs without

---

[3] Men's soccer head coach, Creighton University.

opposition, or at least without aggressive opposition. The tempo and opposition can be increased as the players learn their responsibilities within the respective drills; whenever difficulties arise, the tempo and opposition should be reduced until the problem is identified and corrected, after which they can be stepped up again. The important thing here is to avoid leaping into full-speed, game-intensity conditions before the players understand fully what they're doing. Confusion is a sure sign that learning has been put on hold.

Each phase of the system should be treated in this manner before returning to the whole pattern for practice in scrimmaging or controlled scrimmaging. If the system breaks down, you merely identify the problem and go back to the particular breakdown drill where the problem arises.

And that's it. Admittedly, we're simplifying what in reality may be a lengthy process, but the principles involved really *are* simple if you've taken the time to break down the system into its component parts. That, too, can be a lengthy process, but as our long-time assistant coach, Arthur Graves, likes to point out, "That's why God created the off-season, to give us time to correct this year's mistakes and find ways to avoid them next season."

TIME MANAGEMENT

If we appear somewhat obsessive about how our coaching time is spent, it's because there never seems to be enough time to do all that needs to be done.

When we were young coaches facing the daunting task of building a program from the ground up, we longed for the day when, with a powerful program in place, we'd be able to sit back, take it easy, and watch the wins roll in with little effort on our part. In our youthful naiveté, we assumed that those 18-hour days we were spending building our program would no longer be necessary when we developed an effective feeder program to keep us supplied with skilled players from one season to the next. What we failed to consider was that *staying on top is just as difficult and time-consuming as getting there.* There's always somebody out there who's waiting to catch you if you slow down or slack off. The problems differ at various skills levels, but every team needs thoughtful, careful coaching in order to achieve its potential, whatever it might be.

Time management is the key to team development.

Daily Practice Length

We've already covered the basic concerns regarding time allotments in daily practices: individual fundamentals vs. group activities and competitive drills; drills vs. scrimmaging (or controlled scrimmaging); and offense vs. defense. How you spend your practice time should be determined by your awareness of what your team needs to work on.

Should you highlight a different area for in-depth instruction and drill every day, or should you cover a broad range of areas in less depth? We recommend trying it both ways to see which way works best for you.

Should you make your practices less physically demanding as the season goes on (e.g., by emphasizing technical and tactical aspects of preparation rather than scrimmaging) to save your players' legs for post-season play, or should you have shorter practices? As before, there is no single correct method, but merely the one that works for you.

One coach told us that she once had to confine her daily practices to an hour a day. "It was tough getting everything in, especially early in the year when we had so much to cover," she said, "but all in all, it was a wonderful experience for me as a coach. Every day, working on my practice schedule, I had to look for ways to trim away the fat and make every minute count. It was hard at first because I'd never been what you'd call an organized person, but it didn't take me long to figure out what was important and what was not. I was amazed when I realized how much time I'd been wasting previously in my coaching—not just in soccer but in other sports as well.

"I don't think I'd like to spend my entire career conducting 60-minute daily practices—but I must confess that I learned more about effective and efficient coaching that year than in all my other years combined. The kids loved the short practice sessions—I did, too—and I never had to get on them about hustling in practice, not when every other high school soccer team in the universe was going at it for 2-1/2 hours every afternoon.

"I still like the idea of cutting back our practice schedule to 90 minutes or less as we get closer to the playoffs; it keeps the kids fresh mentally as well as physically, and that's a point I think a lot of us in coaching overlook: the mental staleness that can set in late in the season if you let it. When players get stale, they lose their concentration, develop bad habits, and make mistakes that a more sharply focused team wouldn't make. So whenever I feel it happening, I'll go back to a 60- or 75-minute practice format to get us back on track."

The keys to having successful short practices, she said, are to (a) keep the players actively involved every second, (b) keep a clock on everything you do, and (c) accept nothing less from the players than total mental involvement and physical effort. Regarding (c), the coach explained that she gives her players a choice of how they will proceed: "I tell them, *We can either do it the quick-and-easy way, giving me everything you've got for 60 minutes a day, or we can do it the long, hard way and practice for 2-1/2 hours a day.* It doesn't take Einstein's clone to figure out that going to war for me for 60 minutes a day is better, especially since they already know that, for me, at least, there's no such thing as an easy practice."

The Mechanics of Daily Practice

Some things never change. We *always* allot 5 minutes of practice time for jogging, 10 minutes for stretching exercises, 15 minutes for fast footwork drills and keeper work, and 10 minutes for two-man moving drills involving passing, receiving, heading, and the like. Everything else is negotiable.

With an unskilled or inexperienced team, the bulk of your daily practice time should be devoted to basic skills development. Harking back to our files we find that, in 1984 when we were getting started in soccer coaching, only 20 percent of our typical 2-1/2 hour daily practice session (see Figure 10-1, p. 00) was devoted to team aspects of the game; the rest consisted of warmups, stretching exercises, and conditioning; passing and receiving, dribbling, heading, chest and thigh work, and shooting drills; and 1-v-1 offensive moves and defense.

With a more experienced team, in which fundamental skills range from good to superior, individual skills work can be concentrated into correspondingly smaller time blocks, thereby freeing up time for team and group drills and activities, tactical considerations, and other aspects of team preparation.

FIGURE 11–2
BASIC DAILY PRACTICE FORMAT, GHS VARSITY BOYS' SOCCER

4:00-4:05   Jogging (3 laps around soccer field)

4:05-4:15   Stretching exercises

4:15-4:30   Fast footwork drills (keeper work separate)

4:30-4:40   2-man drills: 1-touch instep, 1-touch inside foot, 1-touch outside foot, thigh-instep pass, chest-instep pass, headers

4:40-6:20   Net drill, 4 circuits (10 min.)
Corner kicks, offense and defense (10 min.)
Dead ball sets, offense and defense (10 min.)
3-v-3 micro soccer w/small goals, 4 games (9 min.)
4-v-4 micro soccer w/small goals, 4 games (9 min.)
5-v-5 micro soccer w/small goals, 2 games (9 min.)
6-v-6 micro soccer w/small goals, 2 games (9 min.)
11-v-11 scrimmaging/controlled scrimmaging (19 min.)
5-v-5 Big Dog soccer w/regulation goals and keeper (9 min.)
Technical/tactical work (e.g., new drills, analysis of opponents' playing style and strategies, walk-throughs, etc.), three times a week
Water breaks (3 @ 2 min. each)

6:20-6:25   Conditioning

6:25-6:30   Cool down

Figure 11-2 shows our basic daily practice format for a recent year with a team ranked No. 5 in the state in preseason polls. Even a cursory glance at Figure 11-2 reveals vastly different practice goals from nearly one and a half decades earlier, especially in its greater emphasis on (and time allotment for) competitive activities in large *and* small groups.

As we noted earlier, much of our practice schedule is highly flexible. In addition to changing the order of activities in the large 4:40-6:20 time block, we may also borrow time from one or more activities or even delete them entirely, if necessary, in order to add new drills or highlight areas such as tactical changes in our playing style or game plan. (We normally do tactical work three days a week.) The key word here is *borrow*, since allowance must be made for whatever we add to our practice schedule. No matter how we allot our time in that slot, it has to total 100 minutes out of a 150-minute practice session.

The practice schedule shown in Figure 11-2 does not include tactical work or game preparations; on those days, we either subtract, say, two minutes from each of the other areas' time allotments or eliminate one of the activities for that day. While either way is acceptable, the latter is easier to keep up with.

A Different Slant on Breakdown Drills

As you'll recall, breakdown drills are used to teach an offensive or defensive system by breaking them down into their component segments for drill and practice. Some coaches take the process a step farther, breaking down their opponents' systems into isolated segments for drill and practice.

"Usually," a coach explained, "we'll pick out one or two of our most important opponents, scout them long before we play them, break down their offense or defense and throw a few of those drill segments into our daily practices. Sometimes, we don't even identify the opponent initially when we practice its breakdown drills, but use the drills merely as breaks in routine from our regular practice activities. And later, when our game with that opponent is coming up, our players will be familiar with that system and will have no trouble understanding what we plan to do to counteract their strategies."

In most cases, the coach hastened to add, the process is not as difficult or time-consuming as it might appear. Since most coaches tend to stay with the same system from one year to the next, the same breakdown drills can be used every year—provided, of course, that the team doesn't change coaches. Whereas new coaches almost always install their own playing systems, returning coaches tend to stay with what has worked for them in the past, because they believe in their system and the players understand it. In 99 cases out of 100, you can bet that, when a coach makes radical changes in his playing system, it's because a radical personnel change has occurred that necessitated the switch. Learning a new playing system from scratch is *not* the sort of thing that coaches want to inflict on their players.

Even a cursory scouting report on the opponent in question will reveal whether the coach has changed playing systems. If you keep detailed files on your opponents—including the breakdown drills you used this year—you'll have no trouble keeping on top of the situation.

DAILY PRACTICE: FINAL THOUGHTS

The brash young coach—we'll call him Coach A—managed to insinuate himself into a private conversation between two well-known soccer coaches at a coaches' convention. "You know," he told them, "I've always wanted to coach a team like yours."

Coaches B and C exchanged brief, *Who-is-this-guy?*, *Is-he-a-friend-of-yours?* glances. Neither seemed to know who he was.

"You know, it's funny you said that: I've always wanted to be an astronaut," Coach B responded quickly.

"Not me," Coach C replied, catching his drift. "I'd get airsick up there where there's no air. I'd rather be a billionaire playboy with a yacht and a private jet."

Coach B turned to the young man, smiling, and said: "We're kidding, of course." Then, lowering his voice to a confiding whisper, he added, "As a matter of fact, you *can* have a team like ours, if you hurry. I get most of my players from a little shop in Baltimore called Soccer Players 'R' Us, and when I was in there last month, they still had a few all-State players in stock."

Coach C shook his head. "Forget it; they're already gone. I was in there the day before yesterday, and all they had left was a couple of all-City players from Phoenix. But maybe you'll get lucky the way I did; I picked up my keeper for practically nothing at a yard sale last year."

Although the veteran coaches were unnecessarily harsh in their treatment of an admiring, envious—and somewhat overzealous—young coach, the fact remains: Unless you believe that superior players arise spontaneously rather than being developed through thousands of hours of concentrated practice, you'll see the wisdom inherent in the old coaching adage *you play the way you practice*. Daily practice is the vehicle through which young players learn to execute the fundamental skills that all superior players possess.

On our freshman and jayvee teams, the coach devotes 80 percent of every practice session to working on individual fundamentals—fast footwork drills, dribbling, passing, receiving, shooting, defense, and the like—and only about 10 percent to team concepts and strategy. The same percentages should hold true for rec league and club-level practices; if you spend your time scrimmaging with 6- to 12-year-olds, you're depriving them of many hours of valuable instructional time.

While a certain amount of learning will occur in your formal practices, most of the players' skills development will in fact occur outside of practice and games, in the informal, backyard practicing they do on their own time. But they won't know what to practice, or how to execute the skills properly, unless you take time *every day* to teach them what they need to know. The enthusiasm, determination, and patience you bring to your teaching will go far in determining how quickly your players develop.

The process of developing skilled players is slow and tedious, and there are no shortcuts. Expecting young players to absorb team strategies and playing styles when they haven't mastered the fundamentals is like expecting students to master differential calculus when they haven't had first-year algebra. That is why many coaches fall by the wayside while others "advance confidently in the direction of their dreams," as Thoreau put it.

If you have the enthusiasm, determination, and patience to teach skills *every day*, especially on those days when you don't feel like doing it, you will, over a period of time, develop highly skilled players and teams while less dedicated coaches will drop out of coaching because, as we once overheard a soon-to-be ex-coach complain, "How am I supposed to coach these kids? They don't know a thing about soccer!"

Finally: Having taken time to prepare daily practice schedules, you should extend the process by (a) evaluating your practices and (b) filing your practice schedules for future reference. Even if you don't use the same practice schedules from one year to the next, you may want to refer to them for various reasons, and you can't do that if you throw them away. (You should also keep drills files, preferably broken down by category; if you do this, remember to keep a record of the bad drills as well as the good ones, so you won't repeat earlier mistakes.)

In evaluating your daily practices, it is important to note, not just what worked and what didn't, but why. It's not enough to chalk up every bad practice or bad drill to "player apathy"—and in our case, at least, it's usually not accurate. Most of our "bad" drills have been those we designed ourselves but either didn't think through properly or failed to teach properly. At any rate, the best time to evaluate your practices is right after they're over, in the privacy of the coaches' office. If you have assistant coaches, solicit their input and *use it* in considering ways to make tomorrow's practice effective.

Chapter 12

GAME PREPARATIONS

There is nothing like a soccer game. A full stadium, thousands of banners, the ball shining white ahead, a sure kick, goal. I love it!

—Pele

SCOUTING

Scouting is time-consuming, and it can be expensive as well, especially if you aren't reimbursed for mileage, meals, and so forth. Scouting is, however, a natural and necessary part of game preparation; the more you know about your opponents, the more likely you'll be to find ways to defeat them. Even if you've scouted or played a team many times in the past, you still must see them in action prior to playing them in the current year—if for no other reason than to verify that their coach, system, playing style, and impact players haven't changed since the last time you played them.

Some coaches feel that, with a strong team that is capable of dominating most opponents, scouting isn't necessary, since they intend to make opponents play the game their way. While we'll concede that the changes in game plans and preparations that strong teams make are generally minor rather than major, we prefer to know as much as possible about *every* opponent in order to be ready for whatever they intend to throw at us. The old adage, "Forewarned is forearmed," is a good one to follow where scouting is concerned.

Scouting a soccer match is far different from scouting, say, a football game, in which every action sequence is planned in advance and announced in the huddle. Soccer is a fluid game involving eleven players using their skills and creativity to make space for themselves or deny it to opposing attackers. You won't see many set plays *per se* in soccer, except in dead ball situations. The number of attackers is likely to vary with every possession, depending on where the ball is and who is in position to attack. Defenses generally don't change much from one possession to the next, but defensive players can and do occasionally join the attack by making runs through the defense.

What Teams Should You Scout?

The answer to this question isn't always as simple or obvious as it may appear. For starters, scout the teams on the current year's schedule. Even so, regardless of whether you do all the scouting yourself or delegate some of the scouting among your assistant coaches, you'll probably have to prioritize your scouting needs. And what might those priorities be?

1. *Scout your early season opponents, with your next opponent having highest priority.* Exceptions exist, but it's not always necessary to scout teams two months in advance of playing them, particularly if more pressing needs exist. Many (if not most) teams are still in the process of finding their identity early in the season; their style and system may expand considerably by the time you play them a month or so later.

   Too, there is the inescapable fact that the most important game on your schedule is the next one, no matter who's lurking farther down the road. And while this isn't to say that you should follow your schedule in lock-step fashion in your scouting, since other priorities may take precedence, we simply remind you that you win or lose games one at a time, and your upcoming opponents should not be overlooked.

2. *Scout the teams you need to defeat in order to achieve your goals for this year's team.* In many cases, traditional rivalries take precedence over other games. We've known of many instances over the years in which coaches have been fired or replaced because they couldn't defeat a hated rival school. It shouldn't be that way, of course, but if it is, then *that's* where your scouting should begin.

   Another consideration in prioritizing your scouting involves the fact that, in most areas, post-season tournament entries and pairings are based on regular season records in region or subregion play. If so, then those opponents should be a higher scouting priority than the nonregion opponents on your schedule. If you don't have enough open dates to scout all of your opponents before you play them—and you probably won't—scout your region or subregion opponents in order to give your team its best chance of finishing as high as possible in league standings at the end of regular season play.

When our program was young and our teams were weak, we seldom bothered to scout the best teams in our region prior to playing them; rather, we used our games with them as scouting reports for future matches and concentrated instead on scouting the region or subregion teams that we had a realistic chance of defeating—or at least competing with.

If you've coached at the same school for several years, you'll generally know who has what and which players you should look for. We coach at the club level as well as coaching our varsity team—and most of our varsity players play at the club level as well—so we (and they) are familiar with the best players on the teams we play. In most cases, before playing a team, we're already familiar with what their best players can and cannot do.

The coaches in our region exchange schedules every year; we even draw up a master schedule of all region and subregion games to be distributed to all coaches. This practice is of inestimable value in coordinating our scouting schedules.

If, in reviewing the upcoming year's schedule, all you can see is two or three possible wins, then *those* games are—with the possible exception of traditional rivalries—the most important games on your schedule. Win them, and your players will gain confidence in their ability to win at least occasionally; lose them, and you may never be able to convince your players that they can defeat *any* opponent.

A veteran coach suggests prioritizing your scouting needs with a team of low to average ability as follows:

1. Scout the opponents on your schedule who are demonstrably weaker than your own team. These are the games you absolutely, positively *must* win (because you're supposed to win them).

2. Scout the opponents who are roughly equal in ability to your team. Assuming that you win all of your matches against weaker opponents, these games probably will determine whether your team has a winning season.

3. Scout the opponents who are stronger than your team. These are the games that separate the superior teams from those of average ability. While you cannot logically expect to defeat superior teams consistently, the ability to do so at least occasionally is a good indicator of the progress your team is making toward what you want it to become.

4. With a strong team, ignore step 1 and scout those opponents who are equal (or superior) to your team first.

   In scouting strong teams (assuming that their system hasn't changed since the last time we played them) we'll focus primarily on individual players—which players they like to go to (or avoid); how they set up their attacks, defense, and dead ball sets; their strengths and weaknesses; who is likely to beat us (and how); and who possesses individual weaknesses that we might be able to exploit.

   Our guiding principle here is that *success is a ladder:* Winning breeds confidence that takes you up a rung at a time, and failure generates doubt that will bring you down. If you win the games you expect to win, your players will gain confidence that will, in turn, elevate their play to higher levels in the future. Lose those same games, and the intensity of your players' efforts against stronger opponents is likely to decline in direct proportion to their expectations of winning those games.

5. With a strong team—one that you can reasonably expect to make the state tournament—scout opponents that you're likely to meet in post-season play.

These guidelines aren't infallible, since your priorities may differ from ours or other coaches'. And that's all right, too, as long as you take time to consider your own priorities in light of what scouting can do for your team.

Indirect Scouting

While it's important to see your opponents play, it's not always feasible. Indirect scouting refers to gathering information about your opponents without actually having seen them play this season. Although such information is likely to be at best incomplete and less valid than that gleaned by direct methods of scouting, it can supplement your other sources of information and give you hints about what to expect and how to prepare your team.

Your first indirect sources are likely to be those closest to home, that is, last year's scouting reports, game plan evaluations, and videotapes. They will, of course, be most helpful when the opponent in question has the same coach and an established playing style and system that doesn't change much from one year to the next. Regardless, however, those sources should provide information about individual players and their strengths, weaknesses, habits, and tendencies, and should indicate what worked—and what didn't work—against that team last year.

Newspapers are another source of indirect information about opposing teams. The sports section of your local or metro area newspaper may carry pre-season previews of all the teams in your area. While you may not want to believe everything you read therein, you can double-check for accuracy by comparing the write-ups to your scouting reports and game plans from last season. At the very least, you'll find out who's returning and who's new to the team.

Finally, you can talk with other coaches about common opponents. This is, in fact, the most popular form of indirect scouting among coaches. While rival coaches may be understandably reluctant to talk about their own teams except in general—and usually negative—terms, most of them will discuss other teams if asked. Be advised, though, that the way they perceive a given opponent will reflect their own teams' relative success against that team. To a coach whose team is exceedingly weak, most other teams are powerhouses. (The same holds true for strong teams, only in reverse.)

Direct Scouting

Being there is the second best way to scout an opponent. (The best way is to videotape them while you're scouting them.)

It's important to bear in mind in direct scouting that what you're watching involves two teams other than your own. The nonscouted team may differ markedly from yours in ability, style of play, and other ways, and what works (or doesn't work) for that team may or may not have any bearing on what your team can or should do when you play the team you're scouting. You should, therefore, approach your direct scouting from two angles.

First, you want to record as much as you can of what the team is doing—its playing system, strategies, and individual and team tendencies. At the same time, keep a critical eye on how your own team and players might stack up against that opponent—what might work, what might *not* work, possible individual matchups, and so on. You can't really guess what they might do against your team since, if the coach knows you're there scouting her team, she may try to hide as many of her strategies and players as she can get away with, depending on the strength of her present opponent. We've known coaches to bench their starters (or play them out of position) against weak teams to prevent us from seeing what they do best—and we've done the same thing ourselves, because it's good coaching to do so when you can get away with it.

We normally spend the early part of the game trying to get down as much as possible while the outcome of the game is still in the balance. We want detailed information here because now, more than at any other time in the game, we're likely to see the opponents' basic game plan—their preferred system for establishing control or dominance of opponents.

Assuming that the game remains relatively close, we'll record changes the team being scouted makes in playing system, style, and strategies—noting when such changes occurred and why they might have been necessary. (In a competitive match, such changes are likely to constitute the team's secondary, or *contingency*, game plan—what they go to when their basic game plan doesn't produce the desired results.) We'll also continue to study individual players, and their strengths, weaknesses, and tendencies that may affect our matchups with them.

Scouting Tips

1. Call the host school or coach on game day to verify the game date, starting time, and location. It may save you from making a trip to a game that's been postponed, canceled, or moved to another playing site.

2. Check your scouting necessities (e.g., road maps, coaching pass, clipboards, sharpened pencils, scouting forms) before going to—and returning home from—your scouting trip.

3. If possible, take someone (an assistant coach, spouse, etc.) along to help you gather information, especially if you're scouting both teams. Two pairs of eyes see twice as much detail, and the other person can help in keeping whatever stats you need. It's also helpful to use the time driving home to discuss what you've seen.

   An alternative to this approach to scouting is to divide your scouting responsibilities among yourself and the assistant coaches on your staff (i.e., by scouting two or more games at different locations on the same night); that way, you can get two or three times as much scouting done in the same amount of time. If you do it this way, be sure to tell your assistant coaches exactly what information to collect—the scouting forms in Appendixes M through P should be helpful here—and how to collect it, especially if they are new to soccer or coaching. The best way to teach inexperienced coaches how to scout is to take them along with you on a couple of scouting trips. It may also prove helpful to have the same coaches scout the same teams every year.

4. Get to the game site early, and find a comfortable seat that is high enough to afford a clear view of the action. We prefer to sit by ourselves and away from other spectators, the band, and the student cheering sections; in most cases, this means sitting on the visitors' side of the field.

5. Purchase a game program and keep it for your files. If the program features photos of the players, it will help you in identifying them later, since you can't always depend on their wearing the same uniform numbers in home and away games. Too, the lineup section of the program may indicate the players' grade levels; such information will be helpful the following year.

6. Sometime prior to the game, review any other scouting reports you have on the team, including the one from the previous year if the head coach is the same one.

   If you don't have any previous scouting reports on this team—or if the team's playing system has changed since the last time you scouted them—you should do a comprehensive scouting report; otherwise, you can merely supplement earlier reports (i.e., verifying previously noted systems and strategies and adding new information as it is noted).

You can also use the time before the game starts to note such things as field conditions, lighting, field dimensions, and individual characteristics (see Appendix M).

7. Treat scouting as a professional responsibility, not as an occasion for socializing with other coaches. The time for socializing is when you've seen all that you need to see regarding the opponents, their playing system, and associated strategies. Until that point is reached, don't be lulled into shirking your responsibilities to your team by the presence of coaches from other schools. Just because another coach isn't paying attention to the game doesn't mean that you shouldn't be.

If the game is one-sided, you may be tempted to leave early in order to avoid the post-game traffic. Our rules of thumb here are *(a) Don't leave before or during halftime,* and *(b) Don't leave while the scouted team's starters are still in the game.* In the former case, the trailing team may stage a terrific comeback; if so, you need to see what adjustments the coach makes; and in the latter case, the coach may want to try out plays or tactics that the team has been working on in daily practice.

The same rules of thumb apply to close games. Additionally, staying to the conclusion may reveal the scouted team's late-game strategies, and indicate how well the players handle pressure situations.

Preparing Your Scouting Report

The forms in Appendixes M-P are meant to streamline and simplify your preparation of a written scouting report. To use the checklists in organizing and analyzing your scouting notes, simply place checkmarks in the appropriate boxes, respond to those questions as fully as possible, and ignore the rest.

Your scouting report should contain the following information:

1. *General information.* Scouted team/opponent, location, date, score of game (by halves), weather, field conditions, lighting, field size (approx.).

2. *Overall evaluation.* A general statement of how the team plays—its strengths and weaknesses, overall team speed and skills level, preferred playing tempo, playing systems (offense and defense), and basic strategies.

3. *Individual players.* Profiles of each of the starters' and mainline subs' strengths, weaknesses, and playing preferences. Be specific and detailed here; this information will guide your players in carrying out their individual matchup responsibilities.

4. *Team offense.* How they set up their fast breaks (if at all), build their attacks, and attempt to penetrate and set up shots in the attacking third.

5. *Team defense.* How they respond to transitions, how well they retreat to cover fast breaks, and how they play their zone or man-to-man defense in their defensive half of the field.

6. *Dead ball tactics.* (i.e., kickoffs, throw-ins, goal kicks, corner kicks, indirect and direct free kicks, and penalty kicks). List and describe all set plays and/or strategies in each category.

If you don't prepare written game plans for every upcoming opponent—or if you combine your scouting reports and game plan into one package to save man-hours of labor on your part—be sure to indicate exactly what you want your team and each individual player to know and to do. It's usually better—but not absolutely necessary—to separate the two, using scouting reports to describe the opponent, and game plans to describe how you stack up against them and what you intend to do against them.

With the exception of point 2, all information contained in your scouting report should be as specific and detailed as possible, with diagrams to supplement the text as necessary. After all, if you don't use written game plans, your scouting reports will be the only study guide available to your players regarding what the team and its individual players do and how they attempt to do it. (You could, of course, use chalk-talks to show and tell your players everything you gleaned from your scouting trip, but a scouting report will last longer and can be studied by the players prior to the game.)

GAME PLANNING

Coaches need game plans for the same reason that generals need battle plans, that is, to remind them of what must be done and how to do it.

With a powerful team composed of experienced and highly skilled players, your basic game plan probably won't change much from one game to the next, but even then, your planning should take into account what to do if Mr. Murphy (of Murphy's Law fame) makes an unscheduled appearance and things fall apart. Called *contingency planning*, this practice of anticipating and preparing for the unexpected can save you untold grief if you apply it to every game you play.

Let's not put the cart before the horse, though; *first* comes basic game planning, and *then* contingency planning.

Your Basic Game Plan

All of us, if we had our druthers, would druther play games *our* way, at *our* best pace and with *our* team dictating the flow of games, if not the final score. That things don't always work out that way goes without saying; still, that's where game planning begins—with your basic game plan for defeating and/or controlling opponents on your terms, not theirs.

Installing your basic game plan should begin early in preseason practice. Ideally, it will conclude prior to your first game; if not, you'll have to use your early-season daily practices to get everything in. Only then can you afford to go on to other priorities, such as refining your offense or defense or considering what to do if opponents are able to take you out of your basic game plan.

How long it takes to install your system will depend on your players' familiarity with it. Obviously, then, your most difficult period will be immediately after taking over a new program or changing to a system that is new to your players.

Conditioning should be your top pre- and early-season priority; assuming that you've properly conditioned your players toward a target goal of, say, playing all-out for two hours rather than 90 minutes, your next priority is installing your playing system. At the same time, the players still must work on individual skills and small-group drills and activities emphasizing soccer fundamentals—starting with the basics and working up to advanced skills levels. Such work should proceed faster at the varsity level than with jayvee or ninth-grade players.

Before progressing beyond the basics of individual and team play, your players should understand your basic game plan well enough to play any position on the field. Only when such mastery is achieved are you and your players ready to proceed to the next phase of game planning.

Contingency Planning

Unfortunately, we have thus far omitted one very large factor in your planning, namely, *the opponents.* They have a game plan, too, and the game will revolve around the efforts of the two teams to impose their will on each other in order to achieve dominance. Thus, your basic game plan must be modified, however slightly, to include, not just what your team does best, but also *what you think the opponents will try to do to stop you from doing it.* These two elements are synthesized by analyzing your own playing system, players, and tactics and attempting to determine, via analysis of scouting reports, how successful the opponents are likely to be in negating your plans or imposing their own plans on your team. If you aren't sure how to proceed, you can always stick with your original game plan and make changes as necessity dictates in the game itself. You should understand that if you make anything more than minor changes in your game plan, such as altering individual matchups, then those changes become your basic game plan *for that game;* and if those changes don't work, your best bet is likely to be going back to your original game plan.

Changes are made to enhance individual and team performances. If the changes don't work, you have the options of going back to what you do best or trying something new and different that the opponents may not be ready for. The latter is likely to work, if at all, only if your players are comfortable with what they're doing.

Either of two factors may arise that require changes in your basic game plan. First, the size—especially the width—of the playing fields you'll encounter may vary considerably from one game to the next; and second, your original game plan may not be sufficient to control opponents or deter them from doing what they do best.

Adjustments for Wide or Narrow Playing Fields

Under FIFA rules, soccer pitches may range anywhere from 50–100 yards wide. Many high schools play their soccer games on football fields measuring roughly 53 yards wide; many others—the lucky ones—use pitches designed especially for soccer. Such facilities are usually much wider than football fields. The difference between the two can be considerable, often as much as 15–25 yards, and will have an impact on the way the game is played. Your team should be prepared for either contingency.

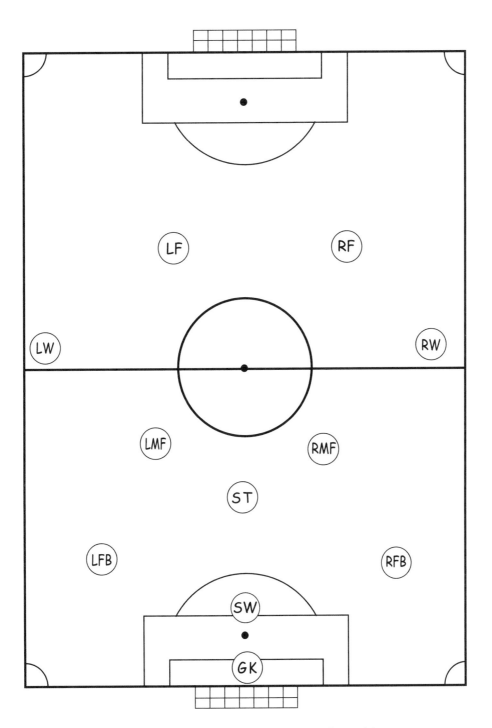

FIGURE 12–1. 4-4-2 on a Wide Field

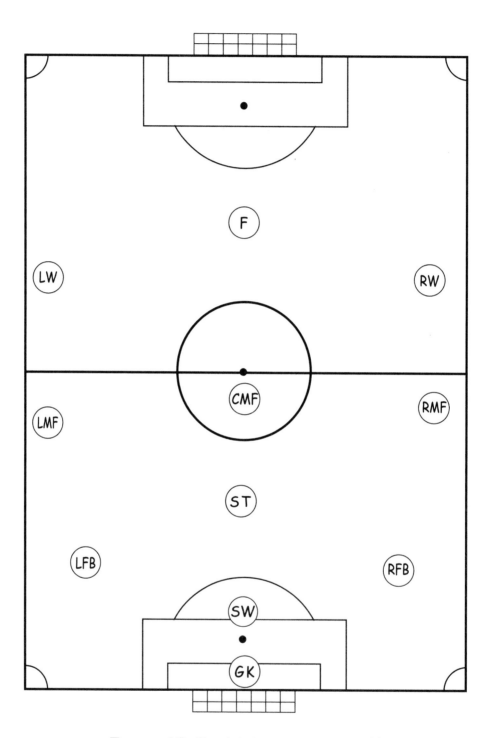

FIGURE 12-2. 4-3-3 on a Narrow Field

Let's assume for the moment that you're fortunate enough to play your home matches on a pitch measuring 120 yards × 70 yards—and let us assume further that, like ours, your basic system of play is a rather conservative 4-4-2, featuring two forwards up front and four midfielders behind them (Figure 12-1). Knowing from scouting that your next game will be played on a football field, you can prepare for it by (a) scrimmaging on a field with cones laid out to mark the narrower touchlines, and (b) adjusting your offensive game plan by switching from two forwards to three and deploying three midfielders instead of four (Figure 12-2). The adjustment may be necessary if you're running a 42 attack, because there's less room between the touchlines to create space using two forwards and four midfielders in your attack. (It *can* be done, of course, since many teams do it that way, but it's not easy to spread a defense on a football-width playing field.[1] We think it's easier to spread the defense and create space for your attackers by changing the alignment from 4-4-2 to 4-3-3.)

Since most of the difficulties associated with playing on a narrow field arise in (but are not confined to) the midfield third, we prefer that our defenders play long balls up to the wingers and forwards on football fields, bypassing the midfield area entirely and forcing the opposing fullbacks to stop us.

Other adjustments that might be made to accommodate a narrow field include treating throw-ins like corner kicks in the attacking and defensive thirds, and giving your goalkeeper additional practice time working on goal kicks, punts, and corner kicks.

Regarding throw-ins on a narrow field, in the attacking third, we want our players to throw the ball into the 18 (box area) and force the keeper to make saves in the air. Since the opponents are likely to use the same strategy against us in our defensive third, it is imperative that our defenders treat throw-ins into our box like incoming missiles, going all-out to win all air balls and clear the ball out of danger.

Here's a sad—for us, at least—reminder of how important throw-ins can be on narrow fields: With the 1996 Georgia AAAA State Championship game being played on a regulation football field, we held a 3–1 lead with 18 minutes left in the game, only to see the opponents score *two* goals from long throw-ins. We actually won the second throw-in that led to the tying score, but our clearing pass went to an opponent, who drilled the ball past our keeper. We eventually lost the game when, with 1:38 remaining, an opposing attacker's shot hit the crossbar and rebounded back to him for an easy header that our keeper never had a chance at. Those two goals that allowed the opponents to catch up with us never would have happened that way on an authentic soccer pitch, since the throw-ins could not have reached the box.

Extending or Adjusting Your System

Which comes first, the system or the players? The players, of course. You have to use a system that your players can master, or nothing else you do will be effective. But what do you do on those (hopefully infrequent) occasions when your players cannot make the system work the way it's intended to? It's simple; you either make adjustments, large or small, in your original game plan, or else you lose games that you might have won.

---

[1] Strategically speaking, this suggests that, if your team is unskilled or inexperienced, it will be to your advantage to play your home matches on a football field.

You want your changes or adjustments to be minor because—almost without exception—a coach's making major changes in playing style once the season has begun is a sure sign of desperation. First, it's an admission of failure; not only is what the team currently doing not working, but the coach is convinced that it won't work in the foreseeable future, even with minor adjustments. Second, major changes represent a significant amount of time already wasted learning a system that doesn't—and won't—work, and additional time spent learning a new system that may not work, either. Your time—and that of your players—could better have been devoted to other things.

A change in playing style or system is "major" if it takes the players far beyond what they understand or are comfortable doing—for example, switching from a conservative to an aggressive attacking style, or switching to zone (or man-to-man) defense if the players have never played it before. Such tactical changes are best made, if at all, during the off-season, and taught from the first day of preseason practice.

In discussing adjustments in playing style with young coaches, we always tell them, *If the urge suddenly comes upon you to make wholesale changes in your game plan that your team might not be ready for, the first thing to do is sit down, take a few deep breaths and count to ten—and then try to find a less drastic solution to your problem.* Like getting married, buying a house, or hiding taxable income from the IRS, tossing out your current game plan in favor of something radically new and different to your players is too risky to be entered into lightly.

On the other hand, every coach makes minor adjustments in the game plan—altering alignments to intensify defensive coverage in certain areas or change points of attack offensively, switching players around in the alignment, or adding new wrinkles to the defense or offense. Sometimes the adjustments arise during game planning or as the result of having scouted the opponent, and sometimes they occur during the heat of the game itself. Sometimes the adjustments work, and sometimes they don't. As carnival barkers tell their customers, *You pays your money and you takes your chances.* The important thing to remember about adjustments in your game plan is that, if they are to be successful, they should be built upon what your players already know.

Late-Season Adjustments

The term *late-season* can refer either to preparations for post-season play or to playing a team for the second (or third, etc.) time in a season.

Coaches are divided in their opinions regarding the need for resting players to save their legs for the playoffs. Many coaches believe that, since the legs contain the most powerful muscles in the human body, once properly conditioned they should be capable of carrying players through a season's worth of games and daily practices without requiring additional rest as the playoffs draw near. Many other coaches contend that, to keep legs fresh (and possibly attitudes, as well), players should be rested whenever possible in late-season games.

Although we don't know which side is right (except in the sense that the team that wins the games evidently made the right decisions), we tend to side with coaches in the latter group since, unlike the "Big Three" American sports, soccer isn't a seasonal activity. Many of our players play soccer all year round. Thus, we offer a couple of ways to save wear and tear on your players' legs if it's important to you.

You can, of course, substitute freely in blowouts regardless of which end of the score your team is on—but if you want to substantially reduce the players' running, you can also shorten your daily practices or cut down on your full-field scrimmaging. Shortening your practice sessions by an hour a day can reduce the players' running by several hours per week, depending on how many games you play in a given week and how often and long you scrimmage. Even if you don't shorten your practices, when you factor in daily time spent practicing such necessities as ballhandling, footwork, dribbling, shooting, and passing drills—as well as conducting walk-throughs of opponents' offenses and defenses and your game plan for countering what the opponents do best—you're likely to conclude that at least part of your normal scrimmaging time will have to go.

The Second Time Around

When you're preparing for a team you've already played, you have in your possession the best possible scouting report you could hope for. Having played them previously in the season and evaluated the results of your game plan,[2] you should know what worked and what needs changing next time around.

The old adage, *If it works, don't fix it*, is good advice if you won convincingly last time. You'll probably want to show the opponents something new this time, though, just to give them something to think about. (That's why you might want to avoid showing them everything you've got the first time around, if you can do so without jeopardizing your chances of winning.) As before, your changes should be related to what you're already doing, or else your own players may be more confused than the opponents.

If your last game with them was relatively close, you can either go with the same game plan and hope that your players can execute it well enough to win, or add such new wrinkles as you can muster that your players can master.

If your team was thoroughly drubbed last time, things get sticky. Obviously, major changes are called for—but if your team is exceedingly weak, major changes are scary since *any* changes you make, even minor ones, will take your players farther away from what they are comfortable doing. The best we can say here is that, if you played conservatively last time and were still thrashed soundly, *play even more conservatively this time around*. Play the entire game as if you were defensing corner kicks if you must, but *don't* play it the opponents' way and at their pace. (Realistically, you might have nine or ten defenders playing deep—and if you're bound to do something major to avoid a second shellacking, switch from man-to-man to zone defense or vice versa.

QUESTIONS AND ANSWERS REGARDING GAME PLANS

❒ *Is it important to prepare a different game plan for every game?* Only if what you intend to do next time is (a) different from what you've been doing, (b) likely to be misunderstood by the players or forgotten by the coaches, or (c) complex.

---

[2] A reproducible Game Plan Evaluation form to be filled out after the game has been played appears in Appendix R.

If nothing more than what you've been doing (including contingencies) is planned—and if your players understand that plan—you may be inclined to use your previous game plan and rely on your scouting reports for information on individual opponents.

We *do* feel, however, that it's important for the head coach to have a written game plan available—whether for use by the players or by himself of herself.

❐ *How detailed should my game plan be? How should it be organized?* Your game plan should be long enough to cover the subject. If brevity is important, use diagrams rather than text wherever possible. As for organization, a simple four-section outline should suffice: team goals; team offense; team defense; and dead ball sets (offense and defense), or you can use the reproducible Game Plan form in Appendix Q. (The blank pitch diagrams included in this appendix are helpful.)

❐ *How should I present the game plan to my team?* Coaches use any or all of several techniques, the most common being walk-throughs in daily practice and audio-visual presentations (chalk-talks or discussions) at team meetings. Your players should be thoroughly familiar with their individual responsibilities within your game plan before they enter the pregame locker room.

❐ *What else should I keep in mind?* Three things: First, if you use a written game plan, have it laminated for use on the field (in case it rains). Second, don't let the game plan out of your sight for a second once you're out on the field (especially at road games), unless you don't mind having it wind up in the hands of the opposing coach. Third, remember that a game plan is a guide to action, not a set of laws that must be followed at all costs. Sometimes you have to follow your instincts.

Chapter 13

FILLING IN THE GAPS

Economists report that a college education adds many thousands
of dollars to a man's lifetime income—which he then spends sending
his son to college.

—Bill Vaughan

Technically, the off-season for a varsity team begins when its participation in regular season and tournament games is concluded. For many coaches and many players, however, the end of the varsity or jayvee soccer season is a transition period, not a time for rest and relaxation. That transition may be either to coaching or playing at the club level or to participating in the ensuing sport season, whatever it may be.

We have mixed feelings about youngsters' playing soccer year-round. On the one hand, the participation itself is wholesome, keeps players in close association with other, similarly dedicated, players, and permits continuous development of their soccer skills under the supervision of experienced, knowledgeable coaches. On the other hand, playing year-round denies players the opportunity to rest and revitalize themselves mentally and physically from the rigors of the season—and it increases the chances of their becoming burned out at an early age.

That's not our decision, though, is it? Kids who want to play soccer in the off-season, *will* play, and we can't really complain about it, given the far less savory alternatives that idle minds might find to occupy their time.

Other players will go from soccer to the next sport in line, and that's not all bad, either. Occasionally, coaches of other sports have tried to persuade our players to forsake soccer for *their* sport, but with little success in most cases. Our players enjoy the familylike atmosphere that exists on our teams. We'd rather our players be involved in soccer or another school sport than for them to lose the Team atmosphere entirely until the next varsity soccer season rolls around.

The problem is even more complex for coaches, for whom financial or professional considerations may take priority. While you'd probably prefer to coach your school soccer team and no others, taking on other coaching responsibilities brings in supplemental income to help you remain at least marginally financially solvent. In many cases it's a moot point anyway, since the conditions for your being hired in the first place may have included coaching sports other than soccer.

Beyond that, the summer months are virtually the only time that full-time coaches can pursue advanced degrees or renew their teaching certification via course work. For other coaches, summertime offers the opportunity to pull in a few extra bucks to pay for things like Dustin's braces, Mandi's class trip, or repairs to the family auto. If you manage to avoid taking summer courses or getting a job, you'll probably be involved in soccer in some manner, whether conducting (or working at) a summer camp, working with your local club teams, officiating rec league games, attending clinics or conventions, reading about soccer, or preparing for next year's soccer season.

One thing is for sure: No soccer coach ever dies of boredom. Boredom is a luxury that most soccer coaches not only can't afford but can't even imagine.

POST-SEASON RESPONSIBILITIES

There never seems to be enough time available for everything that needs to be done. If you coach more than one sport, the end of one season heralds the beginning of the next, and if you aren't organized, things can pile up like unwashed laundry on a holiday weekend. Two organizational guidelines can help to make your post-season responsibilities manageable: *making lists of things to do,* and *doing as much of your post-season work in advance as you can find time for during the season.*

Listing (and Prioritizing) the Work to Be Done

Memories are fallible; lists are not, if you can remember where you put them. As early as possible, begin thinking about what must be done during your post-season, write down everything that comes to mind, and then prioritize your work in terms of what must be done *now* and what can be attended to later. You can (and probably will) add items to your list, and you'll mark off other items as you accomplish them. Prioritizing your list will help to ensure that you don't overlook or forget anything important.[1]

The top post-season priority for most coaches is inventorying equipment and boxing up uniforms.

Preliminary Work. Many of the post-season responsibilities can and should be addressed prior to the end of the season. Those responsibilities might include such things as the following:

❑ Making arrangements for your sports banquet, including date, time, site, and menu; guest speaker; a list of players and guests to be invited; workers to prepare the site, meals, and clean up afterward; awards and recognitions; and invitations and programs.

❑ Writing thank-you notes to everyone who helped you during the season (including the coaches in your feeder program), and inviting them to your banquet.

---

[1] Closely allied to this, the practices of using a "day runner" or personal planner and marking down all important dates and times on a calendar will significantly increase your organizational efficiency.

❑ Scheduling next year's opponents. The sooner you begin your scheduling, the more likely you'll be to find favorable dates for the teams you most want and need to play.

❑ Budgeting for next year. If you're going to order new uniforms and/or equipment for next year, be advised that, like the U.S. Postal Service, sporting goods manufacturers don't operate on regular time like the rest of us. Uniforms should be ordered six to nine months in advance, and equipment three to five months in advance.

Unless you're prepared to pay for your purchases out of your own pocket, don't *ever* make unauthorized purchases to be billed to your athletic department. Follow your school's (or system's) written guidelines to the letter regarding purchase orders (or get the approval of your booster club), and *always* stay within the limits of your athletic budget.

❑ Setting standards for earning varsity letters, jackets, and so on, and ordering them as soon as you've determined who qualifies.

❑ Setting up and supervising an off-season strength and conditioning program. See the "Conditioning" section in Chapter 6, and Appendixes S and T (for weight training).

❑ Compiling and storing your season stats.

❑ Preparing highlight films or videos, both individual and team, covering the past season. Videotaped team highlights provide a wonderful background atmosphere for your banquet meal, and individual highlight tapes will help you in showcasing your players for college coaches in recruitment.

❑ Monitoring your players' grades, academic progress, and classroom conduct. This should be a year-round process, regardless of whether you are actively involved with your players before or after the season. If they play on your soccer team, they're *your* players, no matter how many other sports they play for other coaches—and they're just as ineligible to play for you if they allow their grades to slip below prescribed limits in someone else's sport season. Your players should understand that they are answerable to you for their academic progress and behavior *all* the time, and not just from Day 1 of soccer to the end of the season.

❑ Improving yourself and your program. Coaching and playing are two sides of the same coin. Expecting next year's team to improve without your working to improve yourself during the off-season is no different from expecting it to improve without the players' working to improve themselves during the off-season. Even if you're coaching another sport before or after soccer season, you should find time to improve yourself by reading soccer books and magazines, attending clinics and conventions, renewing professional memberships and magazine subscriptions, and the like. Reflecting on your team's progress during the past season will reveal whether major or minor changes will be necessary. In either case, the off-season is the proper time for initiating any changes you may want to make.

The off-season is a good time to update your playbook, soccer media guide, practice plans—which, like practically everything else, can be stored in a computer for quick retrieval and updating—and any other paperwork you use and save. The off-season can also be used to prepare new motivational posters, signs, and so on, for next season, and to do handyman work like repairing equipment and overseeing the condition of your playing fields.

HELPING THE COLLEGE-BOUND ATHLETE

Many are called, but few are chosen.

—Matthew 22:14

Two often-overlooked facts will help in orienting you and your players in the right direction regarding college. First, many of your players will attend college but will not play soccer at that level, or else they will play on a partial scholarship or none at all; you owe them the same level of guidance through the college selection process that you give your top-of-the-line, sure-fire, "can't miss" prospects. Second, everyone concerned—players, parents, and coaches—should understand that, while in most cases the formal recruitment process doesn't begin until a player's senior year, the college search and informal recruitment process has a much longer time line, reaching back to the player's freshman year of high school.

The Freshman Year

Probably the first and most important thing you can do for your ninth-graders, beyond making them feel comfortable on your team, is to teach them the importance of setting and pursuing long-range goals rather than simply taking each day as it comes. *Carpe diem* (Latin for "seize the day") is a good slogan to live by—but *carpe annum* ("seize the year") is important, too. The freshman year is a season of adjustment, and that adjustment includes laying a groundwork for future success in the classroom as well as on the soccer field. Your freshmen should understand that, just as they are expected to work hard to develop their soccer skills in daily practice and on their own, they must develop good study habits in order to establish themselves as student-athletes rather than simply as athletes.

Regarding college, freshmen should be encouraged to start thinking about whether they might be interested in playing college soccer farther down the line. If so, there are several points for them to consider:

❑ Opportunities exist. Soccer is one of America's fastest-growing sports, and colleges and universities are, in increasing numbers, adding men's—and especially women's—soccer teams to their athletic programs.

❑ Academic performance is important. Regardless of skills, student-athletes won't get into college if they can't meet the entrance requirements. While the SAT and ACT tests are still about two years away at this point (i.e., at the end of their sophomore year), college admissions departments study academic records from the freshman year on. It is far easier to establish and maintain a high grade-point average (GPA) from the ninth grade on than it is to raise a low GPA to acceptable standards as a senior.

❏ Although different levels of college athletics exist (NCAA Divisions 1, 2, and 3; NAIA; and JuCo), *all* college soccer involves the best available players on those levels. To join that large but elite group of athletes, high schoolers must immerse themselves totally in soccer and leave no stones unturned in their attempts to develop college-level skills. Even then, many players won't make it to the next level. The only guarantee players have is that they won't even be considered by college coaches unless they develop the academic and soccer skills necessary to compete at that level. Goal setting is critical in the early stages of player development.

❏ Beyond practicing diligently, freshmen must also put themselves in a position to be seen by college coaches. Aside from their high school teams' reaching the state finals, two of the best ways to accomplish this are (a) playing on a traveling club team that participates in regional and national tournaments, and (b) attending soccer camps. The former has the benefit of affording wide exposure, but can be very expensive in some cases; the latter can also be moderately expensive, but offers contacts with college-level coaches as well as top-level skills instruction. Those coaches can't actively recruit freshmen, but they will notice and evaluate players' potential, especially if a player has previously expressed interest in playing at the coach's school.

The Sophomore Year

The competitive screws begin tightening inexorably during a player's sophomore season. Academically, the player will take the PSAT—and possibly the SAT as well—which can help in determining the level at which the player is most likely to succeed academically.

Sophomores desiring to pursue soccer to the college level should consult their high school guidance counselor regarding the thirteen core courses required of high school graduates to fulfill NCAA academic requirements. The NCAA sends out copies of its academic eligibility requirements to all high schools in the United States every year, so your athletic director and guidance counselor should have a copy. Make a copy for yourself if you don't already have one.

Athletically, the soph season could refer to "sophisticated" as well as to "sophomore," since those players should have become more sophisticated in their approach to playing the game with a full varsity season behind them. (This isn't necessarily so if they played jayvee ball the previous year, or if your senior high school contains only grades 10–12.)

In pursuing the same avenues of development and exposure as in the freshman year, sophs should also become more sophisticated regarding their possible roles as college players. College coaches look closely at skills development, of course, but they are also looking for players who work well within a team context—including leadership ability, team play, and social interaction.

Players should begin compiling a soccer résumé of their athletic qualifications during their sophomore year. That résumé, which will be updated every year, should include personal information (name, address, phone number, height, weight, etc.); educational information (school, grade, GPA, SAT/ACT scores, and intended major); a background of the player's soccer experience (teams played for, individual achievements, honors and awards received, camps attended, etc.); and soccer-related references (name, position, address, and phone no.), whose approval should be enlisted before including them.

A sample résumé appears in Appendix U.

The Junior Year

The junior year is the biggest year of all for many high schoolers, at least in terms of their finding themselves as athletes. Improvements in play tend to take a quantum (and often unexpected) leap forward between players' sophomore and junior seasons, giving them a more realistic sense of where they stand as players than was possible earlier in their playing experience. You can help by taking them to college games so they can both gain a sense of what the game is like at that level and compare their skills with those of the players they're watching. You can have them study their performances in your team's videotaped games—and, by watching the tapes with them, you can teach them how to critically assess their own play in an objective manner.

You can also tell them how to develop a personal videotape for marketing themselves to college coaches who may not have time to see them play. Coach Mike Morgan of the Stone Mountain (GA) Soccer Club tells his players,

> If you don't own a camcorder, it is possible to rent them. (Try your local camera and video store.) Coaches prefer to see game footage for a significant period of time, as opposed to seeing highlights of various events. It is possible, however, to edit parts of the game to show a series of events that present you in the best light possible. Most major cities have companies that will help you with the editing of the videotape, which should allow you to give a realistic showing of your performance while also allowing you to eliminate sequences that might be detrimental to your chances of being recruited.

> In preparing your videotape, open up with a brief introduction, giving your name, jersey number, and team name; this will allow the coach to focus on you rather than having to search through a roster to determine which player she or he should be watching.

While players cannot be actively recruited until July 1 following their junior year, they will begin receiving general information from colleges throughout their junior year regarding the colleges' athletic and academic programs. This informal, feeling-out process gives the players an idea of which schools and coaches might be interested in recruiting them later.

The narrowing-down process continues when the players take the SAT or ACT standardized tests as juniors. Players should understand that failure to achieve satisfactory scores the first time does not automatically disqualify them from being admitted to a given college; they can take the tests as many times as they wish. The NCAA has seven national testing dates for the SAT and five for the ACT.

When players get an idea of the level of college that suits their academic aptitude and athletic ability, they can begin looking at specific schools, considering such variables as location, size, intended majors, and financial needs, and eliminating from further consideration schools that do not meet their needs. They should not be too highly selective, though; at this point, they need to keep their options open and allow for the possibility that none of the schools they are interested in will provide an exact fit for what they want.

During their junior year, players should complete their personal résumés and send them to every college in which they are even remotely interested, along with cover letters that introduce them to the coaches and explain why they are interested in that school. Letters should be personalized, not form letters; having access to a word processor will greatly reduce the work involved.

The Senior Year

By their senior year, players are beginning to see the light at the end of the tunnel. With only one year left in high school, they may want to slack off, take it easy, and have fun—a state of mind commonly referred to as "senioritis." Your task here is to remind your seniors that *this* is the year they've been working toward—the year when coaches can actively recruit them.

Working closely with the school's guidance counselor is imperative for seniors. First, they should ensure that they are in compliance with NCAA Recruiting By-law 14-3 regarding the thirteen core course requirements, and are on schedule for graduation. If necessary, they can and should continue to re-take the standardized tests (SAT or ACT) until they reach a level that will satisfy college entrance requirements. They can also examine possibilities for taking advance-placement courses to fulfill college requirements and exempt them from basic college courses.

Since competition for scholarships is fierce, and funding for soccer is limited in many schools, it is important that players present as positive and individualized an image of themselves as they can manage. Besides updating their athletic résumés to include additional honors received, records achieved, and increases in GPAs or standardized test scores, they should send a copy of their team schedule to every school they're interested in, along with a videotape (if they haven't already sent one) and cover letter expressing their continuing interest in that school.

Politeness, courtesy, and honesty are important in all dealings with college coaches. Brief thank-you notes following up letters, telephone calls, and information received from a school will help a player to stand out in coaches' minds, since many of their prospects overlook this basic courtesy. Telling a coach that one is no longer interested in his or her school can be difficult—but it's the classy thing to do.

APPENDICES

ANNOTATED BIBLIOGRAPHY

Catalogs

Some of the books and videos cited herein are, unfortunately, out of print or production. The catalogs listed below offer a far broader listing of print and video resources in all areas of soccer coaching and training than is possible in these pages.

CHAMPIONSHIP BOOKS & VIDEO PRODUCTIONS
2730 Graham
Ames, IA 50010
Phone No. (toll-free): 1-800-873-2730

SOCCER LEARNING SYSTEMS
P. O. Box 277
San Ramon, CA 94583
Phone No. (toll-free): 1-800-762-2376

Books

❐ Catlin, Mark G. THE ART OF SOCCER. St. Paul, MN: Soccer Books, 1990. 208 pp. Very good analyses of systems of play and organizing attacks. Contains drills and a good section on what to look for in young players.

❐ Chyzowych, Walter. THE OFFICIAL BOOK OF THE UNITED STATES SOCCER FEDERATION. Chicago: Rand McNally & Co., 1978. 253 pp. This was the first and most important book we used in learning how to coach soccer. Easy to read and understand, the late Wake Forest coach's book is excellent for beginners—but alas, it's out of print.

❐ Coerver, Wiel. SOCCER FUNDAMENTALS FOR PLAYERS AND COACHES. Englewood Cliffs, NJ: Prentice Hall, 1986. 184 pp., 700+ photos. Superb photos and sections on fast footwork and drills involving rebound nets. Coerver has also produced several outstanding soccer instructional videotapes. (CB&VP)

❐ Ditchfield, Mike, and Bahr, Walter. COACHING SOCCER THE PROGRESSIVE WAY. Englewood Cliffs, NJ: Prentice Hall, 1988. 238 pp. Especially effective in dealing with principles of offensive and defensive control and support. (SLS, CB&VP)

❐ Dorrance, Anson, and Nash, Tom (eds.). TRAINING SOCCER CHAMPIONS. JTC Sports, 1996. 160 pp. The highly successful University of North Carolina women's coach tells how he developed his championship program at UNC that won 12 NCAA titles (including 9 straight) in 14 years. Covers team organization, training, player management, and tactics. Like Coerver, Coach Dorrance has produced a videotape to complement his book, and other videos as well. (SLS, CB&VP)

☐ _____. FIFA: THE LAWS OF THE GAME. U. S. Soccer Federation. 110 pp. Updated annually, this is soccer's official rulebook. (SLS, CB&VP)

☐ Harris, Paul E., and Harris, Larry R. FAIR OR FOUL? THE COMPLETE GUIDE TO SOCCER OFFICIATING IN AMERICA (6th ed.). Manhattan Beach, CA: Soccer for Americans, 1997. 224 pp. An invaluable aid to understanding the rules of soccer at the high school, college, and national/international levels. A very popular book, and deservedly so. (SLS)

☐ Machnik, Joe, and Hoek, Frans. SO NOW YOU ARE A GOALKEEPER. Manhattan Beach, CA: Soccer for Americans, 1996. Offers valuable insights into how to train goalkeepers. Updated from an earlier edition. (SLS, CB&VP)

☐ Marziali, Floriano, and Mora, Vincenzo. COACHING THE ITALIAN 4-4-2. Very good analysis of Flat Back Four zone defense. The book's companion videotape features Italian World Cup coach Arrigo Sacchi. (CB&VP)

☐ McGettigan, James P. COMPLETE BOOK OF DRILLS FOR WINNING SOCCER. West Nyack, NY: Parker Publishing Co., 1980. 254 pp. Comprehensive, well organized, with ample diagrams to supplement the book's 264 drills.

☐ McGettigan, James P. SOCCER DRILLS FOR INDIVIDUAL AND TEAM PLAY. Englewood Cliffs, NJ: Prentice Hall, 1987. 222 pp. An excellent follow-up to his earlier drills book. The author has had three undefeated seasons in his college coaching career. (SLS, CB&VP)

☐ Reeves, John A., and Simon, J. Malcolm. THE COACHES COLLECTION OF SOCCER DRILLS. Champaign, IL: Leisure Press, 1981. 160 pp. Drills books are always in demand, and this one containing 125 drills is very good. (SLS)

☐ Warren, William E. COACHING AND CONTROL. Englewood Cliffs, NJ: Prentice Hall, 1997. 225 pp. Tells how to achieve your goals in coaching by controlling your program, your players, and your opponents.

☐ Warren, William E. COACHING AND MOTIVATION. Englewood Cliffs, NJ: Prentice Hall, 1983. 201 pp. Written in lay terms, this perennial best-seller tells you everything you need to know about motivating yourself and the people around you toward maximum performances.

☐ Warren, William E. COACHING AND WINNING. West Nyack, NY: Parker Publishing Co., 1988. 180 pp. A definitive, in-depth analysis of what it takes to become a consistent winner in your coaching, borrowing from philosophies, principles, techniques, and strategies employed by winners in all sports.

☐ Whitehead, Nick, and Cook, Malcolm. SOCCER TRAINING GAMES, DRILLS AND FITNESS ACTIVITIES (4th ed.). London: A & C Black, Ltd., 1997. 128 pp. Although we've used this book primarily for its soccer-related fitness activities, it also contains excellent shooting activities among its 60 games and drills. (SLS, CB&VP)

Magazines

SOCCER AMERICA
P. O. Box 16718
North Hollywood, CA 91615-6718

    50 issues/yr., $79 subscription rate.

SOCCER JOURNAL
SUNY-Binghampton
West Gymnasium
Binghampton, NY 13902-6000

    The official publication of the National Soccer Coaches of America, available to members only; 6 issues/yr., $50

SOUTHERN SOCCER SCENE
P. O. Box 19445
Greensboro, NC 27419

    Published monthly, covers high school and college soccer in NC, SC, GA, TN, and VA; $20 subscription rate

Videotapes

❏ _____. GROUP TACTICS SERIES. (Soccer Learning Systems) One 1-hr. videotape on group attacking, one 36-min. videotape on group defending. Covers the basics of team play very well. (SLS, CB&VP)

❏ _____. INDIVIDUAL TACTICS SERIES. (Soccer Learning Systems) Two 40-min. videotapes, one 30-min. videotape. Covers individual attacking, individual defending, and methods of training individual tactics. (SLS, CB&VP)

Both the Group and Individual videotape sets are excellent. Skills are illustrated at game speed, in slow motion and via graphically enhanced footage of international matches. From International Tactics.

❏ _____. THE WINNING FORMULA. (Soccer Learning Systems) Three 1-hr., one 80-min., and one 40-min. videotape. Deals with all phases of offense, defense, and midfield play. Tape 5 covers goalkeeping. From The Football Association. (SLS, CB&VP)

❏ Coerver, Wiel. 1-2-3 GOAL. Four 55-min. videotapes. Excellent video series covering ball control skills, 1-v-1 moves, creating and converting goal scoring chances, and attacking moves of some of soccer's greatest players. (SLS, CB&VP)

❏ Coerver, Wiel. COERVER COACHING DRILL SERIES. Three 55-min. videotapes. Offers 365 drills for improving attacking skills, passing and receiving, mini-games, and more. (SLS, CB&VP)

❏ Dorrance, Anson. DYNASTY: UNIVERSITY OF NORTH CAROLINA WOMEN'S SOCCER. Two tapes. Covers UNC's playing system, player development, challenges of transition to the college level, skills development, motivation, and positional requirements.

Coach Dorrance is soccer's equivalent of the E. F. Hutton stock brokerage firm: When he talks, people stop what they're doing and listen. (CB&VP)

❏ Machnik, Dr. Joseph A. (Joe). GOALKEEPING SERIES. Two 2-hr. and one 30-min. videotape. Covers every aspect of goalkeeping from warmups and stretching exercises to techniques and tactics. Excellent. (SLS, CB&VP)

❏ Sacchi, Arrigo. COACHING THE ITALIAN 4-4-2. One videotape, 45 min. Although we prefer man-to-man Catenaccio defense for our teams, we like the versatility of the 4-4-2 system—and we strongly recommend Coach Sacchi's videotape for anyone who uses the "42." (CB&VP)

❏ van Balkom, Frans. SOCCER ON THE ATTACK: A COMPREHENSIVE LOOK AT ATTACKING SKILLS. St. Louis: Budweiser-Busch Creative Services Corp., 1986. Three 50-minute videotapes in the *Individual Tactics Series*, this set featuring "Fast Footwork and Feinting" (Vol. I), "Dribbling" (Vol. II), and "Shooting and Heading" (Vol. III).

These tapes are out of production—and that's a shame, because they are head and shoulders above anything else we've seen when it comes to teaching fast footwork, ball control, and dribbling.

Appendix B

COACHING TASKS AND PREPARATIONS

Before Practice Begins

____ Order uniforms and equipment

____ Prepare field for practice and games

____ Schedule field use

____ Prepare/update player handbook

____ Verify team physician/trainer/ chiropractor/rehab personnel

____ Estimate expenses

____ Schedule physical exams, flu shots

____ Order soccer shoes (screw-in and molded cleats)

____ Check eligibility requirements (school records)

____ Make travel plans (bus driver, overnight trips)

____ Contract with officials' assn. (send schedule)

____ Check field lighting

____ Check scoreboard clock, control panel, replace defective bulbs

____ Give out managers' duty list

____ Order FIFA rulebook(s)

____ Prepare scouting schedule

Before Your First Game

____ Send in eligibility reports

____ Complete necessary forms (insurance, parental permission, medical, player information sheets)

____ Recheck clock, controls, bulbs

____ Timer, ticket takers, concession stand workers

____ Security arrangements

____ Bring in officials to discuss rules changes and referee scrimmages

____ Plan videotaping of games

____ Mimeograph forms to be used

THE SOCCER PITCH

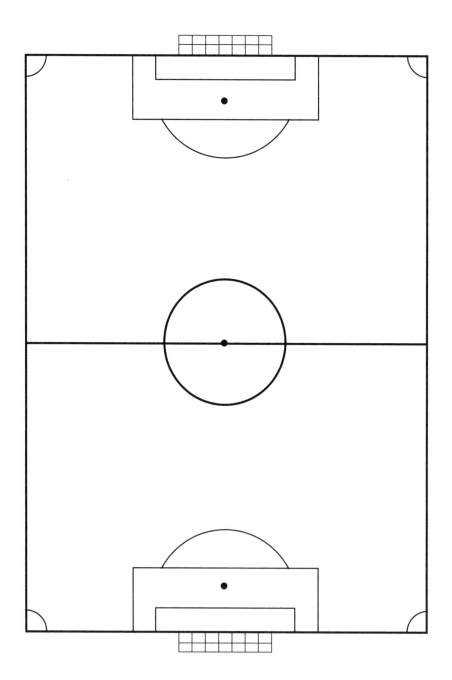

SOCCER STAT SHEET

SOCCER ———→ STATS

DATE _____
OPPONENT: _____
CARDS: _____   OPPONENTS CARDS: _____

#	PLAYER	SHOTS		GOALS		PENALTY KICKS		CORNER KICKS		BAD	FOULS	CARDS		FREE	BLOCKED	OFF
		AT GOAL	ON GOAL	SCORED	ASSISTS	ATT	GOALS	ATT	GOOD	THROW IN		YELLOW	RED	KICKS	SHOTS	SIDES

OPPONENTS TOTALS

SCORES

	1ST	2ND	OT	OT	FINAL
OPPONENT:					

KEEPER STATISTICS

	SHOTS FACED	GOALS ALLOWED	SAVES	PENALTY KICKS	
				FACE	ALLOWED
KEEPER					
OPPONENTS					

SHOT CHART

NAME	ASSIST	TIME

OPPONENTS SHOT CHART

NAME	ASSIST	TIME

PLAYER CHECKLIST—PREPARATION FOR GAMES AND DAILY PRACTICES

To Do:

_____ Be on time (or call in advance if you're going to be late or absent.) The number to call: _____.

_____ Arrange for transportation home from practice.

_____ Arrange for transportation to and from the departure point for road games.

_____ Have ankles, etc., taped before games and practices if necessary.

_____ Contact _____ at _____ regarding
                   MD/phys. therapist   phone no.
      any injury that needs attention or rehab treatment.

_____ Contact _____ at _____ if you
                   MD/chiropractor   phone no.
      experience problems with your neck or back.

_____ Contact _____ at _____ for other
                   physician   phone no.
      medical or physical problems.

To Bring With You:

_____ Clothing appropriate for the weather conditions at practice

_____ Both sets of uniforms, both pairs of soccer shoes (screw-in and molded) to games

_____ Tennis shoes to practice

_____ Special gear (e.g., protector, braces, shinguards)

_____ A positive attitude

_____ HIGH SCHOOL ATHLETIC DEPARTMENT

ATHLETIC PACKET

The athletic packet contains essential information—it is necessary that pages 2 and 3 be completed and returned to the athletic office.

(1) Letter of Athletic Assessment Information to Parents/Guardians
(2) Parent Assessment Choices and Insurance Information
(3) Parent Permission/Release for Medical Treatment
(4) Physical Examination Form

Letter of Athletic Assessment Information to Parents/Guardians:

There will be an assessment on all participants in athletics and cheerleading at _____ High School for the coming school year. The assessment for all participants will be fifteen dollars ($15.00) per year. This is a one-time assessment for all sports and cheerleading for the school year.

All athletes and cheerleaders are required to pay the assessment before the first practice of the sport they are participating in begins. No child will be denied the right to participate because of financial hardship. Arrangements should be made with the coach or Athletic Director.

All athletes and cheerleaders are covered by a secondary accident coverage. Being secondary coverage, it is applied after your primary insurance is filed. This coverage is in effect only with accidents involved during a sports program. This is not school day coverage; however, we do recommend that your son/daughter enroll in school day coverage at the beginning of the school year.

ASSESSMENT INFORMATION/INSURANCE INFORMATION

To: Parents/Guardians of Athletes and Cheerleaders

From: (Athletic Director and School Principal)

All athletes and cheerleaders are responsible for the assessment fee. Please check the appropriate statement 1, 2, or 3 that applies to you. Please complete the entire packet and return to the athletic office immediately.

(1) _____ My son is participating in football. I am enclosing the fifteen dollars ($15.00) for his athletic assessment.

(2) _____ My son/daughter is participating in _____ (sport). I am enclosing the fifteen dollars ($15.00) for his/her athletic assessment.

(3) _____ My son/daughter is participating in _____ (sport). The assessment fee of fifteen dollars ($15.00) was paid at the beginning of this school year when he/she participated in _____ (sport).

_____ HIGH SCHOOL INSURANCE INFORMATION
All athletes and cheerleaders are covered by a secondary accident coverage. Being secondary coverage, it is applied after your primary insurance is filed. This coverage is in effect only with accidents involved during a sports program. This is not school day coverage; however, we do recommend that your son/daughter enroll in school day coverage at the beginning of the school year.

PLEASE COMPLETE THE FOLLOWING INFORMATION:

Parent/Guardian's Insurance Company _____

Insurance Policy/Group Number _____

Policy Holder's Place of Employment _____

PARENT/GUARDIAN PERMISSION FOR PARTICIPATION

I/We do hereby give our permission for my son/daughter _____ to participate in _____ athletics, realizing that such participation involves the potential for injury which is inherent in all sports. I/We acknowledge that even with the best coaching, use of the most advanced protective equipment, and strict observance of rules, injuries are still a possibility. On rare occasions, these injuries can be so severe as to result in total disability, paralysis, or even death.

Such permission is extended to all high school athletics except as noted below. Furthermore, I understand that my child must have a completed High School Association Physical Examination form signed by a licensed physician before he/she will be permitted to try out for athletics. Finally, I understand that such physicals are normally valid from July 1 through June 30 of the following year.

I/We acknowledge that I/We have read and understand the warning presented herein.

_____   _____
Parent's/Guardian's Signature   Date

_____   _____
Student's Signature   Date

Noted Exceptions _____

RELEASE FOR MEDICAL TREATMENT

Dear Parents:

The following is a Release for Medical Treatment form on your child. This form gives our coaching staff the authority to admit your child for medical treatment if he/she is injured and you cannot be reached. This assures your child fast medical treatment in the event that he/she is injured and you are not available to give the doctor or hospital permission to treat your child.

Thank you for your cooperation in this matter.

_____, Athletic Director

I authorize the _____ coaching staff the authority to admit my child, (Student's name) _____ for medical treatment in the event that I cannot be reached.

_____   _____
Parent's/Guardian's Signature   Date

_____   _____
Home Phone Number   Work Place and Phone Number

Your personal physician's name is: _____
Please provide us with the name and numbers of an emergency contact person in case you are unavailable.

_____   _____
Name and Relationship to You   Home/Work Numbers

PLAYER INFORMATION SHEET

Date _____

LAST NAME _____ FIRST NAME _____ MIDDLE

STREET ADDRESS/P.O. BOX   CITY   STATE   ZIP

PHONE NO. _____   DATE OF BIRTH (MONTH/DAY/YEAR)

PARENTS/GUARDIANS NAMES

GRADE LEVEL (CIRCLE ONE)   8   9   10   11   12

NUMBER OF YEARS' SOCCER EXPERIENCE: _____

NUMBER OF VARSITY SOCCER LETTERS EARNED: _____

DID YOU/ARE YOU PLAY(ING) SOCCER THIS FALL? (YES) (NO)   IF YES,
    WHAT TEAM? _____   WHAT LEVEL? _____
    WHAT SOCCER CLUB? _____

WHAT POSITION(S) DO YOU PLAY? _____

HAVE YOU EVER ATTENDED A DISTRICT OR STATE TEAM TRYOUT?
    (YES) (N0) IF YES, WHEN AND WHERE? _____

HAVE YOU EVER PLAYED, OR DO YOU PLAY, FOR THE GEORGIA STATE
    TEAM OR ANY OTHER STATE TEAM? (YES) (NO) IF YES, WHAT STATE
    TEAM? _____

WHAT IS YOUR GRADE-POINT AVERAGE? _____ SAT SCORE? _____
    PSAT SCORE? _____

HAVE YOU FAILED A GRADE? (YES) (NO) IF YES, GRADE AND YEAR FAILED

_____
GRADE   YEAR

WHAT YEAR DID YOU START THE NINTH GRADE FOR THE FIRST TIME? _____

Appendix H

MEDICAL HISTORY FORM

FULL NAME _____
                (LAST)   (FIRST)   (MIDDLE)

DATE OF BIRTH _____ AGE _____ SEX _____

SCHOOL YEAR _____ SCHOOL _____ GRADE _____

HOME PHONE NUMBER _____

HAS THE STUDENT EVER HAD A HISTORY OF:
(Check all that applies and explain below)

___ CONCUSSION	___ OVERNIGHT HOSPITAL STAY	___ OPERATION
___ HEAT EXHAUSTION	___ DIABETES	___ BROKEN BONE
___ HEAT STROKE	___ HEAD INJURY	___ FAINTING
___ CHRONIC COUGH	___ NECK INJURY	___ ASTHMA
___ SEIZURES	___ HEART MURMUR	___ HERNIA
___ SHOULDER INJURY	___ DIGESTIVE PROBLEMS	___ ELBOW INJURY
___ HIGH BLOOD PRESSURE	___ KIDNEY PROBLEMS	___ HIP INJURY
___ WRIST/HAND INJURY	___ HEART DISEASE	___ KNEE INJURY
___ DAILY MEDICATION	___ BACK OR SPINAL INJURY	___ ANKLE INJURY
___ ALLERGIES	___ WEARS GLASSES/CONTACTS	___ DENTAL (TEETH)
___ OTHER MEDICAL PROBLEMS	___ MISSING BODY PARTS	

EXPLANATIONS/DATES _____
_____
_____

HAS ANY PHYSICIAN EVER LIMITED THE STUDENT'S ATHLETIC PARTICIPATION?

YES _____   NO _____

HAS THE STUDENT'S MOTHER, FATHER, BROTHERS, OR SISTERS EVER HAD ANY
HEART PROBLEMS PRIOR TO AGE 50?   YES _____   NO _____

PARENT/STUDENT CERTIFICATION

THE UNDERSIGNED CERTIFY THAT NO MEDICAL INFORMATION CONCERNING
THE APPLICANT NAMED ABOVE HAS BEEN WITHHELD AND THAT ALL INFORMATION
PROVIDED IS FACTUAL AND TRUE.

_____   _____
PARENT OR LEGAL GUARDIAN   STUDENT

THE EXAMINATION PERFORMED FOR THIS PARTICIPATION CERTIFICATE IS LIMITED AND
DESIGNED TO IDENTIFY CONDITIONS OR INFIRMITIES THAT WOULD LIMIT OR PREVENT A
STUDENT FROM PARTICIPATING IN ATHLETIC ACTIVITIES. THIS EXAM IS **NOT** INTENDED TO
BE COMPREHENSIVE AND MAY NOT DETECT SOME TYPES OF LATENT OR HIDDEN MEDICAL
CONDITIONS. ALL ATHLETES SHOULD RECEIVE PERIODIC COMPREHENSIVE MEDICAL
EXAMINATIONS.

PHYSICIAN'S MEDICAL EXAMINATION FORM

FULL NAME _____

DATE _____ NAME YOU GO BY _____

PHYSICAL EXAMINATION TO BE COMPLETED BY EXAMINING PHYSICIAN

HEIGHT _____IN.   WEIGHT: _____LBS.

BLOOD PRESSURE _____/_____

EYES: EARS:

NOSE: HEAD & NECK:

THROAT: ABDOMEN:

CARDIOVASCULAR:

MURMURS:

PULSE: RESTING _____   POST-EXERCISE _____   RECOVERY _____

OTHER:

RESPIRATORY:

WHEEZING: SPUTUM:

OTHER:

ORTHOPAEDIC:

GENERAL CONDITION:

_____ EXCELLENT   _____ GOOD   _____ FAIR

_____ BELOW PAR

COMMENTS:

PHYSICIAN CERTIFICATION

IN REVIEW OF THE ABOVE INFORMATION AND FOLLOWING THE LIMITED EXAMINATION, I CERTIFY THE ABOVE-NAMED STUDENT:

_____ PASSES WITHOUT RESTRICTION

_____ PASSES WITH RESTRICTION _____

_____ FAILS THE EXAMINATION DUE TO _____

_____   _____

PHYSICIAN SIGNATURE   DATE

CHECKLIST OF TEAM OFFENSIVE AND DEFENSIVE PHASES TO BE COVERED IN PRESEASON

I. Installing Your Offensive System: Patterns and Strategies

_____ A. Building attacks

_____ B. Fast breaking

_____ C. Attacking patterns and sequences

    _____ 1. Developing attacking triangles and give-and-go sequences

    _____ 2. Creating space for the dribbler

    _____ 3. Making runs through the defense

    _____ 4. Applying "rubber band" strategies*

    _____ 5. Setting up shots on goal

    _____ 6. Supporting attacks

    _____ 7. Switching the ball

        _____ a. Crossing passes

        _____ b. Overlaps

        _____ c. Working the ball around the perimeter

    _____ 8. Slowdown tactics

_____ D. Situational strategies

    _____ 1. Kickoff plays and strategies

    _____ 2. Throw-ins

    _____ 3. Goal kicks

    _____ 4. Corner kicks

    _____ 5. Direct and indirect free kicks

    _____ 6. Penalty kicks

II. Installing Your Team Defense: Principles and Strategies

_____ A. Man-to-man or zone marking responsibilities

    _____ 1. Aggressive/passive 1-v-1 marking strategies

    _____ 2. Double-teaming and support strategies

    _____ 3. Defensing fast breaks

_____ B. Situational defense

    _____ 1. Kickoffs

    _____ 2. Corner Kicks

    _____ 3. Direct and indirect free kicks

_____ C. Clearing the ball

---

* See Chapter 7 on the rubber band principle.

Appendix K

MANAGERS' DAILY DUTIES AND RESPONSIBILITIES

General

1. Be at the field 30 minutes before practice every day, 45 minutes before departure on away games, and 90 minutes before home games.

Daily

1. Clean the coaches' office, home dressing room, and visitors' dressing room. Sweep the floor. Pick up clothing, trash, and equipment off the floor. Flush the toilets, and be sure that toilet tissue and hand towels are available. Be sure that the coaches' office and dressing rooms are locked during and after practice.

Practice Procedures

1. Get a copy of the daily practice schedule from the coach. Study it to find out where and how you'll be used in practice, and where to place field equipment for practice. Set up goals, rebound nets, and grids with pop-up goals and cones.

2. Inflate balls if necessary; have balls, ball rack/ball bags, portable chalkboard, erasers, chalk, medicine kit, towels, practice vests, video camera, clipboards, pencils, stat sheets, and stopwatch ready for use as necessary.

3. During practice, the senior manager will time drills. Other managers will assist with drills (e.g., by gathering balls and resetting grids, goals, and cones between activities), and keep stats and/or film drills and scrimmages.

4. After practice, the managers will collect all equipment and gear for return to the coaches' office; check the field one last time; collect towels, vests, and so on for washing; and clean the dressing room.

MANAGERS' GAME DAY RESPONSIBILITIES

Before/During Game	After Game	Home Games
_____	_____	1. Clean coaches' office, home and visitors' dressing rooms
_____	_____	2. Visitors' locker room key to/from visiting coach
_____	_____	3. Prepare field
_____	_____	a. Field lined off, corner flags in place
_____	_____	b. Drainage grates covered, goal nets hooked up, trash cans in place
_____	_____	4. Prepare scoreboard clock
_____	_____	5. Have pencils/lineup sheet/clipboards/stat sheets ready (give to coach after game)
_____	_____	6. Fill water containers early, have cups ready
_____	_____	7. Towels, medicine kit for home bench
_____	_____	8. Check ball inflations, adjust as necessary, take to bench area
_____	_____	9. Prepare video camera for filming
_____	_____	10. Unlock home dressing room and referees' room before halftime
_____	_____	11. Take soft drinks to refs, visiting team, and home team at halftime
_____	_____	12. Collect all equipment, clothing, etc., after the match

Before/ During *Game*	*After Game*	*Away Games*
_____	_____	1. Prepare balls, take ball bag to bus
_____	_____	2. Have pencils, lineup sheet, and stat sheets ready for use
_____	_____	3. Prepare water container, have cups and towels ready
_____	_____	4. Prepare medicine kit
_____	_____	5. Prepare video camera for filming
_____	_____	6. Collect valuables for valuables bag (DON'T LET IT OUT OF YOUR SIGHT FOR A SECOND!)
_____	_____	7. Before leaving, double-check to be sure that all necessary equipment and supplies are on the bus
_____	_____	8. Get dressing room key from/to home team's coach
_____	_____	9. Collect warmups
_____	_____	10. After the game, be sure everything is returned to the bus, including ball bags, clipboards, pencils, stat sheets, water containers, towels, medicine kit, video camera and warmups. Return players' valuables to them. Double-check the bench and dressing room areas one last time before leaving, to be sure that nothing is left at the site

Appendix M

PREGAME SCOUTING FORM

_____   _____   _____
Teams (circle scouted team)   Location   Date

I. Field Conditions

A. Lighting _____

_____

B. Field Dimensions/Features (e.g., approximate size of pitch, condition of grass or playing surface, potential hazards such as fences, concealed sprinkler heads, or a track circling the field)

_____

_____

_____

_____

_____

_____

II. Individual Players

(Note such things as players who are absent, not in uniform, or limping; foot preferences in dribbling, passing, and shooting; and effective shooting ranges.)

_____

_____

_____

_____

_____

_____

_____

_____

_____

_____

SCOUTING CHECKLIST—INDIVIDUAL PLAYERS

I. Shooting/Scoring

_____ How many of their attackers are effective scoring threats in 1-v-1 situations? Who are their best (and worst) shooters?

_____ Where do their best shooters and scorers like to shoot from? What is their effective shooting range? How do they set up their shots? (Off the dribble? Or via long, crossing, overlap, or through passes?) Are they effective headers?

II. Speed and Quickness

_____ Who are their fastest players? How does their quickness compare to ours?

_____ Do they play effectively at high speed, or do they tend to play out of control?

_____ Can we neutralize their speed advantage, if any? How? (Can we mark their fastest attackers tightly 1-v-1 and deny them the ball? Or should we double-team them or lay off them and not allow them to get past us?)

III. Attacking

_____ Who are their best ballhandlers and playmakers? Do they have more than one effective playmaker? To what extent does the team's success depend on their playmaking ability? Do they become frustrated if denied the ball constantly? Who do we want to keep the ball away from when the game is on the line? How can we neutralize those players defensively?

_____ Do their playmakers need the ball to be effective, or do they readily give it up to a teammate when challenged? What do they do when they don't have the ball?

_____ Do any of their attackers overdribble? Can we double-team or trap them? If so, where?

_____ Do their attackers want to receive the ball at foot level or into space?

_____ How well do they penetrate 1-v-1 on the dribble? Do they favor one foot or direction, or can they go either way equally well? Can we neutralize their dribble penetrations without resorting to double-teaming?

© 1999 by Parker Publishing Company, Inc.

© 1999 by Parker Publishing Company, Inc.

_____ How effective are they at high-speed ballhandling? Do they dribble and pass well under pressure?

_____ In terms of ballhandling, who are their weakest attackers? Why? (Do they watch the ball while dribbling or favor one foot over the other in dribbling and passing?)

_____ What do the wingers do when the playmaker has the ball? How are their dribbling skills? Can they cross well?

_____ Do any of the defensive midfielders or fullbacks make runs in the attacking third? (If so, how do the other players rotate? Do they cover well, or do they leave areas open?)

IV. Defense

_____ Apart from the keeper, who are their best and worst defenders?

_____ How effective are their midfielders and fullbacks at 1-v-1 play? Are they skilled at playing air balls?

_____ Do any of their off-the-ball defenders watch the ball rather than their marks? If so, who?

_____ Are any of their fullbacks notably weak at dribbling, or at protecting or passing the ball? Can we get the ball back by applying pressure when we lose possession (e.g., by cutting off their support and forcing them to go 1-v-1 with us)?

_____ How effective is their keeper in terms of agility, quickness, and jumping ability? Does (s)he have good hands? Play well in the air? Get down to stop low balls? Will (s)he come out from the goal line or goal box to challenge deep penetrations, or stay glued to the line? Where does (s)he play on corner kicks and free kicks?

_____ What does the keeper do with the ball? Does (s)he have a strong leg on punts and goal kicks? Possess a strong, accurate throwing arm? Is (s)he cool under pressure, or does (s)he tend to panic when attacks penetrate the 18?

V. General

_____ Who are their most effective subs off the bench? How, if at all, does the team's performance diminish when they're in? Why?

_____ Which players are most likely to get rattled in pressure situations?

_____ Of the players who receive the most playing time, which ones are the youngest or most inexperienced?

_____ Are any players sick, injured, suspended, or otherwise not in uniform? Will they be back in the lineup when we play them?

Appendix O

SCOUTING CHECKLIST— TEAM OFFENSE

I. Overall Offense

_____ Is their team speed superior, equal, or inferior to ours?

_____ Do they prefer to build their attacks? Or to go over the top with long balls?

_____ Do they rely on passing more than dribbling, or vice versa? Or are they equally likely to use either method of moving the ball?

_____ How well do they respond to pressure?

_____ What are the weakest aspects of their offense? How can we best exploit those weaknesses?

II. Fast Breaking

_____ Do they fast break relentlessly? Occasionally? Seldom? Or never? How many players do they send in their fast breaks? Which of them are effective high-speed dribblers or passers?

_____ Do they tend to initiate their fast breaks via long passes, by dribbling, or by a series of short give-and-go passes? Do they prefer to bring the ball up the middle of the pitch or along one side or the other? (Which side?) Can we slow their fast breaks by challenging the ball aggressively immediately after losing possession?

_____ How patient are they on attack? If their initial fast break is denied, do they tend to press their attack and go for the first available shot, or to settle into their regular attack?

III. Patterns and Tendencies

_____ Do they run any set plays or patterns in their regular offense? Or is their attack freelance and spontaneous?

_____ How do they get the ball into their attacking third, by building up with short passes and then trying to hit a forward or winger? Or by going long and hoping their front runners' speed will be too much for the defense?

_____ What formation(s) do they operate from? How does the formation change during attacks? Do they prefer one side to the other? Or the middle? Or do they attack randomly wherever the defense is vulnerable?

_____ How many front runners do they send? (If more than one, who is their preferred target? Where do they look for that player? What do the other lead attackers do?)

_____ How do they change fields? With crossing passes? Or by dropping the ball back for a series of safe passes from one support player to another around the perimeter?

_____ Besides the forwards and wingers, who else joins the attack or makes runs through the defense? How do the support players contribute to the attack?

IV. Set Pieces

_____ Who takes the free kicks? Goal kicks? Corner kicks? How do they set up? Who, if anyone, is their go-to player?

_____ How do they align themselves on goal kicks? Where do they go?

_____ Do they use in-swingers on corner kicks, or curve the ball away from the goal mouth?

_____ Is there a lot of movement on free kicks? Or just a straight kick to goal?

_____ Do they use set plays to establish the ball deep in the attacking third on kickoffs?

SCOUTING CHECKLIST— TEAM DEFENSE

I. Overall Defense

_____ Are they basically aggressive or passive on defense? (Do they come out after the ball all over the field and try to take it away? Or do they stay back in position defense and wait for the ball to come to them?)

_____ Do they recover quickly after turnovers? Are they susceptible to long passes and fast breaking? Do they challenge the ball immediately after losing possession? (If not, in what third of the pitch do they intensify their defensive coverage?)

_____ Do they prefer zone or man-to-man defense?

II. Zone Defense

_____ What alignment(s) do they use? Do they double-team or trap? If so, where?

_____ Are they aggressive, passive, or lazy in their coverage and movement? Do they overshift toward the ball side of the pitch? (If so, can we attack them via deep crossing passes?) What, if any, are the most obvious weaknesses in their coverage, and how can we take advantage of them?

_____ Does playing zone defense limit or enhance their attacking potential?

III. Man-to-Man Defense

_____ What alignment(s) do they use? Do they use a flat-back formation with their fullbacks, or a sweeper-stopper formation?

_____ How effective is their 1-v-1 marking? Do they double-team? (If so, where?) How much pressure do they apply to the ball?

_____ In what respects is their defense strongest? Weakest? How can we negate their strengths or exploit their weaknesses?

IV. Set Pieces

_____ Is there anything noteworthy or unusual about the way they defense free kicks, corner kicks, goal kicks, throw-ins, or drop balls?

Appendix Q

GAME PLAN

——————————————————— —————————— ——————
Opponent   Location   Date

I. Overall Aproach _____
_____
_____
_____
_____
_____
_____
_____
_____

II. Individual Players

____(_____)_____
_____
_____
_____

____(_____)_____
_____
_____
_____

____(_____)_____
_____
_____
_____

———(   )————————————————————————

——

——

——

———(   )————————————————————————

——

——

——

III. Team Offense _____

——

——

——

——

——

——

——

——

——

——

——

——

——

——

——

——

IV. Team Defense _____

——

——

——

——

_____
_____
_____
_____
_____
_____
_____
_____
_____
_____
_____
_____
_____
_____
_____

V. Special Situations

KICKOFFS _____
_____
_____
_____
_____
_____

THROW-INS _____
_____
_____
_____
_____
_____

GOAL KICKS _____
_____
_____
_____
_____
_____

CORNER KICKS _____

_____

_____

_____

_____

_____

_____

DIRECT/INDIRECT FREE KICKS _____

_____

_____

_____

_____

_____

_____

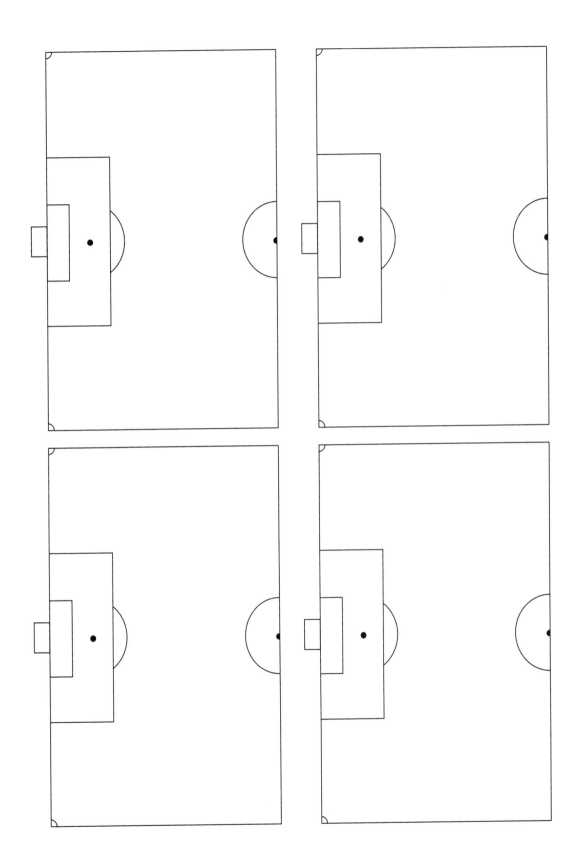

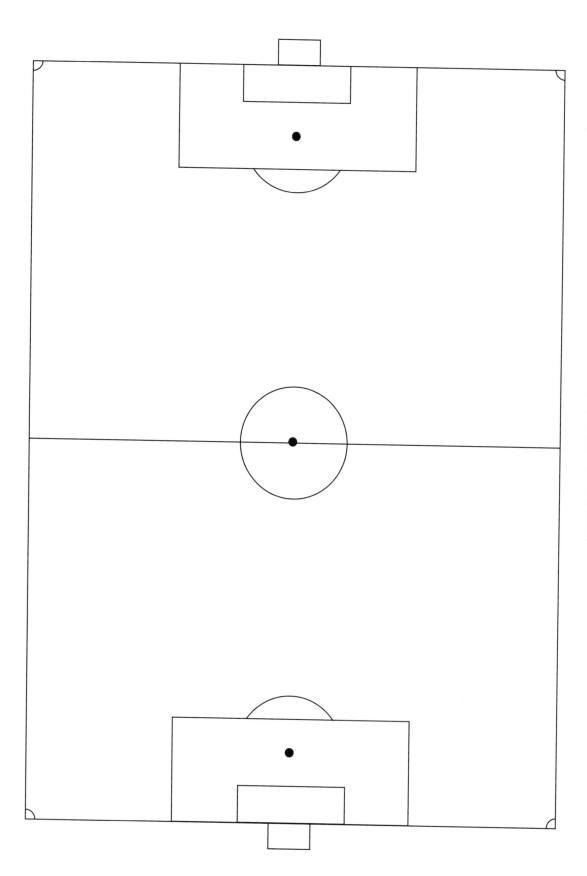

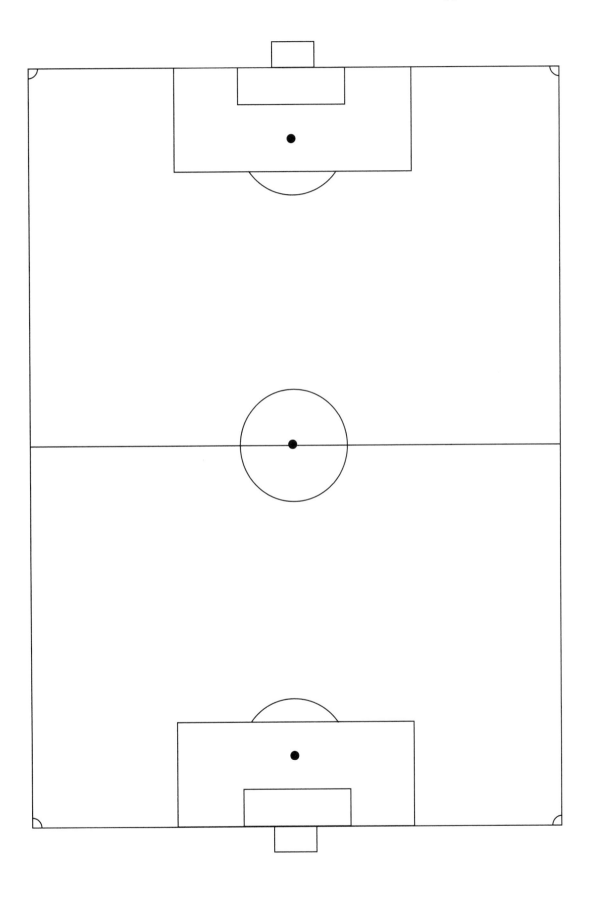

Appendix R

GAME PLAN EVALUATION

_____   _____   _____
Opponent   Location   Date

I. What Worked Best for Us _____
_____
_____
_____
_____

II. What They Did That We Didn't Expect—and How We Reacted
to It _____
_____
_____
_____
_____

III. What Didn't Work for Us and Why _____
_____
_____
_____
_____

IV. Possible Changes Next Time _____
_____
_____
_____
_____

WEIGHT TRAINING

Although many such programs exist, the off-season strength training program we recommend for soccer players lasts for eight weeks and consists of seven exercises. It was developed for us by our assistant coach, Arthur Graves, and fitness specialists Bob and Beckie Bell of Alabaster, Alabama.

Activity	Sets	Repetitions
Squats	4	12
Calf Raises	3	20 (hold for eight seconds, rest for three)
Dumbbell Pullovers	4	12
Upright Rowing	3	12
Pullups/chinups	4	maximum
Situps (crunches)	2	maximum
Alternating arm curls	2	10

Although inappropriately named and somewhat negative in its connotation, the "Training for Failure" workout procedure is excellent for establishing initial resistance and performance standards, and for maximizing strength gains without bulking up players to the point of losing fast-twitch muscle efficiency. What we're looking for here is overall strength and fitness that will complement, not hinder, our players' effectiveness.

To initiate a TFF program, a preliminary session is necessary in order to determine the starting resistance (weight) for each player in each activity, that is, the maximum weight with which they can successfully perform the number of reps in the first set of that activity—12 for squats, dumbbell pullovers, and upright rowing, and 10 for alternating arm curls.

Having established a starting point, the athletes work their way through the prescribed number of sets in each activity, going for the maximum number of reps in each set. When they reach the point where they can do more than 12 reps in the first set, it's time to increase the resistance by adding weight, not reps. Normally, that point is reached and poundages begin to rise after one to two weeks.

You might want to have the players perform pullups and chinups on an alternating set basis—the (overhand grip) pullups working the triceps and lats and the (underhand grip) chinups working the biceps. For situps or crunches, you can increase the resistance by having the players use an incline board or hold a weight behind their heads; otherwise, some of your situp specialists might keep going indefinitely like the Energizer bunny.

Be sure to have your players do a series of stretching exercises prior to each workout—and it goes without saying that no player should work out unless she or he has passed a physician's examination within the past twelve months.

For maximum benefit, players should work out every other day; if that's not feasible, go for three workouts a week—say, Monday, Wednesday, and Friday. Players need a day of rest between strength training sessions (but not between running workouts; players should run every day).

Keeping records of daily progress is motivational and provides a record of the players' progress. A reproducible workout log is found in Appendix T.

Appendix T

WEIGHT TRAINING WORKOUT LOG

Name _____

Sport _____

Exercise

NOTE: The date goes in the empty squares at the top of the page. Pounds lifted goes in the upper diagonal of the other squares, reps in the lower diagonal.

SAMPLE COLLEGE RÉSUMÉ

LISA DOE

Personal

Lisa Doe
123 Main St.
Atlanta, GA 30000
(404) 123-4567

Central High School
000 Peachtree Street
Atlanta, GA 30000

Academic

Class: Junior
GPA: 3.50
SAT: V-510
M-620

Club Level Play

U12–U16 Georgia Soccer Club
456 Maple Street
Atlanta, GA 30000
Coach: Mary Smith

Starting Midfielder — 5 Years
Best Defender — 2 Years
Most Valuable Player — 3 Years

U17–Present SE Soccer Club
1 Pine Ave.
Atlanta, GA 30000
Coach: Ronni Jones

U17 State Champion
U19 State Champion
16 Goals, 12 Assists

High School Play

3-Year Starter at Central H.S.
9th Grade—5 goals, 4 assists
11th Grade—21 goals, 9 assists

2-Year Most Valuable Player
10th Grade—7 goals, 11 assists
NSCAA All Region

Soccer Awards

1990 Most Improved Player, University of Georgia Soccer Camp
1991 Best Goal Scorer University of Georgia Soccer Camp

References

Bob Smith—Head Coach
Little Bopper Soccer Program
999 Broad Street
Atlanta, GA 30000

Joe Martin—Director of Coaching Central High School
000 Peach Tree Street
Atlanta, GA 30000

Jill Johnson
Georgia Soccer Club
456 Maple Ave.
Atlanta, GA 30000

David Dunn
Camp Director, U. of Georgia Soccer
83 Athens Boulevard
Athens, GA 31000

INDEX